◁ W9-COE-022

Later

SYRACUSE BABE

Some of LP's at Syracuse U presumably
all in surrounding area in New York State.
8 cases. Each case "named" with an
outstanding characteristic or more.

The Effective Principal

PERSPECTIVES ON SCHOOL LEADERSHIP

Arthur Blumberg
Syracuse University

William Greenfield
Syracuse University

Allyn and Bacon, Inc.
BOSTON LONDON SYDNEY TORONTO

To Our Kids

Barbara, Lester, and Susie

and

Geoff, Amelia, Ara, and Monica

The people from whom we've learned most about schools

Copyright © 1980 by Allyn and Bacon, Inc., 470 Atlantic Avenue,
Boston, Massachusetts 02210. All rights reserved. No part of the material
protected by this copyright notice may be reproduced or utilized in any form
or by any means, electronic or mechanical, including photocopying, recording,
or by any information storage and retrieval system, without written
permission from the copyright owner.

Library of Congress Cataloging in Publication Data

Blumberg, Arthur, 1923–
   The effective principal.

   Bibliography: p.
   Includes index.
   1. School superintendents and principals.
2. Leadership.   I. Greenfield, William D., 1944–
II. Title.
LB2831.8.B57   371.2'012   79–16780
ISBN 0–205–06812–X

Printed in the United States of America

Acknowledgments

Excerpts from "Doctrines of Administration: A Brief History" by H. W. Button. Educational Administration Quarterly 2 (3) (Autumn 1966). Reprinted by permission of the University Council for Educational Administration.

Excerpts from *Performance Objectives for School Principals* ed. by Jack A. Culbertson, Curtis Henson, and Ruel Morrison, Berkeley: McCutchan Publishing Corporation © 1974. Reprinted by permission of the publisher.

Excerpts from *The Normative World of the Elementary School Principal* by J. M. Foskett. Copyright © 1967 by University of Oregon: Center for Advanced Study of Educational Administration. Reprinted by permission of the publisher.

Excerpts from *Elementary Principals and Their Schools—Beacons of Brilliance and Potholes of Pestilence* by K. Goldhammer, G. Becker, R. Withycombe, F. Doyel, E. Miller, C. Morgan, L. Deloretto, and B. Aldridge. Copyright © 1971 by University of Oregon: Center for the Advanced Study of Educational Administration.

Excerpts from *Staff Leadership in Public Schools: A Sociological Inquiry* by N. Gross and R. E. Herriott. Copyright © 1965 by John Wiley and Sons, Inc. By permission of the authors and the publisher.

Excerpts from *The Sex Factor and the Management of Schools* by N. C. Gross and A. E. Trask. Copyright © 1976 by John Wiley and Sons, Inc. Reprinted by permission of the publisher.

Excerpts from *Administrative Performance & Personality* by J. K. Hemphill, D. E. Griffiths, and N. Frederiksen. Copyright © 1962, Bureau of Publications, Teachers College, Columbia University. Reprinted by permission of Teachers College Press.

Excerpts from *Administration of Public Education* by S. Knezevich. Copyright © 1975 by Harper and Row Publishers, Inc. Reprinted by permission of the publisher.

Excerpts from "Non-Verbal Behavior of Administrators" by J. M. Lipham and Francke. Educational Administration Quarterly 2 (2) (Spring 1966). Reprinted by permission of the University Council for Educational Administration.

Excerpts from *The Principalship: Foundations and Functions* by J. M. Lipham and J. A. Hoeh, Jr. Copyright © 1974 by J. M. Lipham and J. A. Hoeh, Jr. By permission of Harper and Row Publishers, Inc.

Excerpts from "American Public School Administration: A Short Analysis" by J. G. March. School Review 86 (2) (February 1978). Copyright © 1978 by the University of Chicago. Reprinted by permission of The University of Chicago Press.

Excerpts from "The Origin and Development of the Public School Principalship." Ph.D. dissertation by P. R. Pierce, University of Chicago, 1934. Reprinted by permission of the author.

Excerpts from *The Principalship* by W. H. Roe and T. L. Drake. Copyright © 1974 by Macmillan Publishing Co., Inc. Reprinted by permission of the publisher.

Excerpts from *The Man in the Principal's Office: An Ethnography* by Harry F. Wolcott. Copyright © 1973 by Holt, Rinehart, and Winston, Inc. Reprinted by permission of the author and the publisher.

Contents

vi   Contents

Preface

In a sense, this book is the story of a journey that we took, knowing where home was, but not sure of either what roads we would take or where we would end up. It was similar to a Sunday afternoon drive that families take (perhaps less frequently these days given the cost of fuel) to see the countryside, wander around, and possibly have dinner at a good restaurant if they happen to stumble on one—or, more likely, at the first hamburger stand that looms into view around dinnertime. More to the point, our purpose was to take an intellectual trip into the work lives of some school principals who, for one reason or another, were judged to be out of the ordinary by their peers or us. Thus, "home" for us was a rather simple matter—our curiosity about these people. Where we would end up in our travels was quite a different matter; it would depend on the human landscape we encountered.

What we found, as we journeyed through the work lives of these school principals was exciting, reassuring, and humbling. It was exciting for us to come to understand these people better, to see how each, rather uniquely, conceptualized and acted out his/her role. We were excited to learn more clearly than we had known before how directly a determined school principal can affect the form and substance of what occurs in a school.

We were reassured and had our sometimes flagging confidence renewed in the institution of public education. It is no secret—the pollsters and columnists say—that the schools are currently suffering a confidence gap with the public. If the schools only did their job correctly (as they used to), if teachers were more concerned about teaching than how much they get paid, then youngsters would learn more and we would have less trouble all around us—this is the current mythology. There may be some truth to this mythology, but our study confirmed some things we already knew—that there *are* enthusiastic and dedicated people who are trying to make a difference in the educational and emotional lives of youngsters in the schools.

Finally, and most definitely, we were humbled as we came to understand what it meant to be a school principal who was trying to make a difference, who was not content with serving as an organization maintenance person whose main purpose in life was to keep things running smoothly, with "keeping the peace." The amount of time and energy—intellectual and emotional—that it takes for a principal to make an impact on a school is startling. We became convinced that it takes a unique person to help give a school, first, an image of what it can be and, second, to provide the drive, support, and skills to make that image approximate reality.

We (the authors) were the primary beneficiaries of the experience of studying these school principals and writing a book about them. The book, though important, is almost incidental in the long run. What we learned about ourselves and about the schools is of a higher order of importance. In a sense, the act of writing this book together resulted in a renewal of faith for us.

In an odd sort of way then, and by hindsight, we wrote this book for ourselves. Others, however, should find its contents of interest. Professors and students of school administration should find it useful as a further means of understanding both the complexities and ambiguities of the principalship. Practicing administrators may find it helpful as it describes and conceptualizes experiences that most of them have confronted and continue to confront.

This book represents a collaborative effort between the two of us and the people who were the subjects of our study. Not simply inanimate repositories of data, they contributed most willingly to our analysis of the data that they had provided. We thank them for their time and their thinking. Finally, thanks go to Mrs. Marilyn Stauffer, our typist, whose skill and willingness to work under pressure with much good humor was invaluable.

I

Introduction

This book is about the lives and times of some out-of-the-ordinary school principals. Indeed, the "some" of the previous sentence can be narrowed down to a few—eight to be exact. The book is, then, not a broad-based empirical study of the role relationships of school principals, nor is it a review of the research on school organizational climate and the manner in which a principal's behavior may affect that climate. A vast literature on those subjects already exists. Rather, this volume is, initially, an inquiry into the sometimes elegant, sometimes humdrum, sometimes bumbling, sometimes hectic, and many times frustrating lives of several people who happen to be school principals and who somehow seem to be different from most of their colleagues.

The differences are hard to define. There are no "hard" data-based criteria by which one can, in a priori fashion, identify those principals who are making or who have the potential to make unique contributions to their faculties or youngsters. What we do know is that, from time to time, as we talked with teachers, parents, district administrators and our students, a name of a principal would come up as "someone you ought to find out more about." That is, this person was doing something, communicating something, or organizing things in a school in a way that prompted people to say, "That principal is unusual. Something is happening in that school."

As professors of educational administration our interest was aroused by these circumstances. We have a working knowledge of the theories and research related to school administration, leadership in schools, and schools as organizations. But something has always seemed to be lacking, both in our teaching and our research, when questions like these were raised by a colleague or a student: "What makes the difference between school *A* and school *B*? "How come the teachers and kids are excited and having fun in *A* and those in *B* don't seem to be?" "Why do parents, if they have the choice, want their youngsters to go to school at *A* rather than *B*?

Common wisdom suggests that the principal is the key, but the research on the role of the principal does not provide the answer to such questions. In point of fact, they may be unanswerable. Nonetheless, we wanted to talk to some principals who, by reputation, seemed to be different and whose schools seemed to be different. We wanted to ask them about their life as a principal, what they valued, how they related to people, what guided them in their work, what conditions prompted them to action, and where and how they picked up cues about their role. We were curious about what frustrated them, what angered them, and what made them feel good. Mostly, we wanted to learn from them.

The ultimate purpose of this line of inquiry was not completely clear to us in the beginning. That is, although we were intellectually curious about the *zeitgeist* of some school principals who, indeed, appeared to be out of the ordinary or who, it seemed, created or maintained school environments that were somehow different and, in some cases, exciting, the nature of the substance with which we would have to deal was not at all clear to us. Nor was it clear how the book would be best organized or, most importantly, what we would have to say beyond describing these principals.

Shortly after the study began, as our interviews progressed and we started to attain some insight into the work life of these principals, the initial structure of the book became obvious. It was clear that what might be said about each of them could and should stand alone. Thus, Chapters 4–11 are thumbnail sketches of the principals, each sketch portraying the individual in a thematic way that is quite different from the others—and yet with certain similarities. Curiously, in what may seem to be a contradiction, it was the glaring differences that developed among the principals and the way they went about their tasks that lent wholeness and symmetry to the study. That is, although each of the people whom we interviewed was, by some consensus, outstanding, each was also strikingly different. Their idiosyncratic ways of dealing with the problems of leading a school provided the unifying thread for our thinking. Perhaps more importantly, though, our understanding of these idiosyncrasies caused us to recast some of our thoughts about the role of the principal. That is, as we interviewed our eight subjects and started to write about them, it became abundantly clear that the *person* of the principal and the values that he/she communicates via behavior to teachers, parents, and students needs to be resurrected as a legitimate subject of study. Unashamedly, then, and in the face of huge volumes of empirical research that may point in another direction, we were led backward (though it may be forward) to a consideration of some modification of a more or less "great person" perspective on the process of leading a school.

We write in much more detail about this perspective in Chapter 15. A few comments are in order at this point, however. Early thinking about the phenomenon of leadership and the process of leading focused on the personality traits of the leader. This approach gave way to a functional and situational focus as study after study of personality traits of leaders failed to yield replicable findings. The functional and situational focus suggested that the process of leading—the ability to exert influence— was a question of certain functions being performed that depended on the demands of the situation. The notion was also egalitarian in that it appeared reasonable that the necessary functions could be enacted by any member of a group depending on the skill of the individual.

This functional approach to leadership reinforced more philosophical ideas concerning the concept of democratic leadership. It found fertile ground in the schools, one of whose functions, after all, is the acculturation of youngsters to the basic tenets of a democratic society. Why not, for example, train prospective school principals in the concepts and skills of democratic leadership as a step toward democratizing the schools? Further, if leading is a matter of learning and exercising certain skills, then anyone can be a leader—or a school principal.

In point of fact, almost anyone can learn to perform leadership functions—to summarize, to elaborate, to coordinate, for example—and many did. The problem we sensed, however, as we visited schools, observed, and held endless conversations with teachers, is that it all seems not to have made much difference. As Sarason (1971) put it in his brilliant analysis, *The Culture of the Schools and the Problem of Change*, everything changes but everything remains the same. Except—except in a relatively few cases things seem not to have remained the same. And this fact takes us back to our concern with the individual school principal as a person and the possibility that our thinking about leading a school, which is what a principal is supposed to do, needs to be refocused on the people who occupy the position of leadership. This, then, is essentially what this book is about—some principals who do appear to have made a difference in their schools.

As was indicated earlier, the methodology used in this study was a qualitative one. We selected eight principals to be interviewed. Four of them were elementary school principals; three male and one female. Four of them were secondary school principals; two male and two female. The criteria we used for selection were, for the most part, reputational. That is, we asked numerous teachers, principals, and faculty colleagues to nominate principals whom they knew who, indeed, were leading their school and were making a difference. In addition, we had personal knowledge of a few people who, in our judgment, fit the same criteria. It should also be said here that we also knew all the principals we interviewed before we asked them to be part of our work. They had all had some affiliation with our University. Nonrandomness was, then, not an issue. Quite the opposite was the case. We wanted to be highly selective, for as was noted above, this study was not intended to be a broad-based inquiry of school principals qua school principals.

A further word is needed concerning our selection criterion of principals "who were making a difference." All school principals, in point of
fact, "make a difference" insofar as their behavior affects, for example,
the organizational climate of a school. Our interests went much beyond
that notion, however. We were interested in investigating how some
school principals who seemed to have some highly positive qualitative
impact on teachers and youngsters perceived their work lives. "Qualitative impact" is an elusive idea. Given the idiosyncratic differences that are
found among schools (and their sameness, as well) we would be hard put
to define the phrase in any generalizable way. For sure, the selections we
made reflect some of our own biases about what a school should be—a
balance of rather joyful humanism combined with a determined focus
on creating productive learning environments. We think, however, that
our choice of people was influenced by more than our values as, in most
cases, these choices received general ex post facto support, both from
practitioners in the field and from our faculty colleagues.

There is an interesting bit of data that was not available to us when
our study commenced but which, in retrospect, reinforces our decision
to be highly selective about the principals we interviewed. Carroll (1978)
recently conducted a study of the Central Life Interest of school principals. The systematic study of Central Life Interest (defined as the
preferred location for the performance of certain acts in day-to-day
life) was initiated by Dubin (1956). According to Dubin one may have
a CLI that is job-oriented or non-job-oriented, or may exhibit no preference. Carroll's study of 277 principals indicated that only 17 percent of the
sample were job-oriented, 44 percent non-job-oriented, and 39 percent had
no preference. These results were at some variance with studies of other
professional or managerial groups where the percentage of job-oriented
people was much higher. For example, the percentage of job-oriented
nurses was 79 (Orzack, 1959) and for middle managers in an industrial
firm it was 53. In point of fact, the percentage of school principals who
were job-oriented is much closer to that of blue-collar workers and office
clerks than it is to that of other professional groups that have been studied.

The point of this comment is not to suggest that non-job-oriented
school principals or those who have no preference do not do a good job.
Indeed, they may be outstanding, though no data is at hand to enable us to
take one position or another. The point is that our inference about the
principals with whom we talked is that, for the most part, they were
indeed job-oriented. Concerns with the job seemed to involve most of
their working hours. It is not that their lives away from the school building were not satisfactory or fulfilling for them; indeed, quite the opposite
holds. What is at issue, however, is that it appears as though the principals
in the study constitute a rather unique subgroup among other school
principals—at least as far as their Central Life Interest is concerned. It is
almost that for them, "the job was the thing."

Our interviews with these principals were simple and straightforward. We told them what we were interested in and that the primary criteria for their selection was their reputation among their peers. We simply asked them to start talking in an open-ended way, about their life in school. The interviews were unstructured, though as we proceeded from one to the next we would raise issues that might have been touched on by one and not by the other. The interviews were tape recorded and transcribed.

There is a methodological issue in connection with this interview strategy that needs to be discussed here. We deliberately did not create a schedule that might serve as a guide for the interviews, so that each principal could paint his/her own picture of his/her world. Although we did raise points with them that had been remarked on by one and not the other, we did not push very hard. Thus, if one emphasized relationships with youngsters and another did not, we did not push this seeming lack of emphasis. There was, of course, considerable overlap in the circumstances talked about, but at the heart of it all was the notion that the role that these principals saw themselves playing was theirs, not ours. We wanted to get as close to the "eye of the beholder" as we could.

Beyond this desire to let the interviews serve as a projective device that we would interpret was another decision. The study would not be comparative in any systematic sense of the word. Although we do engage in some synthesizing, it was not our goal to compare or contrast the interviewees with one another for two reasons. First, it seemed important (to continue the painting metaphor) to let the picture of each principal stand by itself as do paintings in an art gallery. The issue, from our point of view, was to inquire into the internal dynamics of these self-portraits, not to compare one with the other along predetermined lines.

The second reason for not using a structured interview schedule became apparent to us shortly after the study commenced. The people with whom we talked used different concepts to describe their view of themselves in their role. Each, indeed, seemed to have his/her own theory of the principal's role that stemmed from his/her personality, experience, and training. Thus it seemed wiser to let the individual principal's interests dictate the course of our discussions.

This interview strategy, despite the difficulties it presented relative to our effort to synthesize the results, enabled us to deal with each principal as an individual without regard to anyone else. We became able to trace the themes that they presented of themselves and produce an interesting and informative collage. The collage illustrates the many forms that leadership in a school can take and still produce a productive learning environment.

Part of the study design called for a group interview with all the principals after the individual interviews had been completed. Six of the eight were able to attend. Each had been provided with the thumbnail sketch that had been written about him/her. They were asked, initially, to react to the sketches and tell us whether or not our portrayal of them matched reality as they saw it. With a few minor exceptions, what had been written was congruent with their self-concepts.

The main thrust of the meeting, which lasted about four hours, was not solely to get their reactions to what we had written about them. Indeed, this was a minor part of our goal. Of most interest to us was to inquire into what Levinson (1973) has called the "emotional toxicity" of the work situation. That is, we were interested in the sometimes subtle, sometimes blatant factors in the worklife of a school principal that seem to take a toll on his/her emotional well being. This discussion enabled us to inquire, in a sense, into the "shady" side of their lives, one that rarely gets talked about publicly.

There was also an interesting sidelight to the meeting. The exercise of reading about themselves and discussing their reactions seemed to be satisfyingly confirming for them. It was as though someone understood them in a manner that was helpful to them.

Though the bulk of the book deals with our description and analysis of the views held by these principals of themselves in their roles, a conceptual stage for thinking about the school principalship is set in the next two chapters. Chapter 2, "The Principalship: Past and Present," discusses the historical evolution of that role. It takes note of the increasing complexity of the job of being a school principal, paying particular attention to the lingering and always close-to-the-surface conflict of whether or not the principal's primary task is that of an instructional leader or organization manager. Chapter 3 focuses on some major research concerning the principalship. We hasten to add it is not a complete review. Such would be impossible within the confines of this book. The concern of this review is with some of the larger scale studies that have given attention to trying to develop an understanding of the dynamics of the role of principal. In Gestalt terms, Chapters 2 and 3 provide the ground upon which rests the figure of what follows.

Chapters 4 through 11, as was noted previously, present the sketches of each of the principals interviewed. Each is entitled with the theme that seemed to characterize the individual involved. Although some readers may object to such labeling, the intent was not to develop categories and assign people to them, but to briefly communicate what appeared to be the core of each person's view of self in the principal's role.

Chapter 12 summarizes and interprets the similarities that exist among the eight principals, despite their idiosyncratic goals and styles. It also focuses on the issues that are involved in these principals' relationships with their peers and superiors. Chapter 13 deals with what appear to be three elements of principal effectiveness: vision, initiative, and resourcefulness. Chapter 14, "All That Glitters is Not . . ." is an analysis of the group meeting that dealt with problems of personal emotionality of the principal's job. Chapter 15 is entitled "Toward a Theory of Leading a

School." It proposes a systemic framework for thinking about the process of leading a school in terms that are related to other frameworks but appropriately different, given the insight that developed in our study. Chapter 16 deals with the implications of our findings for both the practice of school administration and the preservice training and staff development of school principals.

The reader will note that we have had occasion, in different chapters, to repeat particular bits of data in the form of quotations from our interviews, that had been used in earlier chapters. This was done when the remarks of a principal seemed to have interpretive application to issues broader than those of special concern to just one principal. In particular, such replications will be found in Chapters 12 and 13.

Two additional comments are in order by way of introduction. First, it may seem to some readers that the observations, explanations, and ideas that are offered here are somewhat hazy and imprecise. Our position is that the act of being a school principal is incredibly complex and that the phenomena we have been studying and attempting to understand do not lend themselves to easy observation or precise conceptualization. This position is in no way an apology. Rather, it suggests that the waters into which we were wading and searching were murky. Precise outlines of objects underneath the surface are hard to make out, and when they do emerge, their silhouettes are not starkly clear.

Second, there is one bit of data that we must share which, though not directly pertinent to what follows, certainly gives food for thought. We started to collect our data in the fall of 1975. The first draft of the manuscript was finished in September 1977. In the interim, four of the people whom we interviewed left their positions. Three of those remaining indicated that they wanted to leave, and one seems satisfied enough at present to stay on. We don't know precisely how to interpret these facts. It may be that there is a certain restlessness or a certain weariness that accompanies being the sort of principal who makes a difference in a school.

2

The Principalship: Past and Present

The American public school principalship has increasingly become a focal point for school critics, university researchers, teacher groups, and central office administrators bent on understanding and improving the quality of educational programs in our nation's schools. Principals frequently take the brunt of multiple and usually conflicting expectations over issues ranging from student discipline to the problems of personnel administration, compliance with increasing numbers of state and federal policy mandates, and maintaining a "smooth-running" educational program that serves the needs of a school community that has become less and less homogeneous in the character of students' abilities and parents' aspirations for themselves and their children. Principals daily face pressures of competing images about what their role should be, and even the best have a difficult time maintaining an appropriate balance between the tasks of managing a smooth-running school and serving as a catalyst for and facilitator of instructional improvement.

While the role of the principal is extremely ambiguous and wrought with conflict, the numbers of teachers aspiring to leave the classroom and take on these challenges continues in spite of a surplus of certified administrators and the shortage of job opportunities that has accompanied a decline in school enrollments. Although many of these prospective school principals are motivated by a sincere desire to expand educational opportunities for children and to improve the quality of life in schools for students and teachers alike, others are lured to the principalship by the opportunity it presents for upward mobility and by the prospect of "getting out" of the classroom and away from the multitude of problems teachers face.

Whatever the reasons for wanting to become a school principal (some are more noble than others), most aspirants to the role have a vague understanding of much that it entails. The loneliness, the conflict, the dullness of the routine, the "busy work," and the anguish that accompany having to solve complex educational and organizational problems with extremely limited resources are usually not part of teachers' conceptions of the principalship. Frustrations that principals experience when their idealized conceptions of themselves as educational leaders become tarnished and frequently dulled forever by the mounting pressures for administrative meetings and for monitoring the growing complex of accountability procedures introduced into their schools, are seldom sensed by teachers wanting to become school principals. Beyond what principals tell their husbands and wives, their sponsors, their peers, their psychiatrists, and some of their friends, there is little to inform would-be principals of what the role is really like. Textbooks on the principalship tend to be more prescriptive than descriptive, and there have been relatively few empirical studies that attempt to describe and explain what school principals actually do on the job.

The purpose of this and the next chapter is neither to remedy the apparent knowledge gap of would-be principals (a task certainly beyond the range of two chapters in any book), nor to describe or explain what principals do in general. However, the following brief review of some of the existing literature on the principalship will provide the reader with a broader context in which to place the sketches and observations that comprise the major portion of this book. The remainder of this chapter, then, reviews the evolution of the role of the school principal as we know it today. It emphasizes changing doctrines in the broader field of educational administration and functional responsibilities prescribed for principals. The next chapter moves from a discussion of the concept of the principalship to a concern with some focal studies of that role.

EVOLUTION OF THE PRINCIPALSHIP

The role of the school principal as we know it today can be traced to its present development from around the middle of the nineteenth century. The essential features of the principalship were established by the turn of the twentieth century and have not changed in any substantial way since that time. While the duties and responsibilities have continued to grow and increase in complexity, the expectation that principals serve the twin functions of providing instructional leadership and managing school affairs had been rooted firmly in the minds of school superintendents and school board members by the early 1900s, particularly in America's larger cities.

At least four important factors contributing to the early development of the principalship can be identified: (a) the rapid growth of cities during the 1850–1900 period and the subsequent problems accompanying the schooling of an ever expanding school-age population; (b) the grading of schools and the introduction of new sets of management problems related to the coordination of pupils and curricula; (c) the reorganization of schools and the consolidation of departments under a single administrative head; and (d) the establishment of the position of a head assistant to free the principal from teaching responsibilities (Pierce, 1934).

Prior to 1850, as Pierce notes, many of the duties that lay boards of education prescribed for principals were of a clerical nature. A sampling of duties shows that:

58.8 percent concerned records and reports
23.5 percent related to matters of school organization
11.8 percent focused on building and equipment
 5.9 percent concerned discipline and care of pupils (Pierce, 1934, p. 211)

These, then, reflect the distribution of duties of what might be termed the "principal teacher." Most of the individuals serving in that capacity also were responsible for some teaching in addition to these clerical duties. However, by the late 1800s the emphasis in responsibilities had shifted from the maintenance of records and reports to matters of school organization and general management. A sampling of duties prescribed by school boards during the period 1853–1900 shows that:

40.5 percent related to organization and general management
15.2 percent concerned equipment and supplies
13.9 percent focused on records and reports
12.7 percent dealt with discipline and care of pupils
 7.6 percent concerned building and grounds
10.1 percent related to miscellaneous duties (Pierce, 1934, p. 212)

Thus, by the year 1900, "the principal had become the directing manager, rather than the 'presiding teacher' of the school" (Pierce, 1934, p. 211). Principals had assumed increasing responsibility for the daily management of schools and had by this time acquired a number of powers which, in their view, increased the prestige of their position as principal:

The right to graduate pupils on the basis of the principal's standards, the right to have orders or suggestions to teachers given only through the medium of principals, and the right to a voice in transfers and assignments of teachers connected with their schools. . . . the right to direct teachers, enforce safeguards to protect the health and morals of pupils, supervise and rate janitors, require the co-operation of parents, and requisition educational supplies. (Pierce, 1934, p. 211)

As schools continued to grow, more and more new and often ill-prepared teachers had to be hired to provide instruction for pupils. School committees, comprised of lay members of the community, soon found that overseeing instructional matters in the schools was becoming increasingly time consuming and complicated, and they, therefore, delegated some of their responsibilities to principals. These factors contributed to the emergence of the instructional supervision dimension of the principal's role. The principal was looked to more and more by superintendents as the medium through which their ideal of "a well graded system of schools" (p. 214) could be realized.

The supervisory role of principals had thus also started to develop by the middle of the nineteenth century. In Cincinnati, for example, principals had become involved with ". . . class visitation, pupil adjustment, measurement of pupil progress, rating of teachers, and instruction in methods—virtually all of the phases of modern supervision" (p. 213). However, these functions did not characterize the role generally and did not become more fully developed until early in the twentieth century. Pierce notes, perhaps reflecting early educational enthrallment with "science," that by the 1930s the supervisory functions of principals had undergone much development:

> They apply the methods of case study to solve the difficulties of maladjusted pupils; they diagnose teaching and learning difficulties; and they classify pupils on scientific bases. (Pierce, 1934, p. 215)

In addition to assuming these increasing responsibilities for the supervision of instruction and for the organization and management of their schools, principals also became more and more involved in matters of school-community relations. In 1894, a large movement in this direction was the establishment of the first mothers' clubs. "The clubs aroused the interests of parents in children's health, recreation, and habits, and in improved methods of parental control" (p. 217).

> These involved meetings of parents in the schools, at which various phases of the work were explained and often illustrated by lantern slides, demonstrations and exhibits, and special visiting days. (Pierce, 1934, p. 217)

Thus, by the early 1900s, three critical and enduring functions of the principalship had been established: the organization and general management of the school; the supervision of instruction and staff development; and the interpretation of the work of the school to the immediate school community. The role evolved from that of a "principal teacher" performing numerous clerical tasks to the prototype of the modern day principal who usually does little or no teaching and is concerned primarily with administrative, supervisory, and community relations activities. The role that emerged during the latter half of the nineteenth century, and which has endured through most of the twentieth century, developed essentially in the larger American cities of the period during a time of expanding school enrollments. Schools had become larger, the student population being serviced was increasingly heterogeneous, and the organization and administration of educational programs became more and more complex.

To a large extent, then as now, the principalship developed in concert with changes in the larger social milieu and reflected, in part, the changing conceptions school superintendents held for themselves as educational administrators. Button (1966) offers an illuminating history of the changing doctrines of educational administration during the past hundred years. He has identified five such "doctrines" and he maintains that these have in large part "served as a justification of administrators and administration to the public and to the school staff, as well as a guide to administrators themselves" (p. 216). These doctrines are reviewed briefly here because they reflect some of the major shifts in the ideal that educational administrators, superintendents in particular, projected for themselves and others during the latter half of the nineteenth century and early twentieth century.

The first doctrine, the "teaching of teachers," characterized the period from about 1870 to 1885. Thomas H. Balliet, a superintendent of schools in Springfield, Massachusetts, during this time, is quoted by Button:

> The superintendent must be, first of all, a teacher of pedagogy. His most important work will be to train his teachers to do thorough and clear thinking in all lines of educational work. . . . The superintendent must do work that is almost identical with that of the teacher of pedagogies in a normal school or college. (Button, 1966, p. 217)

This doctrine served to distinguish the superintendent from lay members of the board of education, and as Button notes, was appropriate to a period in the history of education when teachers were poorly prepared to teach. This period was also characterized by a growing school population in the large cities and the emergence of graded schools, both of which probably added credence to this conception of educational administration as the "teaching of teachers."

Then as schools became larger and as educational programs demanded more attention and direction from superintendents, the doctrine of "administration as applied philosophy" emerged during the period 1885–1905:

> The doctrine asserted that truth, concerning all things and all matters, was eternal and to be discovered. . . . It therefore followed that the learned administrator, who could discover relevant truths, was the best authority on all matters concerning education, and that the problem of administration was the application of philosophical knowledge to schools. (Button, 1966, p. 218)

The need for supreme authority in all matters concerning education, not just the "teaching of teachers," is reflected in Button's quote of W. H. Payne, a professor of education:

> If there is to be a plan, someone must devise it, while others must execute it. As members of the human body execute the behests of the supreme intelligence, so in human society the many must follow the directions of the few. It is not possible to conceive of a state of society in which there are not inequalities based on gradations in the ability to govern. . . . The assignment of the course of study, the examination of the pupils, their oversight and correction, the oversight of teachers, the compilation of records—these are some of the items on which depend the success of the system, and which require the attention of a single head. (pp. 218–19)

The doctrine of educational administration as "applied philosophy" provided superintendents with the authority and the elevated status they believed were needed to direct and develop educational systems during the 1890s. However, a new doctrine emerged during the early twentieth century in a period that emphasized fiscal efficiency above all else. The new doctrine of "school administration as management" reflected the following idea:

> The appropriate basis for decision-making . . . was ideally a fiscal one. Like a business enterprise, the schools were to be operated at minimum cost . . . and maximum efficiency. The child was first the raw material and then the product; the teacher was the worker; and the school was the factory. (p. 219)

Superintendents were coming under increasing pressure from their communities to run schools more efficiently. Button quotes Frank Spaulding, a successful superintendent of the period:

> I know nothing about the absolute value of a recitation in Greek as compared with a recitation in French or in English. I am convinced, however, by other very concrete and quite logical considerations, that when the obligations of the present year expire, we ought to purchase no more Greek instruction at the rate of 5.9 pupil recitations per dollar. The price must go down or we will invest in something else. (p. 220)

The dollar had become a major criterion in the school public's mind, and as Button suggests, the new doctrine not only seemed to "fit" the situation, but also served to align school superintendents with a high status group at the time, the businessmen.

The business management doctrine was abandoned in the 1930s, as the Depression and the New Deal emerged, and although "the techniques of administration (budgeting, accounting, purchasing, plant construction, and maintenance, etc.) had been enormously developed and refined since 1905 . . . the justification for administration was almost unchanged" (Button, 1966, pp. 220–21).

Democratic ideals and the involvement of "everyone" in school decisions usurped much of the control superintendents had previously managed to obtain in the direction of educational matters. "Democracy in the schools . . . left the administrator in a position of diminished power and esteem, although the technical services which he could provide were still required" (Button, 1966, p. 221).

This period lasted until the 1950s when the doctrine of school administration as "applied behavioral science" emerged. This doctrine holds "that much of administration can be conceptualized in the terms of the behavioral sciences, and that a science of administration generally is emergent" (Button, 1966, p. 222). The scientist was given much credence by society during the late 1950s:

In part, the new doctrine was an honest attempt to restore the prestige of administrators. Briefly and approximately, the logic went like this: If the status of administration was to be repaired and improved, it was necessary to "professionalize" it. The first step in professionalization was to improve the preparation of those entering the field and to incorporate "basic" knowledge; knowledge of the behavioral sciences was the best choice. (Button, 1966, p. 222)

Button questions whether this new doctrine is as yet fully accepted, and suggests it might not be. In looking toward the future, to the inevitable emergence of a new doctrine, Button expresses hope that "the next doctrine of administration will be indigenous" (p. 223). That is, that the doctrine will rest on "a knowledge of schools and administration and of educational policy" (p. 223) and that administrators will no longer have to rely for their credibility on the borrowed status of another field or profession.

As we survey the educational scene from our perspective of the 1970s, we sense that many remnants of these earlier doctrines are still reflected in the principalship. Some principals like to think of themselves as "teachers of teachers," others as "applied philosophers," "managers," or "professionals" imbued with the special knowledge the behavioral sciences provide regarding school administration. However, like the period following the 1930s, today many principals seem to lack the clear doctrines that were available to guide them in other eras. A general malaise seems to have come over the principalship in recent years; the present and immediate future hold more uncertainty than anything else.

Expecting school principals to be both strong instructional leaders and effective school managers poses a dilemma which shows no sign of abating. It is heightened in the current conflict among principals themselves regarding whether it is more appropriate to align themselves as a separate employee group or to identify with either teachers or superintendents at the bargaining table. Increasing violence and vandalism in our nation's schools, mandates from federal and state agencies to service special categories of students in particular ways, and pressures to increase teaching effectiveness in basic skill areas present principals with organizational and educational challenges of unprecedented magnitude. Those aspiring to the principalship, and those already struggling with the daily crises and incessant demands of the job, can expect to continue grappling with these and other problems in the foreseeable future.

Principals frequently are expected to be all things to all people, to do all things and to do them well. This might have been a reasonable expectation in days gone by, but it is no longer realistic given the increasing complexity of the role and its demands. Resources are limited. Problems must be put in priority, decision alternatives examined, and some critical choices made in the face of uncertainty.

The next segment of this chapter examines, in more detail, some of the commonly held role expectations for today's principal. A basic understanding of the demands of the role is requisite to a principal's making the choices necessary to carry out that role effectively. Many principals attempt to do everything and, in so doing, often fail to do little well. Those with the courage to make some critical choices about which role dimensions to emphasize tend to be those who believe they are making a difference in their schools. Principals need to feel they are making a difference if they are to remain vital on the job.

RESPONSIBILITIES OF PRINCIPALS

There are numerous conceptions of the functions principals are expected to perform in their role as school manager and instructional leader. Our purpose in these next several pages is not to describe what school principals actually do on the job, but rather, to acquaint the reader with the range of job functions frequently prescribed by writers of textbooks and other materials intended to inform principals of their duties and responsibilities.

Knezevich (1975) suggests that "more and more the principal is recognized as an executive or administrator and the principalship as a constellation of positions" (pp. 394–95). He cites Dean (1960), who has conceptualized the principal's office as providing ten important services for the school:

1. A communications center of the school
2. A clearinghouse for the transaction of school business
3. A counseling center for teachers and students

4. A counseling center for school patrons
5. A research division of the school, for the collection, analysis, and evaluation of information regarding activities and results
6. A repository of school records
7. The planning center for solving school problems and initiating school improvements
8. A resource center for encouraging creative work
9. A coordinating agency cultivating wholesome school and community relations
10. The coordinating center of the school enterprise (Knezevich, 1975, p. 395)

A number of other prescriptions are offered by Knezevich as he details aspects of the principal's responsibilities: "The principal can no longer fulfill the role of the headmaster or of an instructional supervisor competent to counsel all teachers. The instructional leadership role of the principal is one of marshalling resources—human and material—that classroom teachers require to perform effectively" (pp. 393–94). Knezevich offers several other observations:

Nor is there justification any longer for the administrator of an attendance unit to teach one or several classes.

The principal should not be overburdened with clerical work. Clerical tasks are a part of school operations and cannot be ignored, but they should be delegated to clerical personnel and not permitted to drain the time of the professional administrator.

The principal in a public school, whether at the elementary or secondary level, is a counselor of students, the school disciplinarian, the organizer of the schedule, the supervisor of the instructional program, the pupil-relations representative for the attendance area, the liaison between teachers and the superintendent, the director and evaluator of teaching efforts, the manager of the school facilities, the supervisor of custodial and food-service employees within the building, and a professional leader. (pp. 394–95)

Knezevich concludes his brief review of the functions of school principals with this observation: "Little wonder that this is a demanding position as well as one of considerable significance in determining the direction of public education" (Knezevich, 1975, pp. 395–96). While we agree with Knezevich that the position is indeed demanding, we question whether the position as he has conceived of it is of "significance" regarding the future direction of public education. It seems that the most one could expect of a principal, if he/she were in fact able to perform adequately all of the duties and responsibilities that Knezevich has prescribed, would be to maintain the current status quo of the school situation. Although we do not believe this is what Knezevich had in mind, if such were the case it certainly would be a significant determinant of future direction. As in the past, not much would change.

Roe and Drake (1974) conceive of the principal's job in terms of a combined administrative-managerial and educational leadership emphasis. The major duties prescribed by them in this dual emphasis are detailed below:

Administrative-Managerial Emphasis

a. Maintaining adequate school records of all types
b. Preparing reports for the central office and other agencies
c. Budget development and budget control
d. Personnel administration
e. Student discipline
f. Scheduling and maintaining a schedule
g. Building administration
h. Administering supplies and equipment
i. Pupil accounting
j. Monitoring programs and instructional processes prescribed by the central office

Educational Leadership Emphasis

a. Stimulate and motivate staff to maximum performance
b. Develop with the staff a realistic and objective system of accountability for learning (as contrasted to merely monitoring programs and instructional processes in input terms as prescribed by the central office)
c. Develop cooperatively operable assessment procedures for on-going programs to identify and suggest alternatives for improving weak areas
d. Work with staff in developing and implementing the evaluation of the staff
e. Work with staff in formulating plans for evaluating and reporting student progress
f. Provide channels for the involvement of the community in the operation of the school
g. Encourage continuous study of curricular and instructional innovations
h. Provide leadership to students in helping them to develop a meaningful but responsible student government
i. Establish a professional learning resources center and expedite its use (pp. 13–14)

Roe and Drake observe "that it is virtually impossible to assume that the principal can be a real instructional leader and at the same time be held strictly accountable for the general operational and management detail required by the central office" (p. 14). These authors further maintain that the educational leadership emphasis is the one "that most principals profess they dream about but can't achieve" (p. 13). In short, the principal is, on the surface at least, expected to do all of these things, to wear both hats at once. As schools have become larger and educational programs more complex, and as the student body has become increasingly diversified and the teachers more professionalized, principals have found it more and more difficult to satisfy both sets of role demands. The exceptional principal tends to emphasize the educational leadership emphasis, but most principal's jobs, according to Roe and Drake, are dominated by the administrative-managerial emphasis.

This dilemma for the principal—what balance to strike between the pressures for change and stability—is not new. It is reflected in many textbooks on the principalship and in research studies of principals and their behavior. We've also observed, in our discussions with the principals we studied and report on here as well as in conversations we've held with principals during the course of our university teaching experience, that the leadership-administration/change-maintenance dilemma is pervasive and touches all of those acquainted with the principalship.

Lipham and Hoeh (1974), perhaps more clearly than anyone, have drawn a useful distinction between leadership and administration, and define leadership "as that behavior of an individual which initiates a new structure in interaction within a social system; it initiates change in the goals, objectives, configurations, procedures, input, processes, and ultimately the outputs of social systems" (p. 182). The emphasis here is upon change, on initiating new structures, rather than solely maintaining or administering existing structures. School principals generally prefer to conceive of themselves as educational leaders, but frequently these men and women find the bulk of their time and energy consumed by the daily press of administrative detail and the problems of maintaining the school organization, its teachers and students, on an even keel.

Lipham and Hoeh, with leadership as the overriding emphasis, describe five major functional areas of responsibility for principals: (1) The Instructional Program, (2) Staff Personnel Services, (3) Student Personnel Services, (4) Financial-Physical Resources, and (5) School-Community Relationships (p. 203). Further, these writers maintain that effective leadership in these five functional areas will be enhanced to the extent that a principal is well grounded in the behavioral sciences that promote the understanding of school organization and administrative processes. The "foundations" prescribed by Lipham and Hoeh include knowledge of general systems theory, social systems theory, values theory, organization theory, role theory, decision theory, and leadership theory (p. 4).

The conceptual skills grounded in these theoretical foundations of administration, and the requisite human and technical skills needed to fulfill the five general functions noted above, are pointed to by Lipham and Hoeh as basic ingredients to successful performance in the principalship. These writers then suggest that "the competency-based approach to the principalship provides a systematic means for analyzing and synthesizing the conceptual, human, and technical skills required for effective and efficient performance in the principal's role" (p. 351).

While the sixty-six specific competencies that Lipham and Hoeh identify as relevant to the five major functions of the principalship need not be listed here in their entirety, a review of the conceptual schemes they use to categorize competencies within each functional area will provide the reader with a sense of the range of activities included within their functional framework.

1. Instructional Improvement
    Assessing Program Relevance
    Planning Program Improvements
    Implementing Program Improvements
    Evaluating Program Change (pp. 228–29)
2. Staff Personnel Services
    Identification of New Staff
    Orientation of Staff
    Assignment of Staff
    Staff Improvement
    Evaluation of Staff (pp. 262–63)
3. Student Personnel Services
    Student Values
    Student Involvement
    Student Guidance Services (p. 294)
4. Finances and Facilities
    Financial Resources
    School Plant Resources (pp. 317–18)
5. School-Community Relations
    Community Analysis
    Communicating with the Community
    Utilizing Community Resources (pp. 344–45)

Lipham and Hoeh emphasize that these comprise the *major* areas of functional responsibility for principals. They suggest that while the seven bodies of administrative and behavioral science knowledge they cite hold great potential for helping one understand the role, they note that these by no means exhaust all the knowledge relevant to the principalship. They suggest, for example, that "learning theory and curriculum theory, as well as the history and philosophy of education, might well be added as foundational areas in which the principal must be well informed" (p. 4). The principalship, given the framework suggested by Lipham and Hoeh, is indeed complex and prescribes a broad range of conceptual and technical competencies one might expect a school principal to draw upon as he/she faces the daily challenges of the role.

While the three general conceptions of the principalship that have been briefly reviewed here suggest fairly similar areas of functional responsibility for the principal, they can be differentiated in terms of the relative emphasis they give to the principal as general manager, instructional leader, and scientific administrator. Knezevich's view presents the principal as an executive manager facilitating the work of teachers and students through a broad range of services provided by the principal's office. Roe and Drake offer a more integrated view of the role and present the principal as having a dual emphasis in managing the school and providing direct instructional leadership to the work of the school staff. Lipham and Hoeh view the principal primarily as a leader conceptually well grounded in the administrative and behavioral sciences.

Three responsibilities that are often associated with the principalship, but which have only indirectly been referred to, concern the management of conflict, the making of decisions, and the introduction of organizational changes in the schools for which they are responsible. Our work with educational administrators at all levels leads us to believe that school principals spend much of their time on the job actively engaged in making decisions related to the management of conflict and organizational change, and frequently the mark of the "effective" principal from the central office perspective is that "things are calm" and "policy changes are implemented smoothly."

In the climate of today's school environment, with increasing pressures from all sides, and with each participant claiming some legitimacy for his/her viewpoint, conflict in schools is inevitable. The conflicts that arise could potentially be used as the basis for initiating new structure in the school social system. However, as the basis for educational leadership, conflict is more frequently viewed and treated as a threat to the on-going stability of the organization. Conflicts thus tend to be managed with the aim of maintaining the existing order. Indeed, a successful principal is frequently perceived as one who keeps things "cool." Disputes between teachers, the demands of a group of students, or the complaints of a vocal parent minority, and the like, are usually dealt with in a manner that permits a bargain or compromise to be reached that does not alter the organizational status quo.

Superintendents generally prefer that conflicts arising at the school level be managed by the principal. While there's often no explicit mandate by the superintendent or other central office personnel for the principal *not* to manage conflict in a creative way that would permit the initiation of structure that would yield some educational or organizational improvement, the culture of schools (Sarason, 1971) seems to be such that conflict is managed so that things don't change much, if at all. That is, conflicts are usually managed by principals so as to permit the least possible disruption of the current school situation. "Keeping the lid on" is usually the criterion applied in assessing the success of principals conceived of as "conflict managers."

The individual as decision maker is another common conception of the role of principal. This view, reflected in the literature on principals, tends to paint a highly rational picture of the individual charged with the responsibility to execute the school principal's duties and obligations. The actual practice of decision making by school principals frequently does not, however, reflect a systematic, ordered approach to problem solving.

Lipham and Hoeh (1974), for example, maintain that "decision making is a central responsibility of the principal" (p. 149). These authors refer to decision making as "a process wherein an awareness of a problematic state of a system, influenced by information and values, is reduced to competing alternatives among which a choice is made based on perceived outcome states of the system" (p. 155). Lipham and Hoeh identify three analytical dimensions related to the principal's primary role as decision maker. These include decision behavior, decision role, and decision involvement. This tripartite concept of the principal's role as decision maker suggests a variety of relationships between the behavior of the principal, as well as other actors in the school social system, and areas of functional responsibility associated with the principalship.

The value orientation of the principal becomes critical in executing his/her role as a decision maker. As Lipham and Hoeh point out, "the sacred, secular, and operational values of the society, the organization, and the decision maker are inextricably entwined in the making of all decisions" (p. 158). This conception of the principal as a decision maker thus presumes that a set of value premises guides the choices, the decisions, that are inevitably made.

What values principals hold as central or peripheral to executing their role responsibilities are thus important to understanding the principalship. Frequently, organizational norms and the expectations of superiors become the central point for principals as they make decisions. The values of the individual principal, to the extent that they deviate in a substantial way, or even in only a minor way from organizational norms or superior's values, are often not prominent in the decisions made by principals. To make a decision that runs counter to the norms of teachers, students, the central office, or the school community is likely to upset the equilibrium of the system, and may have severe consequences for the principal who dares to be different.

Values have a crucial influence on both the ends and means of schooling, and we believe it is the exception rather than the rule for a school principal to analyze critically the value premises underlying his/her decision choices. Usually, organizational norms and the values of superiors take precedence over the individual principal's values unless, of course, both value sets are congruent. While it may be useful to think of principals as highly rational decision makers with a strong sense of personal and professional integrity, and we have no quibble with the fact that principals do make decisions on this basis, the conception on the surface seems to suggest that principals have more freedom in their decision making than is usually the case.

The concept of principals as organizational change agents suggests that principals are, in some sense, "leaders." That is, principals might be expected to initiate new structure in interaction with others in the school social system, or at the least, to act as facilitators of changes initiated by others. The literature on school organizations indicates that principals can be a decisive element in determining whether organizational change efforts succeed or fail. While an implicit assumption in that literature is that the principal is more often a facilitator than an initiator of organizational change, Small (1974), in a discussion of how school principals initiate and respond to change, identifies a number of other role options for the principal as organizational change agent:

1. *Initiator.* The principal makes changes according to his perception of the need. . . .
2. *Stimulator.* The principal . . . provides the opportunity for the appropriate constituencies to develop recommendations. . . .
3. *Reactor.* The principal . . . responds directly to the situation.
4. *Implementor.* The principal is required to implement changes decided upon by central administration.
5. *Conduit.* The principal . . . may then plan an intermediary role and seek to connect those requesting change with the appropriate party.
6. *Orchestrator-Mediator.* The principal may seek to create the context in which change can be negotiated among the parties concerned.
7. *Persuader or Dissuader.* He may . . . persuade those proposing change not to push for the change they have proposed, to push for something else, or to change the timing of their efforts.
8. *Advocate.* He may choose to support those pushing for the change and join them in attempting to bring the change about.
9. *Ombudsman.* The principal . . . voices the concerns of any group whose point of view might otherwise not be given adequate consideration.
10. *Nonactor.* He may choose to make only minimal response to the change proposal and not actively pursue any of the above roles. (pp. 21–22)

Conceiving of principals as organizational change agents thus may include a fairly wide range of role options. Which option is enacted depends on many factors including the knowledge, skills, and values of the principal, the organizational context in which the change is to occur, the nature of the change itself, and the character of the larger social milieu in which the organization functions.

How principals think of their role, and the conceptions held by others of the principalship, can be a crucial determinant of their on-the-job behavior, their frustrations and satisfactions in the role, and their failure or success as principals. To be sure, principals are often expected to be all things to all people: to be an instructional leader; to maintain the status quo; to be a decision maker or an organizational change agent, or to fulfill some other set of expectations regarding the principalship. Most principals can point out that, to a greater or lesser degree, each of these conceptions reflects some of what they do as principals. Others, probably the exceptions, think of themselves as being dominated by one conception or another.

While principals themselves may aspire to the traditional ideal of principal as instructional leader, most find themselves beseiged on a daily basis with the nitty-gritty administrative tasks involved in keeping the ship on an even keel, in maintaining the existing order in their school. If they perceive of themselves as organizational change agents, we suspect that the "conduit," "reactor," and "implementor" are the most frequently enacted role options vis-à-vis organizational or educational change.

We do intend neither to paint a gloomy picture of the principalship nor to criticize principals, but rather to present our view of the situation. While all principals are decision makers and managers of conflict, and some certainly live up to these role demands more fully than others, few are effective instructional leaders or organizational change agents in the broader sense of those ideas. The pressure on principals to maintain the status quo, to keep the ship running smoothly on a daily basis, is enormous. We believe this maintenance emphasis is as much, if not more, a function of the organizational environment in which the principal must perform his/her role, than a consequence of the intentions of individual principals. While many principals might dream of being effective instructional leaders by enhancing the activities of teaching and learning in their schools, in reality, their experience is shaped by the press of administrative and managerial functions that mitigate against that dream becoming fact.

3

The Principal as Administrator:
Some Focal Studies

Large-scale systematic study of school principals began with the initiation of the National Principalship Study at Harvard University in 1959. Prior to that research effort, studies of the performance of school principals were limited essentially to status surveys that chronicled various static dimensions of the principalship. These studies focused on the characteristics of principals, their experience and preparation, working conditions (terms, hours of work, distribution of time, etc.), number of full- and part-time staff in their schools, resources available to the school, and a host of other variables, which could easily be quantified and collected by means of a mailed questionnaire.

Perhaps the best examples of these on a large-scale basis are the national surveys of the elementary school principalship, sponsored by the National Education Association's Department of Elementary School Principals, in 1928, 1948, 1958, and 1968. Other examples are the 1965 and 1978 surveys sponsored by the National Association of Secondary School Principals. While the opinions of principals and demographic data associated with their principalships are useful and informative for some purposes, these data do not provide much understanding about administrative behavior and on-the-job performance of principals per se.

There are many practical problems associated with researching the principalship, not the least of which is the fact that there is usually only one principal assigned to a school building. Studies of the principalship are thus usually both time consuming and expensive to undertake on a large-scale basis, particularly if one's aim is to describe and understand the dynamic aspects of the role.

Another source of difficulty confronting the researcher is the complexity of the role itself, wherein the principal to be studied is caught in a complex web of frequently conflicting expectations that press him/her to be responsive to a wide range of role demands. They may include everything from fixing toilets, disciplining children, and monitoring the lunchroom to developing curricula, evaluating teachers, and working

25

with parents and other members of the community. Pool's (1974) compilation of principalship competencies represents a good example of the complexity of the principal's role as well as the divergent views among educators of what principals "ought" to be doing in the schools.

The studies reviewed here have been selected for the general understanding they offer regarding the administrative behavior of school principals. They are all empirical studies guided by well-conceived theoretical frameworks, and the data collected reflect many of the dynamics associated with the principalship. The bulk of research on the principalship has focused on the elementary school. While many of the results of those studies are suggestive of, if not exactly reflecting similar conditions inhering in the secondary school situation, it is unfortunate that there have not been more studies of middle, junior, and high school principalships. It would seem to be abundantly clear that many of the issues and problems associated with the elementary principalship may be compounded by the larger size, diversity of curriculum, and older students characterizing middle, junior, and senior high schools.

Note that the studies reviewed here focus on rather broad and general issues. In addition to these, however, are a multitude of doctoral dissertations and other studies, which are smaller in scope and tend to examine rather specific problems or investigate relationships among a particular set of research variables. These are not included in this review, but are mentioned here to provide the reader with a glimpse of what has *not* been reviewed. It should be noted, for example, that many of these smaller studies reflect refinements and further elaboration of the problems and relationships examined in this review. Two recent studies not included, but which offer many useful additional insights into the principalship role, are those by Gorton and McIntyre (1978), a three-part study in which one part is an in-depth interview study of sixty effective high school principals, and Ellett (1974), representing a major effort to examine the role of elementary, middle, and high school principals in Georgia. A major contribution of Ellett's work is a content analysis of the literature in terms of statements descriptive of the roles, and an empirical investigation of what principals actually do. The studies reviewed below are ordered chronologically.

In 1962, Hemphill, Griffiths, and Frederiksen published the results of a study in which they sought to: (1) determine dimensions of importance in the elementary school principalship related to understanding the nature of the job of the school administrator; (2) provide information helpful in the solution of the problem of selecting school administrators, and (3) provide materials and instruments for the study and teaching of school administration (pp. 7, 8).

Their approach in this investigation attempted to deal with problems historically plaguing research on administrative behavior:

(1) The lack of useful criteria by which to reliably differentiate good from poor administrative behavior, (2) the paucity of concepts with which to describe administrative behavior, (3) the operational difficulties inherent in actually attempting to observe the on-the-job behavior of administrators, (4) the reality that every administrative situation differs in some respect from every other situation, and (5) the problems of ordering and analyzing large amounts of data that are difficult to quantify. (pp. 4, 5)

To cope with these problems the researchers constructed a standard administrative situation in which administrative behavior could be carefully recorded and observed. A simulated principalship and organizational context were designed that would permit them to observe the ways in which study participants responded to a wide array of school problems, administrative tasks, and issues related to instructional supervision. Several means were employed to do this: (1) "in-basket" tests in which subjects responded to a collection of items simulating the range of paperwork, memos, etc., a principal might be likely to confront; (2) visiting the classes of probationary teachers via standardized kinescope recordings of teachers at work in their classrooms; (3) actually preparing a speech to the PTA; and (4) participating in a small group discussion (pp. 8, 9).

A national sample of 232 principals, 137 men and 95 women, participated in the study. It's interesting to note that of these, only two spent some time each day in classroom teaching as part of their usual principalship duties (p. 64). Each principal participated in a week-long simulation at one of twelve test centers located across the nation, beginning with their arrival on a Sunday afternoon and lasting until the completion of the simulation on Friday afternoon. On their arrival they were briefed regarding features of the simulated situation: the Jefferson Township community, its school system, and the faculty of facilities of Whitman School, the locus of their simulated principalship.

The dimensions identified in this study included two second-order factors related to exchanging information and discussing before acting, and eight first-order factors related to complying with suggestions, analyzing the situation, maintaining relationships, organizing work, responding to outsiders, directing others, preparation for decision, and amount of work accomplished (p. 328). Analysis of the results yielded a large number of observations bearing on principal selection, preparation, and practice. Ten of those discussed by Hemphill, Griffiths, and Frederiksen are summarized below:

1. Aspects of administrative performance most characteristic of women were (a) exchanging information, (b) maintaining organizational relationships, and (c) responding to outsiders.

2. Aspects of administrative performance most related to men were (a) complying with suggestions made by others and (b) analyzing the situation.
3. In evaluating their performance, both teachers and superiors tended to be somewhat negative toward men principals and generally positive toward the women principals.
4. Women, more often than men, tended to ask subordinates for information.
5. Women tended to do more work, discussed problems more with superiors, and used information provided in available background material somewhat more frequently than men.
6. Men made more concluding decisions, followed pre-established structures more often, and took a greater number of terminal actions than women.
7. Superiors' ratings on knowledge of instruction and teaching methods and techniques tended to be higher for women than men.
8. While no extreme differences in mental ability were found, women scored higher in verbal fluency and number facility, and men earned higher scores on tests of reasoning and visualization.
9. Principals who have little administrative experience tended to follow suggestions made by others and to discuss with others before taking final action; those with more experience respond to outsiders, direct the work of others, and analyze the situation.
10. Principals of high general mental ability are characterized more by preparation for decision than by taking terminal action, and tend to also be characterized by higher work output. (pp. 330–44)

The results summarized above do not reflect the complete set of findings reported by Hemphill, Griffiths, and Frederiksen but they do provide insight into some of the dimensions of administrative behavior characterizing the performance of elementary school principals. A taxonomy of administrative performance may be inferred from the two first-order and eight second-order factors identified, and it seems clear that discernible differences occur between men and women principals, and between those of high general mental ability and those of lesser ability.

Gross and Herriott (1965) studied the Executive Professional Leadership (EPL) of 175 elementary school principals in forty large school systems. They defined Executive Professional Leadership "as the effort of an executive of a professionally staffed organization to conform to a definition of his role that stresses his obligation to improve the quality of staff performance" (p. 8). The theoretical framework guiding their inquiry was based on two major assumptions:

First, that administrators of professionally staffed organizations internalize to some degree a staff leadership definition of their role during the period they formally prepare for it, and second, that when they serve as formal leaders of these organizations such administrators encounter certain obstacles that will make it difficult for them to conform to such a definition of their role. (p. 7)

In addition to testing hypotheses derived from their theoretical formulation, Gross and Herriott also tested a number of other ideas commonly thought to influence the performance of principals. These included the sex of the principal, the amount of educational training, salary level, school size, and number of administrative assistants.

Several major findings are reported and discussed by Gross and Herriott in terms of their implications for principals:

1. A positive relationship was found between Executive Professional Leadership and staff morale, the professional performance of teachers, and pupils' learning.
2. The stronger the professional leadership offered by the principal's immediate superior, the greater his/her own EPL.
3. Principals participating in the evaluation of teachers applying to work in their schools demonstrated considerably higher EPL than those who did not.
4. Principals whose administrative superiors strongly endorsed their efforts to improve teaching methods exerted more EPL than those whose superiors did not.
5. The smaller the school enrollment, the greater the principal's EPL.
6. Principals who had the greatest amount of formal education did not provide the greatest professional leadership to their teachers.
7. Several conditions may stand in the way of a principal desiring to serve as the leader of his/her professional staff. Among these are:
   (a) his/her unwillingness to allow teachers to participate in decisions about central school issues;
   (b) his/her stress on distinctions of status in terms of his position in relation to teachers;
   (c) his/her unwillingness or inability to offer social support to his teachers;
   (d) the lack of managerial support teachers receive from the principal; and
   (e) the principal's failure to stand behind his/her teachers when their authority over pupils is questioned.
8. More experienced principals do not generally demonstrate greater EPL than their less experienced colleagues.
9. Neither type nor length of previous teaching experience discriminated among principals as to their EPL.
10. There was no relationship between the strength of a principal's EPL and previous experience as assistant or vice principal.

11. The weakest EPL was exerted by principals appointed to their first principalship at age 45 or older. Those appointed between the ages of 36 and 40 exhibited the strongest EPL; the professional leadership of this last group was only slightly higher than that of principals appointed when they were 30 or younger.

12. Four personal characteristics of principals may have some predictive value in selecting principals who promise a high degree of executive professional leadership:
    (a) a high level of academic achievement in college;
    (b) a high degree of interpersonal skills;
    (c) the motive of service; and
    (d) the commitment of off-duty time to one's job.

13. Sex and marital condition showed no significant relationship to the executive professional leadership of principals. (pp. 150–57)

Several other observations illuminating the school manager-instructional leader dilemma mentioned earlier in this chapter are offered in a concluding note by Gross and Herriott:

> Our findings bear upon a basic controversy over the role of school principals. For years they have been exhorted by their state and national associations and their superiors to make the most of their position; but recently the leadership conception of their role has been challenged as unrealistic and inappropriate. Principals, say the critics, should not engage in efforts to influence teachers' performance but simply should provide routine administrative services; otherwise school administrators invade the teachers' professional autonomy.
>
> On the vexing problem of the respective rights and obligations of principals and teachers, our findings have some bearing. If there is no basis in fact for the widely held assumption that administrators who provide a high degree of professional leadership will have schools that are more "productive" and staffs that enjoy higher morale, it would be a telling argument for abandoning the conception of the principal as one who plays a leadership role. But if there is empirical support for this common assumption, then to confine the principal to routine administrative tasks would be to eliminate a force conducive to improved teaching and learning. The positive relationship between EPL and teachers' morale, their professional performance, and the pupils' learning justifies the staff influence conception of the principalship and strategies to increase the principal's professional leadership. The findings, in short, offer empirical support for a leadership conception of the principal's role, and they undermine a major argument for abandoning it. (p. 151)

Foskett (1967) studies the norms, or rules, surrounding the elementary principalship. His objective was to understand "(1) the way principals view their own position; (2) the perceptions that principals have of the views of other populations within the community; and (3) the actual views of each of the other populations of others" (p. 9).

A forty-five item role norm inventory was administered to twenty-two full-time elementary principals, 367 elementary school teachers, the seven members of the school board, 603 community members, a selected population of parents of elementary school children, and fifty-six community leaders in the school district in which the study was conducted. Each participant responded to each of the statements on the Role Norm Inventory as follows: definitely should, preferably should, may or may not, preferably should not, and definitely should not (p. 13). The inventory measured expectations held for the principal in regard to his/her actions toward teachers, pupils and parents, the profession generally, and the community. The study resulted in these general findings regarding agreement among actors' expectations and accuracy of perceptions of others' expectations:

1. There is a wide range of levels of agreement from one norm to another, and the mean level of agreement is approximately 50 percent.
2. Agreement among principals themselves is only somewhat higher than the amount of agreement among members of the community.
3. Principals and teachers are in highest agreement, principals and the school board and superintendent are in lowest agreement, and lay population and principals are in median agreement.
4. Principals are most accurate in their perceptions of the views of teachers, intermediate in the accuracy of their perceptions of the lay community, and least accurate in their perceptions of the views of the superintendent and school board.
5. Relative to the categories of responses on the Role Norm Inventory, about one-fourth of all responses by principals and each group of others were either "definitely should" or "definitely should not." (pp. 88–93)

Thus, Foskett determined there is a great deal of ambiguity associated with the position of elementary principal. As Foskett concluded:

The evidence suggests that the position is not clearly defined. In part, the principal is identified as an administrator and in part as a member of the teaching staff. Similarly, the principals sometimes see themselves as administrators and sometimes as members of the teaching staff. However, there is a tendency for the principals to see themselves as administrators more frequently than do the several populations of others. This ambiguity is heightened by a low level of agreement among the principals themselves and among others for a number of norms that appear to be critical. (p. 95)

The greatest difference between the principals' viewpoints and those of others concerned expectations about pupils and parents; the least differences concerned expectations about acting toward the community. In Foskett's terms, the principals he studied "appear to identify more with the parents and the lay world in general than with their administrative superiors" (p. 86). Foskett's comment on the similarities and differences in the views of principals and others is instructive:

> If the actual views of the central administration are different from what the principals think they are, the behavior of the central administration may appear capricious and unpredictable. The result can be a sense of insecurity and frustrations or even an antagonistic attitude. When the opposite is the case, as with teachers and to some extent the lay populations, a feeling of mutuality and support may result. If principals can predict teacher behavior and find it consistent with their perceptions they may feel more comfortable in their presence and hence maintain a more positive attitude toward them.
>
> Stated otherwise, to the extent the principals are not aware of the views of the central administration the influence of the central administration will be minimized. The principals may feel they are giving full consideration to the views of the administration but cannot do so if they do not know what the views are. Conversely, the teachers and the lay population may exercise relatively more influence by virtue of the principals being able to perceive their views and hence able to take them into consideration. (p. 93)

Finally, a particularly important result of Foskett's study was the finding that in addition to the mandatory dos and don'ts typically associated with the normative structure shaping a role, the work world of the school principals contains an especially large number of "conditional" rules. As Foskett points out, "roughly 40 percent are either 'preferably should' or 'preferably should not' and 35 percent 'may or may not' " (p. 93). Thus, while principals may appear to have some freedom of choice in acting out their role, depending on the actors and the characteristics of the situation at a particular time or place, certain penalties may accompany this fluidity:

> Whenever a position is interstitial and no well defined guidelines exist for the occupant and for others with whom he interacts, morale may suffer, performance may be less effective, and others may become critical. The data gathered in this study point to such a state of affairs as regards the elementary school principalship. (Foskett, p. 95)

In a rather unique study, Lipham and Francke (1966) investigated the nonverbal behavior of administrators. The theoretical framework employed by these researchers classified nonverbal behavior into three dimensions:

1. Structuring of self: includes such variables as self-maintenance, clothing, physical movement, and posture.
2. Structuring of interaction: includes such variables as greeting of others, placement of others, interaction distance, and interaction termination.
3. Structuring of environment: includes such variables as environmental decor, working order, environmental noise, and the use of status symbols. (p. 103)

Because of the limitations inherent in the taxonomy itself and in the research design they employed, Lipham and Francke decided only to record observations in the categories of structuring of interaction and structuring of environment.

The subjects participating in the study were forty-two principals and eighteen naval executives. The principals were classified into groups of twenty-one promotable and twenty-one nonpromotable principals on the basis of effectiveness ratings by superiors. The eighteen naval executives were classified into two groups of nine innovators and nine noninnovators according to each individual's receptivity to innovation.

Regarding the structuring of interaction, both the promotables and the innovators differed significantly from the nonpromotables and noninnovators. While nonpromotables and noninnovators tended to greet visitors only verbally and to remain behind their desks, the promotables and the innovators tended to greet visitors at their office door or sometimes in an outer office, having on both occasions walked some distance and left the security or comfort of their chair and desk. Both the promotable and the innovator took pains to be courteous and to see that the visitor's hat and coat were properly cared for, and they tended to seat the visitor in a chair either alongside the desk or at the administrator's side of the desk, at a distance of three or four feet. In contrast, the visitors to the nonpromotables and the noninnovators often had to ask where to put their coat and hat, and usually were placed in a seat that was five to seven feet, and sometimes as much as twelve feet, from the person they visited. In addition, promotables and innovators sought to make the visitor comfortable during the interview, and afterwards frequently offered to take the visitor on a tour or to have lunch. The nonpromotables and noninnovators rarely extended any of these courtesies, and generally were less active in escorting the visitor from the interview.

The environments of promotables and innovators also differed from that of the nonpromotables and noninnovators in terms of evidence of personal items in their offices:

The offices of promotable, as contrasted with non-promotable, principals contained numerous personal items. Photographs, paintings, mountings, citations, figurines, and assorted curiosa not generally available in

an office supply store were found in the offices of promotable principals. On the desk of one principal, for example, was a stuffed doll sock,
complete with paper eyeglasses, which bore a striking resemblance to
the principal. (pp. 105–06)

In terms of "working order," promotable principals were as likely to
be characterized by messy desks as by clean ones. However, the innovative naval executives tended to have desks characterized by a state of
disarray. Regarding environmental "noise," nonpromotable principals
tended to be interrupted more often than promotable principals (inter-
com, knocks on the door, telephone, etc.). The status symbols of non-
promotable principals tended to differ from those of promotables. "Name
plates were generally larger, more expensive, and displayed more promi-
nently in the offices of nonpromotables" (p. 106).

Although Lipham and Francke are critical of the limitations of their
study, they stress the importance of these nonverbal indicators and how
important they can potentially be in projecting "images" of self to others.
Given the high degree of face-to-face interaction characterizing the
principalship, the matter of the authenticity of behavior is a serious
problem. The inferences one draws, whether right or wrong, can play a
crucial part in the communicative effectiveness of administrators.

In another study of elementary principals, Goldhammer, Becker,
Withycombe, Doyel, Miller, Morgan, Deloretto, and Aldridge (1971)
focused primarily on principals' perceptions of their problems. A national
sample of 291 elementary principals representative of all states and strati-
fied according to their rural-urban orientation was interviewed. The
interviews were structured around six major categories: (1) school and
society, (2) pupil personnel, (3) instructional program, (4) administrative leadership, (5) organizational texture, and (6) finance and facilities
(p. 48).

The results of the study enabled the researchers to discriminate between two general kinds of principalships, based primarily on conditions
characterizing their schools. They labeled outstanding schools as "beacons
of brilliance" and poor schools as "pot-holes of pestilence."

In the "beacons of brilliance," the principals are charismatic leaders;
they seem to instill enthusiasm in their teachers. The teaching staffs
seemed to be working as teams because their morale was high, their
services extend beyond normal expectations. Teachers and principals,
along with parents, constantly appraise the effectiveness of the schools
in an attempt to devise new programs and strategies to overcome de-
ficiencies. Programs of study are adaptable and emphasis in the instructional program is placed on children's needs. Principals are confident
they can provide relevant, purposive learning without having to lean
on traditional crutches. "Beacons of brilliance" are found in all of the
different types of communities studied, but not in sufficient numbers.

The "pot-holes of pestilence," on the other hand, result from weak leadership and official neglect. The buildings, dirty and in disrepair, are unwholesome environments for learning and child growth. The schools are poorly staffed and equipped. The morale of teachers is low; where control is maintained, fear is one of the essential strategies employed. Instructional programs are traditional, ritualistic, and poorly related to student needs. The schools are characterized by unenthusiasm, squalor, and ineffectiveness. The principals are just serving out their time. (pp. 1, 2)

Further, it developed that the principals of the "beacons of brilliance" shared several important characteristics in common:

1. Most did not intend to become principals.
2. Most expressed a sincere faith in children.
3. They had an ability to work effectively with people and to secure their cooperation.
4. They were aggressive in securing recognition of the needs of their schools.
5. They were enthusiastic as principals and accepted their responsibilities as a mission rather than as a job.
6. They were committed to education and could distinguish between long-term and short-term educational goals.
7. They were adaptable.
8. They were able strategists. (pp. 2, 3)

Finally, the results of the study yielded several general observations regarding the elementary principalship:

1. Teachers, central office personnel, and parents each exert some influence in shaping the role.
2. Principals feel they are viewed by superiors and citizens as subprofessionals rather than as administrators with full professional status and prerogatives.
3. Principals increasingly feel isolated from involvement in group decision-making affecting their leadership and operating patterns in their schools.
4. Principals feel their once close association with the teaching staff has been compromised by growing teacher militancy; should they represent the board or the teachers?
5. They are concerned about the imbalance of managerial and educational responsibilities inherent in their position.
6. Many principals admit they do not have the necessary skills to develop adequate supervisory programs within their buildings.
7. Principals say the needs of the elementary school are often ignored in favor of the secondary school. (pp. 4-6)

Principals indicated that the largest number of problems they experienced concerned the instructional program (35%) and finances and facilities (21%). The responses in the other major problem categories were: school and society (14%); pupil personnel (14%); administrative leadership (8%); and organizational texture (8%) (pp. 66–67).

Regarding foreseeable problems associated with the elementary principalship, respondents in the study expressed a range of concerns:

We must become more competent in evaluating how effectively we are doing what we are doing. The public needs and wants to know how effective our program is for their children. They are questioning what we do and why we are doing it. We need to make decisions on the basis of facts rather than a subjective-type judgment. (p. 147)

Inservice programs for principals and teachers must change. They are too vague and not specifically helpful. There is no way to evaluate the effect of these programs. Most of it is busy work. (p. 148)

The role of the teachers' union will have tremendous effects upon the school. The role of the principal will become more highly structured and I will have to consult teacher union representatives rather than the teachers directly. For example, if a teacher has a grievance against the principal in a decision which he has made, during a conference she may bring a union representative with her. This requires a drastic change in operating procedures on the part of the principal. It seems that the principalship is becoming more of a pivotal position, and by that I mean, this position has pressures from all sides, from the community, from the board, from teachers, and from the students; and I find myself in the middle. (p. 152)

Because of unionization, the principal will become more of a staff officer for the superintendent. The superintendent will need his support because of the insecurities of the superintendency. As a result, the principal will become a greater part of the administrative team. (p. 162)

It is difficult for the principal to keep informed and to know how to bring about change. Part of the problem may be our own laziness or lack of knowledge. Maybe we don't create the right climate for change. Maybe we don't know how to work well with teachers. (p. 154)

The principal of the future will be much less responsible for the evaluation of instructional staff but will have to focus more upon the facilitation and coordination of staff. Principals must learn to identify the needs of teachers in order to provide more relevant inservice activities aimed at promoting teacher growth and effectiveness. (p. 157)

If the principal ever identifies what his role is going to be, which is almost impossible to identify at this time, there will truly occur a tremendous change in the character of elementary schools. Until this happens, however, the ambiguity of the entire situation will continue and elementary education will continue to exist largely in a state of flux and apprehension. (p. 159)

As reflected in the results of this study, the elementary school principalship is in a state of confusion. Principals find themselves caught in the middle of multiple and often conflicting and unclear expectations from superiors, teachers, and the community their schools serve. Many of the observations by Goldhammer et al. parallel and serve to reinforce the findings reported by Gross and Herriott (1965) and Foskett (1967). Role expectations are not clear and principals find themselves caught in the dilemma of wanting to be effective instructional leaders but find themselves beleaguered by the press of routine administration and by their own lack of knowledge and skill in these areas.

Wolcott (1973), in his ethnographic investigation of one elementary school principal, highlights in greater detail many of the trials and tribulations associated with the principalship. While it is impossible to include here the depth and full range of detail described by Wolcott, those excerpts that follow provide a useful glimpse into the everyday work of the elementary principal. As the editors say, however, his work is a case study of "a comfortable suburban elementary school in a lower-middle to middle class, predominantly white, American community. It is not intended to be a study of a wholly typical elementary school because there is no such thing" (p. viii).

The study itself describes the principal as person, the school and community, the formal and informal encounters that comprise the bulk of the principal's daily life, the annual cycle of the principalship, the socialization of the principal and his socialization of the teachers in his school, and the impressions held of the principal by the school secretary, the superintendent, pupils, teachers, and parents. Selected segments of Wolcott's analysis of the rich data associated with the principal's (Ed Bell's) formal encounters during the school day exemplify the diverse and continuous series of personal interactions characterizing this principal's work day:

> The greatest part of a principal's time is spent in an almost endless series of encounters, from the moment he arrives at school until the moment he leaves. Most of these encounters are face-to-face, tending to keep the principalship a highly personal role. Electronic devices, including not only the telephone but the "intercom" systems widely prevalent in public schools, eliminate the face-to-face aspect of some encounters (about 10 percent of Ed's total time at school was spent in talking on the telephone or the intercom), but even these transactions tend to be held between persons frequently in face-to-face encounters at other times during the day. (p. 88)

Wolcott found at least three categories of formal face-to-face encounters warranted by his observations: "prearranged meetings; deliberate but not prearranged meetings; and casual or chance encounters" (p. 88). Ed Bell spent almost one-fourth of his day in prearranged meetings. These encounters include parent conferences, faculty meetings, central office meetings, or other meetings with faculty or students that are prearranged, sometimes formally and at other times only informally.

Another fourth of Ed Bell's day was spent in what Wolcott terms "deliberate but not prearranged" encounters. Deliberately stopping a teacher in the hall or walking to a teacher's class to discuss an item of business are examples. Another example of such a deliberate but not prearranged meeting might be a parent dropping in to school to get "a moment" of the principal's time; another might be the talk he has with a pupil sent to his office by a teacher for misbehavior.

Finally, another 15 percent of Ed's day was spent in what Wolcott called "casual" or "chance" encounters. These include all the face-to-face interactions that Ed Bell had during the school day, but which could not be classified as either prearranged or deliberate but not prearranged meetings (p. 90). Ed spent much of the remainder of his time alone:

> Ed's gregarious nature probably resulted in his spending less time alone, particularly alone at work in his office, than many principals. Some of his teachers commented explicitly that Ed was not an "office sitter" like some principals they knew. The average amount of time recorded in which he was alone and stationary was 15 percent. A separate category for the time he spent alone as a consequence of going from one place to another, whether walking from his office to the teachers' room or driving from school to the bank or to a meeting across town, accounted for another 9 percent of his average day. (p. 90)

A summary of those with whom Ed Bell interacted, and the percentage of total time spent with each category of persons, is noted below:

teachers, individually and collectively	22.1%
other adult school personnel	29.3%
pupils, singly and in groups	19.3%
other principals	7.8%
central office personnel	6.3%
parents and other adults in the community	9.8%
others	5.5%
	100.1% (p. 92)

Ed Bell, then, spent much of his time (about 65%) in face-to-face interaction with teachers, parents, central office staff and others, and much of his day was given over to formal meetings of one kind or another.[1]

---

1. Ellett, Pool, and Hill (1974) have also found that principals tend to spend the majority of their time in the pupil and staff personnel areas, and spend minimal amounts of time during a work week in activities related to curriculum and instruction.

Wolcott comments on the manifest and latent functions of many of these meetings, and calls attention to how their real purposes might differ substantially from their stated purpose:

> The manifest function of school meetings was to facilitate communication and to make collective decisions . . . these ideal functions were not accomplished to any great extent. Even in parent meetings, where the formal school organization exerted little control and the schoolman had to proceed with utmost patience and tact, communication tended to be one-way. Participants were generally called upon to concur with decisions already made rather than engage in significant decision-making of their own. Within the formal confines of the educator group, communication was almost exclusively unilateral, decisions more often revealed than reached. . . . the principals devoted one entire meeting to assuring that a document they had been preparing for weeks would not communicate any controversial information upward within the administrative hierarchy.
>
> The latent functions of meetings, especially those within the educator subculture, accomplished rather different purposes. First, they served to validate role—to give visible evidence of being engaged with the "problems and issues" of schooling. Secondly, and more importantly, they served to validate existing status hierarchies and to provide a continuing process for reviewing each person's position in those hierarchies. What actually transpired at any of those meetings was never as important as the underlying issue of who could call a meeting for what purposes, who felt obligated to attend, and what kind of priority was adequate for an excuse. (pp. 121–22)

In addition to describing the substance of these formal encounters and the character of the face-to-face interaction comprising the larger portion of Ed Bell's time, Wolcott provides a rich view of the diverse range of activities comprising this principal's "daily routine." Although all of the descriptive detail recorded by Wolcott cannot be included here, some of the activities can be listed:

Receiving Requests and Handling Problems

    Listening to the school cook's milk shortage problem
    Covering a teacher's class until the substitute arrives
    Answering the phone (when no one else could)
    Conversations with concerned parents
    Handling staff requests of all kinds
    Monitoring school accidents and children's injuries
    Sorting and responding to mail and other written messages
    Disciplining pupils
    Handling lunchroom problems
    Problems with stealing, defacing school property

Investigating fights among students
Monitoring student "business" activities
Requests for room transfers

Orienting and Greeting

Keeping staff informed of daily activities
Announcing schedule changes to parents and staff
Showing newcomers "the ropes"; employees and others
Orienting new pupils and parents
Conferring with and greeting supervisors and other visitors

Taking Care of the Building

Seeing that everything is "working" properly
Being "keeper of the keys"; building and special rooms
Keeping the building clean; supervise janitors
Inspecting physical plant conditions; constantly (pp. 123–74)

While these are certainly not all of the issues and activities comprising
the principal's activities, they reflect the generally diverse set of responsibilities that Ed Bell, and we suspect most principals, must deal with on
the job. And Wolcott, in commenting on them, suggests that:

A principal who cannot cope effectively with the range of strangely
diversified demands described here would be ill-suited to the principalship. Some principals become meticulous about and obsessed with the
details of running a school. Ed's response was to try to elude some detail on the assumption that pressing problems would catch up with him
eventually. (p. 177)

We suspect this is not an uncommon approach to the principalship.

In a highly oversimplified statement, but one that principals can identify
with, one might say the job's a matter of dealing with "people and their
problems." While this is certainly not the whole of it, this is largely what
Ed Bell did. Remember, he spent about 65 percent of his day in face-to-
face encounters with a wide range of people, dealing with problems that
run the gamut from solving the milk shortage to conferring with parents
about a pupil's behavior or discussing an instructional problem with a
teacher or supervisor. Wolcott nicely captures the essence of the principalship for Ed Bell:

The consequence of Ed's problem-centered orientation brought his
actual behavior into harmony with the expectations of those about him.
It also provided him with a practical goal against which he could
personally measure his administrative success. This goal was the im-

mediate containment of any and every actual and anticipated problem that might possibly disrupt the "smooth" operation of the school. More than this, he also attempted to give at least token recognition to virtually every event, comment, or complaint that came to his attention. Unable to draw on any special body of knowledge or set of unique skills to a position in which he had to perform adequately but wished to perform exceedingly well, Ed brought instead a conscious, almost tangible quality of super-dedication to try to do anything for everybody. He remained ever on-call and available for action, as evidenced by long hours spent at school each day, numerous responsibilities and assignments accepted, new programs tacitly encouraged, and an endless procession of new staff, pupils, parents, and outsiders inducted patiently into the operation of the school. Remote as these functions may be from a ritual quest for a more professional role, they nonetheless present a job description of infinite duration that render service to the institution and provide a man some personal sense of having done a day's work. For whether Ed was engaged in a twelve-second encounter with a hurt thumb, a twelve-minute search for a record player for a substitute teacher, or a twelve-day administrator's workshop with his colleagues attempting to define an ideal elementary school, his behavior seemed to be guided by an unwritten rule that is at once the raison d'etre for the role of the elementary school principal and the perfect obstacle to ever achieving a radical change in that role: every problem is important. (p. 316)

In 1976, Gross and Trask completed analysis of data collected as part of the National Principalship Study (Gross and Herriott, 1965), specifically focusing on the sex factor and the management of schools. The four major objectives were to: "(1) examine the impact of the sex factor on important career decisions of principals; (2) determine if the sex factor influenced their orientations and reactions to work; (3) ascertain if men and women principals perform their roles differently; and (4) examine whether the functioning and productivity of their organizations were related to the principals' sex" (pp. 1–2).

In addition to examining relationships among demographic, professional career, and role variables, Gross and Trask were also concerned with larger issues of organizational performance. Toward understanding the larger impact that sex of the principal might have on school participants, five major questions were posed:

1. Would teachers perform in accord with professional standards with greater frequency in schools administered by women than in those managed by men?
2. Do schools administered by women surpass those managed by men in terms of the academic performance of pupils?
3. Is sex of principals related to the morale of their teachers?
4. Do women principals worry less than men about their work?

5. Is the occupational aspiration level of men principals higher than that of women principals? (pp. 172–216)

The major findings of Gross and Trask's study are:

1. The sex factor does influence the timing, context, and motivation of the career decisions of elementary principals, and it does bear upon the nature and amount of educational experience brought to the principalship.

2. The women principals' occupational aspiration level was lower than that of their male counterparts, and the women tended to worry less about their work than the men.

3. While no sex differences were found regarding the importance principals placed on pupils' academic performance or a school's ability to maintain pupil discipline, women did place a greater emphasis than men on three criteria for evaluating a school: its concern with individual differences among its pupils, the social and emotional development of its pupils, and its efforts to help "deviant" pupils.

4. In evaluating teachers, women placed more emphasis than men on the technical skills of teachers and on teachers' fulfillment of their organizational responsibilities.

5. While there were no differences between men and women regarding the importance attached to supervising instruction, women on the average evaluated their performance more highly and derived more satisfaction from supervising instruction, than did men.

6. Both men and women principals did not differ substantially in the importance they assigned to the management of routine administrative affairs, but men derived more satisfaction from this component of their work than did the women principals.

7. No sex differences were found for the sample regarding: support of teachers in situations involving teacher-pupil conflict, stress placed on teachers offering maximum service to pupils, social distance from teachers in school, and involvement of parents in school affairs.

8. The professional performance of teachers and pupils learning were higher on the average in the schools administered by women than by men, but staff morale was not associated with the gender of the principal. (pp. 217–19)

These findings are discussed by Gross and Trask in terms of their implications for the selection and assignment of elementary principals. They note the common practice in many school districts of giving preference to men in selecting principals, and they argue that the data reported in their study undermine and strongly challenge the validity of the three assumptions on which this practice is often based:

1. Schools with men principals outperform those in which women serve as their administrators.
2. The elementary principalship should be reserved for men in order to meet the need of men teachers for occupational advancement and to make public education a more attractive vocational area for men.
3. Teachers, whether male or female, generally prefer to work in a school administered by a male rather than a female principal. (pp. 219–20).

Gross and Trask respond to these three arguments by offering the following analysis of the import of their study:

> In short, our findings undercut the arguments generally used to support the male preference policy in selecting elementary school principals. They also imply that one of its unanticipated and unrecognized educational consequences has been that the learning of pupils and the quality of performance of teachers has been adversely affected in many school districts throughout the nation. (p. 220)

In concluding their report, however, Gross and Trask make a special point of emphasizing that their "findings have reference to *group*, not *individual*, differences between men and women in the principalship" (pp. 226–27). In other words, to conclude that women *invariably* outstrip men, regarding certain aspects of the principalship, would be a serious misunderstanding and misinterpretation of their findings. Gross and Trask's results are concerned with the performance of men and women principals, *on the average*.

SOME CONCLUSIONS

These studies suggest the principalship is a highly ambiguous role characterized by much face-to-face interaction with diverse others having multiple and often conflicting expectations for what principals should do on the job. Men and women principals themselves are not clear, as a group, regarding their role priorities. While many seem to aspire to enacting a conception of themselves as instructional leaders, relatively few appear satisfied that they are performing well in this area, and many recognize they lack the skill and knowledge needed to be effective in this domain. Principals generally complain that they are overburdened with the many administrative and clerical details involved in running a school, but few seem to have found any viable way to free themselves of these demands. The ideal state, which many principals seem to long for but are not frequently able to achieve, is captured in Joseph Featherstone's (1970) description of what exemplary principals in England see as their primary role:

They see themselves first and foremost as supporters and catalysts for the continued growth of their teaching staff. Many teach classes; those who can't, spend much of their day working in classrooms with teachers and children. They were chosen, among other things, for their ability to provide good examples of ways of working with children, for their talent in leading a teaching staff, not administering a plant. (p. 305)

While such a concept seems worthy, and in fact may be achievable by some individuals in specific school environments, it is not likely that the average American school administrator will achieve this state in the foreseeable future unless some major changes occur in the school environment. While the following recommendations of the Senate Select Committee on Equal Educational Opportunity (1970) are not the complete answer, they attempt to grapple with several obstacles that stand in the way of realizing this ideal in the American school principalship:

First, the school principal should be unburdened from as many of his present administrative burdens as possible and given greater autonomy and responsibility for the improvement of instruction and other activities involving students within the school. . . .

Second, in exercising these responsibilities, principals should consult fully and directly with parent-citizen committees. . . .

Third, in order to relieve the school principal from his present administrative burdens, he should have the resources to select a school administrator or manager to fill a position with the rank of assistant principal. . . .

Fourth, states and local communities should review the criteria under which principals are selected. More attention should be paid to those essential traits which refine a principal's capacity for educational leadership. . . .

Fifth, consideration should also be given by states and school districts to the publication of an annual evaluation of school performance. . . . (p. 306)

The Senate Select Committee clearly believes that providing instructional leadership is the primary responsibility of the school principal:

In many ways the school principal is the most important and influential individual in any school. He is the person responsible for all of the activities that occur in and around the school building. It is his leadership that sets the tone of the school, the climate for learning, the level of professionalism and morale of teachers and the degree of concern for what students may or may not become. He is the main link between the school and the community and the way he performs in that capacity largely determines the attitudes of students and parents about the school. If a school is a vibrant, innovative, child-centered place; if it has a reputation for excellence in teaching; if students are performing to the best of their ability one can almost always point to the principal's leadership as the key to success. (p. 305)

While this conception of the principalship dominates the literature on schools and principals, it is one infrequently borne out in practice. Principals and schools like those described in the preceding passages are the exception, not the rule. Why this is so seems fairly easy to understand given the context in which most school principals find themselves functioning. A recent account of public school administration by March (1978) describes some of the conditions prevailing in American schools:

Educational administration is hierarchical. School systems use conventional bureaucratic forms of organization with standard ideas of authority, administration, and control. Personal prestige and perquisites are associated with position in the hierarchy and (within levels) by size of the administrative unit (school or district) (Austin and Brown, 1970). Individuals are presumed to rise in administrative ranks on the basis of relatively impersonal criteria of merit (National Association of Elementary School Principals hereafter cited as NAESP, 1970; Department of Elementary School Principals hereinafter cited as DESP, 1968; Knezevich, 1971). Leaders are fired if the organization does poorly.

Educational administration is small in size and simple in structure. Compared with other major bureaucratic institutions, schools devote a relatively small part of their resources to administrative expenses (School Management, 1974). The hierarchy is typically quite flat and (except in a few conspicuous cases) uncomplicated (Freeman and Hannan, 1975). The degree of specialization within administration is modest.

Educational administration is only loosely coupled to educational activities in the classroom (Weick, 1976; Meyer and Rowan, 1977; March and Olsen, 1976; Peterson, 1976). School administration is primarily the management of accounts about people. These include financial accounts, pupil progress accounts, and personnel accounts. Account management is authoritarian, standardized, and centralized (Cross, 1971). The accounts are important for the presentation and social justification of the school system; they are less important for the classroom process of schooling.

The time of an educational administrator is subjectively misallocated. Educational administration report that they do not spend time the way they should (DESP, 1968). In particular, they see themselves as spending too much time in clerical work, routine administration, report writing, and attending meetings called by others; they report too little time spent on educational leadership, general planning, supervision, and curriculum development. In general, they believe they do a better job in those areas in which they spend their time (e.g. financial management, plant management, personnel) than they do in those areas in which they think they should spend their time (American Association of School Administrators, 1952; Gross and Herriott, 1965). (pp. 223–25)

School principals are, for the most part, managers; their work environment gives most of them little choice in this matter. While this situation does not prevent a few committed and talented individuals from achieving excellence as instructional leaders, most principals find themselves frustrated by their inability (be it skill, knowledge, or time allocation) to move beyond the management functions inherent in the role of principal as it has evolved during the past hundred years. To the extent that this work environment remains unchanged—the effects of declining school enrollments coupled with increasing bureaucratization and formalization of work roles will exacerbate and not ameliorate those conditions—principals will experience increasing difficulty in realizing the instructional leadership conception of the principalship.

Perhaps, as Button (1966) suggests has occurred with some regularity in the past, a new "doctrine" of educational administration will emerge to replace the lingering but perhaps inappropriate ideal of the "principal teacher." Although a new conception of the principalship may be just around the corner, we don't claim that the eight principals we've studied represent this new doctrine, but they may well be forerunners of a "new" kind of principalship (Wayson, 1971), perhaps a synthesis of the applied philosopher, school manager, and behavioral scientist.

With the exception of Wolcott's study, the research reviewed in this chapter has focused on a broad view of the school principalship. The next several chapters become quite specific and, in a way, narrow. Their concern is with eight individuals and how they see their job.

This chapter (with the exception of Wolcott's study) and the previous one have focused on the school principalship broadly viewed. Such a view is appropriate and essential to the development both of a sense of history concerning the evolution of the principalship and of an empirical knowledge base concerning the structure and function of that role. What is missing from this discussion, and dictated by the nature of the inquiry on which it was based, is a feel for the individual. That is, both of the preceding chapters spoke, in the main, to the role and function of some rather anonymous group of job-holders called school principals. They did not address (with the exception noted) questions that involve the human and seemingly idiosyncratic part of the enterprise—being a school principal, in particular being one who has been judged out of the ordinary.

In some way, then, the next several chapters start to fill in that gap. Rather than dealing with social phenomena that are broad and general, their content is more narrow and specific. Their concern is with eight individuals and how they see their job. They provide some deeper insights into the behavior of principals and, thus, the "behavior" of schools.

4

The Organizer: A Whirling
Dervish of a Problem Solver

40   2 CHILDREN

Talking with Joan about her work as principal of an urban fringe-area
elementary school is an exciting experience. It is one that we wish many
more people than ourselves could have. She speaks quickly, pausing every
so often to think, and then rushes on with her ideas. She is not hesitant
to relate her successes and, in a fascinating way, her intellectual excitement with her failures leaves the listener wrapped up in her story. We
were left somewhat in awe of both the volume and high tempo of her
activity level. Not the least reason for our awe was our wonderment at
where Joan, a forty-year-old mother of two children, a principal who
works a twelve to fourteen hour day (she is also a doctoral student), gets
her energy. She really doesn't know either. All that she knows is that she
has it.

> You know, I don't stop all day. I work at a pace that is very fast, but
> I don't ask other people to do that. My energy level is enormous. When
> I leave school and I think I've left something unfinished, as happened
> today, my mind just doesn't focus on new things.

Her mind did focus on the interview, however, and she provided a
large volume of information about her style, her values, and her working
hypotheses about engaging the diverse public with whom she must deal
as she plays out her role as principal. The theme that seems to guide
Joan's personal life and the manner in which she conceives of a school—
thus her role—are the same. This theme is that one makes the most out
of life by learning how to solve problems as they occur. Joan believes
that schools, particularly the elementary schools, provide an excellent
opportunity for youngsters to learn good problem-solving skills. This
emphasis doesn't deny the importance of learning the traditional skills. It
simply puts the school program in a different frame of reference, one
that, from her point of view, is more relevant to what life is all about.
But it wasn't always that way. Joan had been trained in a rather tradi-

tional teacher education school and had first gone to work in a school system that was noted, likewise, for being traditional. However:

> About ten years ago, I knew I had started to change. Maybe one of the things that started it all was an experience I had at Jackson School. I had forty-seven kids in the sixth grade with desks that were bolted to the floor. You couldn't move a muscle in the room. I asked the custodian if he'd please remove the last two rows of desks, but he refused to do so because he said that there wouldn't be a seat for every kid. I said we could live with that but he still wouldn't do it. We didn't even have a permanent principal to whom I could appeal, so I was totally frustrated. It was then that I realized that I wanted very different things for kids than what was expected of them at that point. I expected kids to be thinkers. I trusted kids and I wanted them to be able to walk around the room and do different things.

The story continues and has an interesting ending, which is really only a beginning. Joan was frustrated at Jackson Elementary. The way out of her frustration came unexpectedly from a local university which was starting a special program to train urban teachers. She was asked if she would like to join the staff as a supervisor. She did and her horizons started to expand as she came in contact, collegially, with new and exciting people.

> I was really impressed. I sat in awe most of the time. I was really learning lots of things and not knowing I had learned them because I couldn't put them into practice right away. But I knew I liked what I heard.

But, nirvana came crashing down. The colleagues whom Joan found most exciting took other positions and the situation became less attractive for her. Again, though, her dissatisfaction and frustration were alleviated from an unexpected source. The same college professor who became principal at the elementary school of which Paul (Chapter IX) is now the administrator asked Joan if she would like to join his faculty. Again, she did, thus setting in motion, unwittingly, the circumstances in which she and Paul would become co-assistant principals and which would ultimately lead to her assuming a principalship of her own. Lest it be misunderstood, though Joan has changed positions several times, these shifts have not been made with the primary motivation to advance to a higher organizational position with a higher salary.[1] She seems, rather, to be motivated to change positions by a desire for new and different learning experiences. Time and again during our interview, for example, she talked about learning new

---

1. As a matter of fact, at this writing, she has applied for a university position as a coordinator of administrative field training that would entail a sizable reduction in pay.

things, about what certain people had taught her and about what she had learned from one or another set of circumstances, including those that she classified as unsatisfactory. Joan is a consciously insatiable learner.

After having served two years as an assistant principal, Joan was offered a principalship. The school, as we noted previously, was in a fringe neighborhood that had not stabilized with regard to its racial balance. Blacks were moving into the area in increasing numbers and whites were moving out. It wasn't a crisis situation, but the school, according to Joan, was in a state of turmoil.

> The parents were revolting; the kids were revolting; and the teachers were all upset. I spent the whole summer meeting individually with parents, teachers, and as many others who were interested in the school as I could. I wanted to know how they saw the problem, how they conceived the school, and what they were looking for. What I found out was this: teachers avoided other teachers not because they didn't like them but because they didn't know them. They never came out of their rooms and didn't know what anybody else was doing. They were terribly threatened by parents coming into the school. At the same time, the parents were incredibly threatened by the teachers. The kids hated school and I didn't know whether they got it from their parents or because they were so negatively reinforced while they were there. It was a mess!

The way in which Joan described the school and her initial activities speak quite graphically to how she conceives a school and the role of principal. The school doesn't exist only in a building in which there are teachers, it exists also in the minds and homes of the parents and the students. Its character exists in the relationships the teachers hold toward each other and in the relationships that are held among parents, teachers, and students. One gets the feeling, indeed, that the building is almost irrelevant to Joan's concept of a school. What's important is the character of the relationships that obtain within its walls and between it and the outside community.

Joan's high work tempo style and problem-solving thrust also come through in her comments about her initial activities as principal. She didn't wait until the end of August to go to work on the school, but instead spent the whole summer talking with people. She doesn't wait for problems to come to her. Rather, she seeks them out. She knew the school had problems, but wanted to get the facts for herself and diagnose the situation in her own way.

Interestingly, while Joan was telling about her early activities as principal, she displayed no feelings of ambiguity concerning her role. For Joan the issue was simple: there were organizational and educational problems to be solved and one might just as well be about solving them because they weren't going to solve themselves. If issues of role or role conflict arose they would be dealt with like any other problem; get the facts, look for alternatives, and act. Always the theme for Joan is problem solving and action. But first get organized, get the facts.

A more abstract way of describing Joan in her role as principal is that she is almost a pure practitioner-empiricist. Her strength seems not to rest with her ability to conceptualize, a priori, her role and her school as an organic social system. Indeed, when confronted with questions that focus on the way she conceptualizes things, she appears a little uncomfortable, feeling more at home with a problematic situation to which she can apply her energy. This does not mean, of course, that the way she acts is not guided by some sort of philosophical or theoretical set. It clearly is, but that set seems to derive from the nature of the data she collects and not some preconceived notion of what ought to be. She clearly is a situationalist, organizing her actions and program proposals to the demands of the here and now, and not to some grandiose educational plan for the future. Instances of this style were plentiful, many of them stemming from her own fact-gathering efforts of that first summer. For example, relative to the teachers:

> The place was so uptight. No one talked with anyone else. So I spent the whole first year knowing that what I was going to do was work on plain old human relationships. I taught a lot that first year with other teachers. I simply wanted to show people that there were other techniques, that there were other relationships that one could build with kids without holding the reins so tightly that they couldn't get up from their seats to move around.

If the problem, then, was that teachers weren't talking to each other, one solution was to model different behavior, and start talking. But not talk for talk's sake; and, this is where Joan's values come in. Although the desks weren't nailed to the floor as they were at the school she taught in several years before, she saw the teachers dealing with their classes as if the chairs were indeed nailed down. So, she worked and taught with them in an effort to induce some change in teaching styles, and to open up the communications system. In the process, Joan gained credibility among her staff because they became aware that she could not only manage the school, but also function very effectively as a classroom teacher.

An additional clue concerning how Joan sees herself slipped in almost unnoticed in her comment above. That is, she said that she taught a lot with "other teachers." This comment ultimately tells the story about Joan and what she is all about. She is basically a teacher, and it's through teaching, whether with youngsters or adults, that most of her personal and professional satisfaction derives.

Another example of Joan's problem-solving thrust, this time with the faculty as a group, becomes clear as she went to work on the learning environment of the school:

We all got together and listed all the kinds of problems that stopped kids from working in a really acceptable learning environment. We then brainstormed the different kinds of ways we could alleviate those problems. What we decided was really important was to make problem-solving skills an integral part of the instructional program. If we didn't help kids learn how to problem-solve there were lots of things they wouldn't be able to do.

And, by problem solving, Joan meant:

To start with, just to be able to identify the problem. What we first found out was that kids would be arguing and they wouldn't even know what they were arguing about. So we helped the kids define their problems. We helped them to learn to separate problems from symptoms and now most kids are really fantastic at that. Then we sat down and talked with them about all the things that come into play with their problems and all the solutions. But we never told a kid which way to solve a problem.

It's difficult to hold Joan to a specific point. She races on, but in the process she reveals more about those things she holds to be of value. More importantly, perhaps it seems clear that there is little incongruency, if any, between her values and her behavior. What she says she believes in, she implements or tries to implement. And she tries to implement, it appears, not by exhorting or making new policy, but by engaging with other people—on a one-to-one basis or in groups—and teaching, always teaching.

The style of teaching in which Joan engages is not the stereotypical classroom variety. It is here-and-now problem oriented, and the teaching methodology she employs gets people working together on the problem. Her school, in a way, is an experiential learning laboratory. Thus, sensing a need to change the character of the school learning environment, she did not promulgate a new policy or develop a lofty goal statement. Rather, working collaboratively with the faculty, she was able to help them identify, own, and commit energy to an issue that affected their lives every day—the very humanity of their school.

One of the things that Joan quickly found out about the nature of the humanity of her school was that the primary mode of dealing with behavioral problems of the youngsters was a punitive one. The school had an aura of negativism. It was cyclical in nature, usually starting at the beginning of each week. What seemed to occur was that numbers of youngsters would arrive at school on Monday morning, upset and sometimes angry. Their behavior in their classes would become disruptive, and teachers' dominant mode of dealing with them was one of negative reinforcement—punishment. The teachers and students became aggravated. Teachers didn't teach and students didn't learn. The result was a disrupted school at the beginning of each week, not a pleasant prospect to confront for principal, teachers, youngsters, and ultimately, parents. The framework within which Joan chose to view this problem provides additional insight into her concept of the role of the principal. A stance that she could have taken, for which no one would fault her, would have been to view each problem that developed as an independent, unrelated matter. This stance would lead to individualized action—dealing with the child, and with the teachers, or both. Hopefully, the problem would be solved for the moment, at least, and the process would be repeated at the next eruption.

Joan chose not to take this point of view that called for isolated remedies. Rather, her position was that, although it was clear that the problems were caused by individual actions and reactions, the ultimate consequences of it all were borne by the school as an organization. She said:

> If *we* (i.e., the school) didn't take care of those problems, then the teachers would have to keep on dealing with them and the result would be a disruption of the whole instructional atmosphere.

It is extremely important to note that the *we* referred to in this statement did not refer to the transfer of behavioral problems out of the teacher's hands and into those of the principal, which would have meant maintaining the individual focus in the principal's office instead of the classroom. The meaning of *we*, then, was the school as a system that had an identity of its own that included but was not the sum of the identities of all the individuals involved. The conceptual import of this for the situation Joan described is that human problems that impact and affect an organization as a system demand resolutions that are organizationally based, and not resolutions that deal with the problems as isolated phenomena.

In this case, the steps taken to work out the problem of behavioral disruptions in the classroom took the form of a structural change that had two different but related facets. Joan's words describe best the action that was taken:

> First, we instituted what we call a parent "drop-in" time two days a week and at different times so that parents who couldn't work it in one hour might be able to at another. We wanted them to feel free to come in and talk and not even necessarily about kids, but anything. We also asked them about problems that may have occurred over the weekend and if they would take the initiative to tell us about this so we could be prepared to deal with them. This has been pretty successful.
>
> The other thing we did was to make the first hour of each day available for any kids who wanted to come down to the office and check in with us to talk a bit. Sometimes a kid will say, "I had a

problem with so and so and I think it's really going to be a bad scene today." Other times they will say, "It worked out, everything's okay, the problem's over." We try and bring the kids together and talk about problems. Sometimes all they want is somebody to listen while they talk. We don't have any hard data about how this is working. But, we do know that teachers feel a lot better.

Patterns in Joan's style, then, repeat themselves. Recall that the first thing she did upon her appointment as principal was to start by reaching out to the community, even before school started. She did this because she needed information and wanted to establish healthy relationships with parents. When another situation developed that seemed to require help from the community, she was back there again, reaching out both to get information and build relationships. The recurrent emphasis on "problems" is also there. And, lest the reader get the wrong impression, we hasten to add that Joan is not a "down in the mouth" problem-burdened person. To meet her results in precisely the opposite picture—an image of a person who looks for and sees opportunities for growth and learning in practically all *problematic* situations with which she is presented. One might say, indeed, that her orientation is not to focus on problems qua problems but to concern herself most centrally with the process of problem solving; of organizing facts and resources in a way that gets the problem identified and eventually solved. We came to think of Joan as "The Organizer."

Joan's comments relative to dealing with disruption in classrooms offer another form of insight into the way she sees the role of principal. At issue is her willingness to create new organizational structures for problem resolution, her willingness to step outside the regularities (Sarason, 1971) of school life in order to fit solutions to the demands of the problems. For example, the curricular pattern of schools does not typically provide for the first hour of the day being devoted to youngsters who have personal things they want to talk about. In fact, many principals would negate the idea because "it isn't done" or "there is no precedent for this" or, "the children should be in the classroom." Concern for what is or isn't done, or for whether or not there is a precedent to a particular action seems not to be central to Joan's thinking. What does appear to be central in her thinking is the idea of organizing the resources of the school and community to do things. If these "things" require changing accepted routines and patterns of structure and interaction—well, they'll have to be changed, because that's what has to be done.

But things don't happen overnight and Joan is the first to acknowledge the slowness of change. Much as she would like changes to occur "yesterday" she is a realist with regard to the time it takes to induce meaningful normative changes in a school. In speaking about the success of the daily hour devoted to kids who have things on their minds, she said:

We are talking about three years of training when you've been working with kids, teachers, and parents. We've tried to help kids understand that there are acceptable ways of dealing with problems at school and ways that are unacceptable. And we've tried to help parents learn to problem-solve with their children. Sometimes the kids have even helped their parents learn skills. We hear sometimes of kids taking their parents over to other parents to see if they could bridge some gap that's developed between them. But it all takes time. It's taken three years, but in that time the idea has become a really important part of our school.

The teachers also had to be part of the problem as well as part of the solution, for both common wisdom and the results of research clearly indicate that programs in schools don't succeed unless the teachers are involved and lend their support. To gain support from teachers she involves them in their own learning. Joan's position is clear as it applies to the problem of disruptive behavior in the classroom:

I never try to hold a conference with a child who has had a conflict with an adult unless the adult is present. There are two reasons for this. First, I don't think you can solve the problem without the person being there. Second, when the teacher is there, it's an inservice session for that teacher on problem solving. The focus is on building relationships. Kids can learn to build relationships with teachers and teachers with kids if they solve problems together and are open with each other and don't behave impulsively. For example, a teacher grabbed a kid who appeared to be misbehaving. The kid said, "You grabbed me and you didn't even ask me first." And the teacher said, "Yes, you're right. I had other problems on my mind. I had no right to do that." And we do the same thing with parents when they have problems with teachers over their youngsters. We inservice the parents.

So, once more, Joan is always teaching. Curiously, though, it seems that the people with whom she works in problem situations feel less that they have been "taught" and more that they have "learned." At least part of the reason for this impression is that one gets the feeling that Joan sees these situations as opportunities for her own learning—and that attitude gets conveyed to others—as well as opportunities for her to teach others. Her enthusiasm and energy seem to spread to others who work with her. Probably one of the primary reasons that this contagion effect takes so well is that, as was noted earlier, her behavior communicated centrally that "First, I, too, am a teacher."

Some effects of Joan's ideas, energy, and enthusiasm seem to have occurred in her school in an unplanned-for way. Recall that her initial observation of the climate of the school was that it was punitive and negatively reinforcing. Further, there was little communication among staff. Her first goal as principal was, as she put it, to work on "plain old human relations" so that the degenerative cycle in which the system was caught could be reversed; so that the total school community—teachers, students, and parents—could start to experience success instead of failure; so that school could be a place where something good happened and not merely a place where people—particularly teachers and students—tested their survival and endurance capabilities. Within the context of this chapter, some bits and pieces of evidence suggest the reversal has taken place. For one thing, the disciplinary problems:

> The first year I walked in, the first month, in September, I had 127 kids referred to me for discipline problems—in my office. This last September (the third of her tenure as principal) there was a total of nine for the whole month.

And, with regard to changing from a negative to a positive reinforcement model:

> Teachers and kids come down to the office now with notes that say "Yippee" or "Hooray" or "Good News" for example when a particular problem kid has passed a grade level test. Or, I'll get a note saying, "Come to my classroom. We've got a great thing going!" Or, they're free to say, "Hey, I tried something in my room today and it didn't work. Do you have any ideas?" And, they're also quick to say, "Look, I've got a really tough home visit today and I don't think I can make it alone. Is there anyone who can go with me?"

Things have changed, indeed, in Joan's school, though she would be the first to say it is only on the surface, or perhaps just beneath the surface, that scratches have been made. The system that was once closed seems now to be quite open. Teachers seem unafraid to talk with each other, and with the principal, about their successes as well as their failures and their anxieties. What was a distasteful social climate three years ago appears today to be quite tasteful.

The ingredients of the change recipe? Some are matters of personal style, including a bit of charisma. Some seem to be matters of intuitive organizational pragmatism for, as was indicated earlier, Joan is fairly atheoretical in any deep academic way. On the style side of the coin there is her energy, enthusiasm, problem-solving skill, optimism, her sense of fairness, and her sense of what is needed in a wholesome learning environment. Relative to her pragmatic side, what comes across strongest is her intuition to reach out to the affected parties and their problem and to involve them in its solution. There is another facet of Joan's way of working with her faculty, however, without which the learning and change that have occurred in her school would not have taken place. It amounts to a creed, and is spelled out best in her words: "I will not do it for you but I will help you learn it."

As one listens to Joan talk to this point, it is almost as if the words were tatooed on her forehead. She learned it from her primary role model, her former principal.

> The *one* thing he taught me was that you don't do things for other people. You sit there and help them learn. That's what he did with me. He would sit in my kitchen, if need be, until two o'clock in the morning to help me learn. If I had a program idea that needed money, he'd say, "I'll show you how to go about raising the money, but I won't do it for you."
>
> But when I became principal, knowing I wouldn't "do it for them," for a while it was awful. I would confront a teacher about a problem and say, "Could it possibly be your problem?" I'd watch the teacher get very offended, and instead of dealing on the factual level, deal on the emotional level and say things which were very cutting and hurt. I would sit there and grind my teeth so as not to get caught in the game, the game that they were always losing with the kids. But it hurt and after the teacher left I cried. I cried a lot that first year.

Trying to do what Joan was doing takes its toll on a person. If a school principal chooses to embark on a design to change a school in ways that matter, the energy, enthusiasm, and skills of the principal need to be combined with a certain toughness—a toughness that lets a person take the hurt, but not engage in hurting back, a tactic that would be self-defeating. Joan's thinking seemed to go like this: "In this confrontation, what is happening could develop into the same kind of situation that occurs between the teacher and the kids—an emotional win-lose game where, ultimately, the issue is, who has the most power? I don't want that to happen here, I don't want to win. I want the teacher to learn." Ergo, Joan refuses to play the game, does not respond in kind, waits, and grinds her teeth. And she also cried a lot, but things did start to change.

The change that Joan started to induce can be described in organizational terms. Briefly, it was an effort—and a conscious one though it did not appear to have a carefully planned action design—to move the locus of decision making in the school from the principal to the teachers, on all matters in which they played a central role. Included were such things as curriculum, instruction, and discipline. Joan's role in all this was that of an initiator and, most focally, a problem-solving organizer and consultant. She refused to play the role of problem solver qua problem solver. She also had a build-in support system in the form of a small cadre of teachers (one of whom became her assistant principal) that moved with her from her former school when she assumed the principalship. They understood and supported her goals and value system. They were able to communicate together quite openly and thus served her as alter egos who helped her maintain contact with realities of the situation that might escape her, particularly when she wanted to have things happen quickly. For example,

Joan's first encounter with her new faculty as a group was a shocker for her:

> From the first words out of my mouth I knew that they didn't even understand the difference between cognitive and affective. I was appalled when I first talked to the staff, used those words, and looked across a room of blank stares. I knew I had to back up twenty paces. Mary and Susie got hold of me and said, "Look, here is what we see and we just want you to think about this. You can't move too fast because if you do you'll lose people. They'll become dissatisfied and frustrated. You won't even get a chance to test out your ideas." It was good for me to hear that and I asked them to pull in the reins whenever they saw we were running too fast.

Besides the potential for "losing" people because of Joan's needs for quick action, there were two other unintended consequences of her high energy and pace. One was the possibility of her staff becoming exhausted and "burned out" and the other, as the exhaustion set in (as it did from time to time), was becoming involved in a curious type of self-induced organizational trap.

> It's hard. We get one hour a week for team planning. Teachers are with me every single week night. And anywhere from ten to seventeen of them are there on weekends. I'm concerned about getting burned out and I'm concerned about their getting burned out. I've seen it happen and watched teachers fall by the wayside. We're trying to find ways of dealing with that.

And, her description of the trap:

> All of a sudden, in February, I found I had to get out of there for a while. I was getting into a bind, falling into a trap. What it was, was that the teachers were getting exhausted and fell back into their old ways of sending problems down to me. And I was exhausted, too, so without even knowing it I started to deal with the problems myself. I was not liking myself and I wasn't helping the teacher because the problems kept recurring. It was a bad scene.

Fortunately, this situation occurred before a vacation, but the vacation was only part of the solution. What Joan did was to ask the staff if they'd mind coming to an unscheduled staff meeting. At that meeting she leveled with her staff about her own feelings of exhaustion, and what she saw as the consequences, the kind of trap she had fallen into and what it all meant for the school. The staff responded in kind and talked about how low they felt and the reasons they felt that way. This sharing had an important impact because it removed temporary feelings of isolation from each other that faculty members had developed. As the meeting progressed, a sense of relief became apparent, and tension was reduced as the total staff came to realize that it was "all right" to be temporarily burned out, to be angry, and to wish desperately for a vacation.

Joan's problem-solving style is evident, once more, though perhaps in a subtle way, in this situation. The dominant strategy of most administrators faced with similar circumstances would probably be to ignore it or to be paternalistically exhortive to the faculty: "I know you're all tired but give it all you've got. Vacation is next week." Joan acted differently She disclosed her own feelings because they were facts that were important to the situation. By that disclosure she enabled her staff to do the same and, in the process, get more facts. But most important, this mutual revealing of self enabled all involved to build a more solid sense of community. The difference in feeling tone after the vacation, in Joan's words, "was incredible." People knew that they had been understood as people.

We sensed through listening to Joan and writing about her, that she is almost totally immersed in her school. As she talked, we felt almost physically transported from the place of our interview (a university office) to the school building, such was the involvement we felt with her teachers, students, and parents. The contagious effect of the behavior that was described earlier spread to us, as well. Joan's job as principal, however, like all principalships, requires interaction with certain relevant others within the school system—the Central Office, other principals, and the cadre of curriculum specialists and supervisors employed by the Central Office.

The impression usually gained from talking with most school principals is that the best strategy to employ in relating to the Central Office is to maintain distance. The existence of the Central Office cannot be denied, of course, but principals seem to see it, at best, as a rather bumbling bureaucracy. Each will acknowledge that there are some individuals in the bureaucracy who can and desire to be helpful, but that, by and large, it is best to avoid dealing with that part of the system whenever possible. One only gets bogged down in unmanageable policy or political constraints. Joan can see this side of her relationship with the Central Office as she said:

> Well, a policy decision will come out. You know that it's something that's absolutely ridiculous. We have to decide, do we ignore the policy and go on doing what we've been doing or pay attention to it? Probably we'll ignore it because nine times out of ten they are not going to know you're ignoring it anyway.

In a sense, then, one aspect of Joan's dealing with the Central Office is to play the role of practicing bureaucrat herself. She's aware of how the system works, seems to feel that the bulk of policy decisions that emanate from "downtown" are either unworkable or don't make any sense in the day-to-day operation of the school, and is keen enough to sense the one time in ten that she has to pay attention.

There is another side of Joan's dealings with Central Office, though, that seems reflective of her reaching-out, energetic problem-solving style of running her school. The following rather lengthy comment tells an interesting story:

> The first year they were extremely helpful to me. I used them for transportation purposes, for gathering information about policy that was unclear to me. I used them to find out how to get around policy. Amazingly, there are people down there who tell you how to circumvent policy without getting hurt. I spent a lot of time meeting with secretaries, particularly the secretary of the supply person because I wanted to know who I was talking to on the phone when I needed something. I spent half a day at the maintenance shop getting to know the carpenters and painters. Mainly, I wanted to become familiar with people, finding out what they could do because you never find it out from the manual. This has all paid off.
>
> The second year I learned whom to trust and whom not to trust. The first year that didn't seem to matter, getting clarification and getting to know people was more important.
>
> Everyone is willing to help a new administrator if you just say, "Look, I'm new, I need your help." It works. It's beautiful. and I wasn't just playing at it. I was kind of helpless in terms of not knowing how things worked.
>
> About the trusting. It had to do mainly with which people passed along different kinds of information and to whom. For instance, I'd go down there and say that I really would like to solve a problem with James Jones and ask how I should go about that. Before I ever had a chance to find out how I should go about it, James Jones knew I had a problem. I didn't like that. I also found out whom I could count on to be "too busy," and who would see me when I needed help. It hasn't happened too often but enough so that I know what to do.

Like almost everything else related to being a principal, then, for Joan the circumstance of her having to establish relationships with the Central Office constituted a problem to be solved. And she employed her typical proactive style, once more, which seems to go something like this: First, don't wait for the people to come to you. Go to them, reach out, as she did with the parent community and teachers of her school. Second, get the facts and get as many different kinds of facts as you can. Go to the people and ask them—and don't be afraid to tell them that you don't know how everything works. Third, become familiar with people as people so that you can relate to them not just as principal to carpenter, for example, but as Joan to John.

But Joan is not naive. Much as it seems that her preferred style of relating to people is one of openness, it becomes clear through her dealings with the Central Office that it was unwise to be as open as she wished if she wanted to maintain control over her prerogatives. She had to become circumspect about her openness, to strategize a bit about whom to talk to and about what. One must play the bureaucratic game, at times. She dislikes doing this but it appears that her contacts "downtown" are infrequent enough so that "playing the game" does not become a major problem. In any event, the battles that would have to be fought to create a more open system in the Central Office would be too costly for her, relative to any pay-off she might receive. It seems sufficient for her to be aware of the politics involved, thus leaving her free to pick and choose her avenues of entry into the system.

If the basis of mutually satisfying and productive collegial relations is a giving and receiving of help and counsel, from Joan's point of view her relationships with her peers—other principals—seem to be out of kilter. That is, it appears that she gives a great deal more than she gets. Things are out of balance.

> I have contact with certain people for certain things. When someone has a problem they come to me. For example, if they're developing a new report card. Well, we already did ours. They'll say, "Hey, can I have a copy of your report card?" Okay. Or, "I understand you are working in teams. Could we come over and see your teams?"
>
> But if I want to get ideas or talk about roles or other things, administrators always seem to be so overinvolved and they tell you they don't have time.

The curious thing about these circumstances is that, although Joan apparently does have the time to give to other administrators, even though she seems to be incredibly busy all the time, she believes it is true that most of her colleagues don't have the time to give in return. She believes that, indeed, they are as overwhelmed with work as they say they are, but for reasons of their own making. Her notion about this constitutes a dreary indictment of the manner in which leadership and management are exercised in the schools with which she is familiar.

> I think principals have done themselves in. They don't know if they have any power, don't feel they have a lot of administrative power, and yet feel the responsibility is overwhelming. So, they can never get out of the building because in order to feel good, in order not to be feeling guilty, they feel they've got to be running the whole show.
>
> And, they do it. No wonder they don't have the time. For example, if the teacher's contract says that teachers can't do hall duty. So the principals say, "I'll have to do it." Well, I don't do hall duty and I don't intend to unless everybody does it.

Another thing. I don't think principals are very good problem solvers. Maybe they solve problems for teachers by taking on the problems themselves, but that doesn't help them as principals. It just takes more of their time and makes the teachers more dependent on them. The whole point is that they take on so many kinds of responsibilities that are not theirs, from hall duty to solving teachers' problems. No wonder they don't have time!

These comments relate directly to those Joan made earlier about getting herself in a trap of her own making. Her point was that it was precisely at the time that she started to take on role responsibilities that were outside of her definition of what she should be doing that the job became overwhelming. Further, she sees most principals doing this and almost guaranteeing for themselves a situation that they will find extremely burdensome. Put another way, Joan sees most principals behaving as if their schools were Catch 22 situations—no alternatives, no exits. But the life of a school principal need not take on a Catch 22 character if he/she seeks alternatives and has some problem-solving skills, according to Joan.

If Joan seems to be less excited about her relationships with other principals, the opposite conditions hold for what transpires between her, her school, and the cadre of curriculum specialists/supervisors that is based in the Central Office. This is a bit unusual; most principals and teachers would prefer to hold these people at a distance, perceiving them harmless at best or insensitive evaluators or spies at worst. Joan describes the situation at her school in the following way:

First, I know that we couldn't do all that needed to be done by ourselves. The outside people could be helpful to us if we knew exactly what we wanted. If we were straight on this then they would be responding to us and not us to them. If they brought us stuff we didn't want, we realized we hadn't communicated well.

Supervisors, by the way, are very seldom asked to come in and support schools. And they are very, very eager to do that if you are inviting them in to participate. It's just incredible. They are so eager to come to our school, and that's because everybody wants them there. The teachers don't see them coming in to evaluate. Sometimes I would like them to because there are times when we get so close to a problem we don't know when we're making big, gross mistakes.

Elements of Joan's organizing style and outlook become clear again, almost sentence by sentence. First she has to sense the need, recognize that there is a problem. Then she tries to get the facts, which lead her to knowing what kind of help she needs. Then she reaches out for help and people respond because they know that they, their resources, and their involvement is wanted and that no political game is being played. This process involves a certain feeling of fallibility, illustrated by "If they brought us stuff we didn't want, we realized we hadn't communicated well." The sense of fallibility is also illustrated in Joan's comments about wishing the outside people would, at times, evaluate. That they don't evaluate may be reflective of their feeling that if they did they would no longer be welcome.

There is another part of Joan's world view as a principal that leaped out at us as we analyzed her comments about outside supervisors that seems to account for a good bit of her success. It is implicit in the number of times she uses the words "we" or "us" when she refers to the school. In the first paragraph quoted above, for example, these words accounted for 20 percent of all the words she used. The point is, of course, that they are not used in an editorial sense. On the contrary, they communicate a sense of community and of involvement. When Joan says "we" or "us" she appears to mean that, precisely.

Finally, and in a somewhat different vein, with regard to the relationships of supervisors to schools in general, Joan may have put her finger at the crux of the problem. The outcome of supervision in the schools is not an overwhelming success story; far from it (Blumberg, 1974). Mostly, it seems, the mythology associated with supervision suggests that supervisors are not very helpful, and that the best strategy for teachers to employ with supervisors is one of avoidance. But many supervisors, according to Joan, have a lot to offer, and the best strategy then becomes to get them to respond to your needs, which, apparently, they are eager to do. The way to develop this mode of response, thus eliminating a potential defense-inducing situation, is to know what is needed and then reach out for help. We doubt that Joan conceptualized the relationship this way, but that's the path in which her intuition led her.

It's difficult to know where to end this discussion of Joan, or if indeed, there can be an end. The infectious enthusiasm, the sharpness of insight, the huge amount of energy that she communicates all seem to lead us on. It is like trying to find an end to perpetual motion. There's much about her as a principal and as a person that we've touched on only lightly, and much that we've not mentioned at all. In the latter category, for example, we did not mention that she makes sure she's in at least two classrooms every day to observe what's going on. Additionally, she makes a dozen or so home visits every week. Where does she get the time to do these things? Aside from the commitment and desire, it seems clear that the time becomes available because of her concept of her self as principal. We paraphrase her sense of her role in the following way: "I am an organizer of problem solving. I want to help people learn how to solve the problems that confront them. I will not solve their problems for them, because when I do that, I treat them like children, not adults."

Perhaps, then, this last comment provides the key to it all. Implicit in it is the notion of an unfinished task; a task, in fact, that will never be finished because the learning of adult behavior is not a finite thing. Rather, the learning of adult behavior would seem to imply, as its core, an open-ended spiral of ability to confront and deal with human problems that are increasingly more complex in nature. And that seems to be what Joan, The Organizer, is after—for herself and for others.

5

The Value-Based Juggler: Up Front with Kids' Interests

George is a principal of an eight hundred student high school in a small town in a rural area. He is in his early thirties and has been principal there for about three years. Prior to holding that position he was the assistant principal in the same school, charged mostly with the discipline function —for which his well-over-six-foot sturdy frame seems to be rather ideally suited. High school youngsters would probably think twice before they decided to buck George because of his size, if nothing else. In addition to his disciplinary duties, he shared a great deal of responsibility for inducing a change program in the school that moved it from a rather traditionally programmed school into a flexible-modular schedule mode. He believes this experience had a great impact on his learning and development. His principal became a valued mentor and the experience itself was a "hands-on" learning opportunity for him to translate theory into practice. In addition to his full-time job he is also a doctoral candidate in educational administration.

In the course of our interview with George, one thing fairly leaped out at us. It was the continual and strong reference that he made to his value system—will it be good for kids?—when it comes to making decisions affecting both the substantive education of youngsters, the quality of their life in the school, and the quality of his relationships with the faculty. When George saw that an issue under discussion was related to his values—as different from one that required simply collaborative effort to resolve a problem in which his central values were not at stake— adherence to these values became the point from which he would rarely give ground. He held this position even though it meant, in some cases, the violation of policy or incurring the ire of his superintendent. He characterized his guide for making decisions by saying, "I think a lot of it comes from right inside." And "from right inside" applies to matters as *seemingly* mundane to the outsider as whether or not to hold graduation exercises out-of-doors and risk the threat of rain, to the question of how and under what conditions to integrate special education students into regular classes, to dealing with bomb scares. For example, George said:

> If I get an idea in my head, right or wrong, I tend to pursue it and try to convince other people or groups regardless of whether or not it's the faculty, parents, kids, central administration, or what have you. Let me give you an example. It's been my worst experience ever as a principal. Graduation has traditionally been held outside on the football field which is a beautiful setting. (The school is nestled in a scenic valley.) Four out of the last seven years have been rained out. A year ago I attempted to switch graduation indoors. The students said "NO!" and against my better judgment I gave in. Not only were we rained out, we were flooded out. We regrouped two hours later in the gymnasium, and then that area of the building was hit by lightning. It was a bad scene.
>
> My judgment on it was that *that* was not the way to conclude thirteen years of education. If graduation is at all meaningful, then let's do it right. The following year I made a dictum—come hell or high water it's going to be inside. I told the superintendent and the president of the Board of Education, "Next year you are going to have to get another principal if you want to hold it outside. It's going to be indoors." And they both concurred.

It's important to note that the central issue was not that the rain and lightning created a mess. Rather, the upset in the physical setting was terribly disruptive, as well, to George's values. Recall the comments above, ". . . that was not the way to conclude thirteen years of education" and "If graduation is at all meaningful, let's do it right."

George's value system comes into play with a vengeance when he perceives bureaucratic regulations (by inference, irrationality) going counter to the educational philosophy of his school. A case in point occurred when a county-wide educational service organization wanted to change the basis upon which special education students from George's school would be admitted to its program. George's school had long been committed to total mainstreaming. The service organization wanted to screen youngsters because their teachers "did not want these retards in their classes." At issue was whether or not George would go along with this new procedure, which he learned of upon returning to his office from a meeting late one afternoon. He didn't. "I went right to the superintendent and met, until 5:30 that day, with the superintendent, the special ed teacher, and the director of special ed. We changed the procedure for screening. If they hadn't, I would have put the kids on the bus that next Monday morning and let *them* send the kids back to our school."

It would be wrong to gain the impression from these two examples that George is an administrative trouble maker who thrives on seeking out opportunities to fight the authority structure. Nor is he a person who seems to need to assert his power in a startling manner. Quite the contrary, he comes across in a very soft, often quizzical way, giving the impression that as he takes positions he is also mulling over alternatives. He juggles things around, balancing values against each other. But once he has taken a stand, it seems clear that he is ready to deal with the consequences. "What's right is right, particularly when the kids are involved." Put another way, when his primary reference group, that is, the group that will be most directly affected by his decisions, is the student group in his school, George's administrative stance appears to be a strong one buttressed by his internal value system, or, as he puts it, "some general statements about education." Indeed, we've come to think of George as "The Value-Based Juggler."

"Some general statements (values) about education" also serve George well as he plays the educational leader role in his school, as distinguished from his managerial role. For example, he is opposed to grouping or tracking students on any basis that would have the effect of separating them and thus creating an intellectual elite. When he sees a department or a faculty member making a move that is going to result in greater tracking, "I move in the opposite direction." George, then, or so it appears, is clearly different from the commonly held stereotype of the school principal who is concerned mostly with routine administrative matters. His fingers seem to be on the pulse of all areas of school life. But his activity doesn't stop with pulse-taking. The latter seems to be a prelude to action, particularly if he doesn't like the rhythm or direction of things.

What has made George different? Two factors appear to be prominent. First, he has had, as have all of us, some very important role models in his life. Perhaps the most important of these was the principal under whom George assumed his first administrative position. His style was very different from George's. Whereas George comes across in a soft and rather quizzical way, his former principal was seen by many people as brash, dominating, and exceedingly active. They were as unlike as apples and oranges. It seems that George, probably in an unplanned-for way, abstracted from his mentor's world view those things that could conveniently and comfortably fit into his own internal system. Thus, there was simply no way that he could emulate the brashness or the aggressiveness of his model's behavior. In current parlance, he would have "bombed-out." What happened is best described in George's own words:

> When I came on board with Frank, theory to me was highly impractical. (My whole master's program was a series of seminars with experienced administrators—real old-time superintendents. And they were not theory oriented. But it was a good experience.) I was a person who was interested in the practical aspects of running a school; implementation, getting the job done, and to hell with theory. Frank and I argued about that for a couple of years, until we implemented flexible modular

scheduling, and I saw how theory was like being there at the birth of the earth. I mean, you saw things happen the way the theory predicted they would. And so I began to get highly interested in what moves people in organizations, what are their needs, how do you meet their needs, and how do they vary from time to time.

George's experience with his principal was a critical turning point in his professional life. It marked a change from his initial conception of the principal's role, which was "How to Keep the Machine Running Smoothly," to one that had its base in conceiving of a school as an organic system that made some sense intellectually. This latter conceptualization gave George a sense of power to influence things. Rather than conceive of himself as concerned mainly with and sometimes overwhelmed by administrative routine (though he acknowledges that a good bit of the job is just that), he began to see that by understanding the nature of the school, of teachers and students, and of the dynamic interaction among them, he could make things happen in ways he had not thought of previously.

The most telling sentence of his comment is, "I saw how theory was like being there at the birth of the earth." The comment seems to fit in with his basic, pervading concern with values. It is not so much that the theory is value oriented, although it may be, as much as it is that sound theory (if there is such a thing in education) can provide an anchoring point for action, as much as values can. Thus, in George's case, it seems the dynamics of his concern with values and with theory as action take-off points appear complementary. Each provides him with a solid reference system for his behavior and decisions.

It would be a mistake, of course, to make the interpretation from the preceding discussion that George's only guides for action stem from his internal system. Quite the contrary, he relates to, uses, and seems to be continually aware of the variety of reference groups with which he is in almost daily contact. In a general way, his strategy for dealing with these groups is summed up in the following comment:

One of the things I learned from my former principal is that I put the knife in the ground and see which way the herd is running. Then I either build a stone wall or a bridge depending on which way I want them to go. But first I get the rumblings from different people— teachers, faculty, students. When they come from all around me, I usually try to find out what is the central direction from which they come. This searching out gives me more time to plan rather than just react impulsively.

This statement is a revealing one. First, it should leave no doubt in the reader's mind concerning who he sees as controlling the school. It is George! And this appears so whether the issues are clear cut or vague. In the former case his actions are quick, i.e., the graduation problem or that concerning the special education students. Where the situation is not so clear his actions are quick and firm, but they are of a different nature. They are process, not content, oriented. Thus, he "puts the knife in the ground" not with the view of being a spectator to whichever direction the "stampede" may take, but to enable him to control things in the school.

The statement is also illuminating in another way. His use of the "herd" and "putting the knife in the ground" metaphor presents an interesting speculation about the way he, and perhaps many principals, see events in their schools. That is, it seems likely that, particularly in high schools, things may start to happen that have herdlike and stampedelike character- istics. Clearly, when circumstances such as these start to occur they tend not to be initially amenable to rational discussion. To use another meta- phor, what George seems to be saying is that when a flood is imminent, one must gauge its direction, crest, and the weak points in the dike, lest sandbags are put in inappropriate, useless places. It would be a mistake, to think that George conceives of all the human problems and movements in his school as having an undifferentiated, stampeding, herdlike quality. But, probably, sometimes they do.

In a way that is not conceptually neat and tidy, George conceives of his role as split between that of the educational leader and the organi- zational maintenance man. These two roles carry with them a different set of behavioral demands, according to George. To be an influential educa- tional leader in his school, to effect change, to move his teachers to grow and become better, the requirements are to be a salesman who knows how to make trade offs. In order to get something you have to give something. To maintain the organization in a stable condition, it's necessary to per- form a balancing act between and among the various competing groups pressuring the principal to support their primary interests.

An interesting and realistic picture is given by George relative to the demands placed on him as a principal (possibly most principals) to be the educational leader of his school. He says:

> I think in the area of leadership, real leadership, the principal has a free hand. For example, nobody's pushing the principal to a new cur- riculum, nobody's pushing for a new schedule or a new program for students. There is no push for new budgeting techniques. You don't have a parent group come in and say, "Hey, let's get X program started at the high school." The faculty doesn't push you either. Even if one department has an out-of-proportion slice of the budget, there's very little pressure to change it from other departments because they see it as just too big a task.[1]

1. It's important to remember that George is talking about *his* situation. Although we are aware of some circumstances where building principals do receive pressure from the superintendent or from parents, but rarely from teachers, to develop new programs, our experience suggests that the lack of such pressure is much more the rule rather than the exception.

The case seems to be, then, not so much that there is a leadership vacuum as there is a lack of any strong concern by potential pressure groups that acts of leadership—suggesting new structures, proposing new programs, and so forth—take place. From George's perspective, then, his job would be secure and the school community would offer him positive feedback if he did little else but focus his energies on maintaining the school in a stable condition, handling discipline problems evenly, and keeping the faculty happy. In other words, keep the peace! There is little pressure to lead.

There is, in fact, a lot of peace keeping to be done if that notion is interpreted as paying attention to keeping the school routine well oiled, so that the parts will mesh with as little friction as possible. And to do this, as was noted above, requires that George perform a balancing act between competing forces, a different role for the principal from when he is interested in promoting an innovative educational idea where he sees himself as a salesman whose sales ability stems from his power to make trade offs. Operationally, there are differences between the kinds of behaviors required. When George wants to get a teacher or a department to try something new, or to think through the efficacy of a particular program, for example—anything that deviates from the normal faculty function of teaching qua teaching—he must offer something in return. Sometimes it might involve an extra period of planning. In large matters, it might mean giving the teacher as much as four weeks of summer work for which the teacher would be paid. In other words, it seems clear that he perceives the success of his leadership initiatives as being in large measure related to the extent to which he has access to and control of the organizational reward system.

The situation relative to the demands placed on George for organizational maintenance is much different—up to a point. That is, as long as the school is running smoothly, as long as the scene is relatively peaceful, no specific demands are made. It is only when something disruptive occurs, stemming either from the faculty or the students, that the pressure comes on. The force of this pressure, of course, depends on the extent and longevity of the disruption. And it is in these situations that he goes into his balancing act.

This reference to the balancing act is not an unreasonable one, raising as it does the image of a tightrope walker needing to counteract the forces of gravity on either side of the wire. This image particularly fits the discipline situation in the school. George steps off a stable platform and starts to walk the rope in September. The close of school in June represents the stable platform at the other end of the rope. As he walks the rope, trying to keep his balance and thus maintaining stability in the school, two major "pulls of gravity" are tugging at him to fall to one side or the other. One pull is the pressure from the faculty not to loosen up on controlling students through disciplinary actions—the one thing, according to George, that would really irritate the faculty. The other major pull, naturally enough, comes from the students; to tighten things up would really irritate them. To continue the image, it's probably hardest to maintain the balance when the rope is slackest, at about the middle —during what principals refer to as the February slump.

There are, of course, times when George has to engage in short-term balancing while he's in the midst of selling and trading off. For example:

> We have a college English program in lieu of senior English. It was taught by teachers from Jones College when it was first established. We would get sixty kids signed up for it, send them to class, and the next day thirty would come in and drop it. What was happening was that the faculty was killing the idea, because we were using teachers from Jones, thus implying that our own teachers weren't good enough. To counter this, our teachers would say, by one means or another, to our students, "You're a good academic student. You're going to get a lot more from my senior English class than you'll get from Jones College."
>
> What we did was to go to Project Upward at Calhoun University. They trained our own teachers who also received inservice credit for the summer training. Our faculty then did the teaching and our kids still got a college level freshman English course. Our teachers were no longer under the threat of not being seen as smart enough, and they also received status in our own organization.

In terms of the trade off/balancing act notion, then, here is what appears to have happened. A new program had been established which, by its very being, and despite the fact that it made no demands on the faculty, had started to throw the system—stable faculty-school relationships—out of kilter. The system was being disrupted, and it appeared that the fall-out of the disruption would signal the demise of the program. This was the prospect even though all parties involved agreed that an advanced English program for superior students was a good idea. The problem was to bring the system back into balance and to maintain the *concept* of the program at the same time, which was done by trading off. In effect, what was communicated to the teacher was, "If we invest in Project Upward and all that it entails, including your time, will you support the program?" The answer obviously was in the affirmative. Trading off, in order to keep the system in balance, paid off.

It seems clear that, for the most part, George is and primarily conceives of himself to be in the business of dealing with groups that have different needs and points of view. Whether by compromise or by rebuff, George wants to accomplish at least three things: (1) to maintain the system in balance; (2) to create new opportunities for learning for youngsters; and (3) to enhance his own self-image as a value-oriented administrator whose primary concern is students.

The remainder of this chapter offers a glimpse into the perceptions that George has of the groups with whom he has to work, which affect his decision making, or which affect his behavior in more subtle, sometimes hardly perceptible ways.

Through the course of our interview with George he identified nine different groups that, in one fashion or another, he relates to as he administers his school. It's important to note, though, that his initial response to questions about his reference groups indicated that he had no formal way of thinking about and dealing with them. Indeed, the idea of having a role set (Katz and Kahn, 1966) composed of a variety of disparate groups, sometimes with conflicting interests, was not something that was central to his understanding of his role performance. This is not to say that he doesn't see himself dealing with different groups. Indeed, he does. But, at the time of our interview, the formal notion of a reference group theory of administrative behavior was not at all focal to George's thinking, even though it seemed clear that he operated on the basis of just that sort of theory.

George, either through his own initiation or as a result of our questions referred to nine different groups: (1) faculty and department heads; (2) parents; (3) students; (4) the "C" students; (5) close colleagues; (6) the community; (7) the Central Office; (8) other administrators in his system; and (9) the School Board.

The faculty group, of course, is most salient in George's thinking, but in an interesting sort of way. The faculty is a group to be served, but more importantly, to be used. Used in the sense that he understands that there will be no movement in the school, no program development, no innovation unless the faculty is supportive, which is not a new idea. However, George's clear articulation leads him to a basic strategy for working with the faculty: the power of the faculty to block or support the implementation of new ideas requires him to maintain the faculty in a state of receptiveness. This strategy gets translated, behaviorally, into a nonunilateral conflict-resolving stance. This stance calls for openness and a careful weighing of the costs and benefits of each particular issue so that stability of relationships can be maintained and so that the faculty has an image of George as being a fair-minded administrator. But he does not back off from making decisions that might upset the faculty. Indeed, he is not the faculty's pawn, but the question that seems to be continually in the back of his mind is, "Is it worth it?" A case in point:

> I remember sitting down with the assistant principal to talk about a specific kid. He was bad news. Nothing we had done with him— befriended him, nurtured him—had worked. The question was whether or not we were going to keep him in school or move him out of school. We made the decision to squash him for the betterment of the system. In other words, we decided that the cost of keeping him in school, in terms of faculty reaction, would be too great.

Don't get the impression from this illustration that George's main concern with the faculty is conflict avoidance. Quite the contrary, he seems not to shy away from conflict, nor to be unable to make decisions contrary to faculty wishes. The essential question, to repeat is, "Is it worth it?" both in terms of short- and long-term fall-out on faculty-administrator relationships. Put another way, the question is, "How big a withdrawal from the faculty 'goodwill account' will result from a decision that runs counter to the direction the faculty desires?"

George is also aware of and uses the power structure of the faculty—the department heads—in a rather straightforward manner in matters of personnel problems or program concerns. "If you want to get something going in your school, you want to get people involved who are part of the power structure. If you had a committee functioning without any department chairman on it, they would find it a hard row to hoe." Not many principals would argue with the "rule of thumb" that's implicit in this statement—involve the people who will be concerned with the decision and who have the power and influence to implement it. George, in this respect, seems not to be out of the ordinary. But what may be at odds with most administrative practice is his position on termination:

If you are firing a teacher, there's a whole bunch of groundwork that has to be laid (so far there is nothing unusual in this). The department chairman, the teacher in question, and the *other people on the team*.

The parenthetical expression and the italics in the above comment are ours and need explanation. Indeed, any school administrator will support the proposition of needing to lay a lot of groundwork if a teacher is to be fired, particularly in this day of increasing militancy of teachers' unions. As ironclad a case as possible needs to be made, even in situations involving nontenured teachers. What caught our eyes, however, were the words we italicized—*other people on the team*. At issue here is the concept of an open, disclosing organization (Steele, 1975). In his delightfully pointed book *The Open Organization*, Steele raises time and time again the problems that are generated by organizations whose norms are generally of a nondisclosing, play-it-close-to-the-vest nature. Such organizations (and unfortunately this probably includes the majority of schools) typically develop taboos against discussion of certain types of problems. Usually among these tabooed discussion topics, at least in the formal system, are problems related to career decisions about personnel in the organization—promotions, hiring, firing, and so forth. Most discussions having to do with such things are carried on in secret with only a select few being privy to them. One of the results of taboos such as these is that an inordinate amount of emotional, nontask-oriented behavior is channeled into maintaining them.

Back, then, to George. As he thinks about such a critical personnel decision as terminating a teacher, it seems that part of the strategy for laying the necessary groundwork also involves his breaking the taboo that is involved. But he probably doesn't have breaking the taboo on his mind, nor does he even faintly realize that this particular way of working helps to break down unproductive taboos. But, it is safe to predict that in George's school it is possible to hold public (or quasi-public) discussions on topics considered *verboten* in many others.

The theme of George's concern for students as students, their welfare and learning, has been communicated on several occasions in the previous pages. We find nothing unusual in that and, indeed, would have been surprised had it not been present. Two more specific comments, however, clarify his concerns about and relationships with students. The first was given during the discussion of the way his value system, beliefs, and ideals affected the decisions he made and directions he took. In response to questions about the origin of some of his educational values, George said:

If you want to, you can trace it all the way back to concern for the "C" student in high school.

The "C" students, the "average" ones, the "silent majority"—in a way the great mass of students that he sees as neglected, even though that neglect may be benign, appears to be salient in George's mind. There are programs for the educationally handicapped and, sometimes, advantage piled on advantage for the educationally gifted (the rich get richer). But no one, or so it seems to George, pays much attention to students who are just "average." "What a contradiction we are faced with," George seems to be saying. "On the one hand the 'C' student body is huge, the most potentially powerful group of students in the schools. On the other hand, we ignore them, for the most part, and simply assume the system will take care of them. They will put in their time, leave, and school will probably have had little effect on them." George would like to change this, and many of his decisions have that "average" student as a reference point.

The second student condition to which he responds has little to do with the academic side of school. This condition is apt to occur when students are agitated and:

When they are organized. When they have power. When they are going to be sitting up on that hill across from the school if you don't do something.

George, then, is not an unrealistic educational reformer. Although his concern for high quality learning opportunities is a thread that ran continually through our discussion, he is also fully aware that the needs of the adolescent culture often run contrary to those of the adult culture.

Further, there is always a possibility that this frequently covert and passive conflict may quickly turn overt and active, a situation he wishes to avoid or at least channel productively. He seems to have his communications networks open, and is rarely caught by surprise by student action. He is not beleaguered by students, rather, he seems to acknowledge that there is always the possibility that he will be, so he stays on top of things in order to forestall that possibility's becoming a reality.

In George's perceptions of and relationships to parents he used them as a source of both passive and active support. By passive support, he means working and communicating with the parent group so that their reaction to change, curriculum innovation, in particular, is minimally resistant and, hopefully, very supportive. He clearly does not use or intend to use parents as a source of new ideas, and his perceptions are that they don't want to be used that way.

George seeks out the active support and problem-solving skills of parents on issues that may or may not be related to curriculum. The drug problem, for example:

> The parents did a fantastic job in helping out on the drug policy. We had no policy on drugs and one of the big issues was the search and seizure of drugs that students might have on them in school and in their cars in the parking lot. It was a touchy problem even though we were legally within our rights. We ended up with parents saying, "Yes, we want that" and so we were able to get signed releases from anybody who parked in the lot with no problem.

But George indicated that organizing the parents and getting them involved does present a problem, particularly in secondary schools. The PTA seemed ineffectual, as is commonly the case. Another feature complicating the situation was that George wanted to have students in on school committee action and he was hamstrung by the attitudes of some teachers who said, "When students walk into this committee, I walk out."

> The answer to this situation was an end run. We formed a Parent-Teacher-Student Council, which was outside the formal organization of the school, but it wasn't a tea and cookies PTA. We met to discuss problems that involved parents, teachers, and students. Primarily, it was a sounding board for faculty meetings and department chairmen. It worked.

Despite what appears to be the viability of this group, the impact of parents on the school, and on George, seems to be a hit-or-miss phenomenon. It is difficult to get them involved because "they are satisfied as long as nothing bad seems to be happening to their kid or as long as the school isn't blowing up." How to get them involved? George's caveat is:

> When there's a situation in which they have an interest, do something they don't like.

This is an interesting comment. It suggests that, at times, he plays the role of Agent Provocateur—rather deliberately, it seems. But that role isn't recommended for a principal who feels insecure in his position and who, at times, does not enjoy a good fight.

Other reference groups seem to minimally affect the world view that George has of himself as a school principal, or the nature of his decision making. He sees the Central Office primarily as a force to be coped with in order to insure his freedom of action. On occasion he has used the superintendent as an arbitrator of differences between himself and another administrator, but usually he prefers to keep the superintendent at a distance. As far as other administrators in his system are concerned, George gives them rather short shrift. Directly, and to the point:

> I find it difficult to relate to other administrators, how they act or how they feel. I don't respect the way they operate. They are different than I; dull, dumb, noncreative, authoritarian, not open, mainly concerned with how to survive in the system. My concerns are decreasingly survival oriented and more and more directed at getting some personal satisfaction out of what I'm doing.

This facet of George's work life is clear. The price he pays for his attitudes toward his colleagues may cause him to be a bit lonely. However, it seems to be a price he is willing to pay in order to avoid being bored and angry with associations he doesn't desire.

George's relationship and feelings about the School Board are similarly direct and unequivocal. Responding to a query about the importance of the School Board to his work, he said:

> Not really, I'm long over being frightened of the Board. I think it's important they understand what we're doing, but that's about it.

In a fashion complementary to the earlier part of this chapter, on the way George's value system continually acted as his guide for decisions, George talked about his relationship with community groups. No Rotary Club for him! Because " . . . they didn't ask me until I became principal and I figured if they wanted a principal they could get somebody else." But:

> My personal involvement is with the ministerial association, which I find to be kind of powerful for me. I feel like God is living, you know, to have on your side. That is kind of Machiavellian, I guess, but that's the way it is.

And that is what George is all about!

6

The Authentic Helper: I Am
Myself—and Comfortable about It

Unlike the stereotype of school principals as presenting an imposing and determined physical image of themselves, Ed—an elementary school principal—is in his early thirties, is not too tall and rather slightly built, has dark hair, and has dark eyes that communicate a certain kind of laughing intensity about what he does. When we interviewed him he was in his third year as principal of his school, which is situated in an industrial suburb of a medium-sized city in Connecticut. We requested the interview because we had heard, of all things, that he was introducing Gestalt therapy techniques into an elementary school setting—unusual, to say the least. It is not that Ed is bent on turning his school into a mass, five-day-a-week therapy session. Nothing could be further from the point. He indicated that his primary concerns are with the quality of the curriculum and instruction that is carried on, not therapy. But the therapeutic focus comes out in a number of ways. For example, some of the goals of therapy (in this case, the Gestalt variety) are to enable people to become more aware of themselves as human beings and to be open to their own emotional awareness of self and others, which fits well into the way Ed conceives of and deals with himself and others. For example, here is Ed responding to a question about how he plays out his role:

> I guess, if anything, I don't perceive of myself as being in a role. I try to be as natural as possible, and natural means to me being as authentic as possible, or as genuine as I can be. It means being aware of what I'm feeling, and, if appropriate, letting people know how I feel in terms of both positive and negative responses. I really enjoy my humor. I use that a lot with children and teachers. I'm very comfortable with the warmth I possess and I will physically show warmth to children and teachers. I think that's very important. My primary identity is that of a human being who happens to be principal of a school.

The tone, then, is quickly set, and rather unequivocally at that. He rejects, first of all, the notion that merely because he happens to be the person who has responsibility for the operation of a school that he should behave differently with people. The key concepts that seem to guide him in his behavior are authenticity or genuineness, and being comfortable with what he sees himself to be. These concepts stem directly from the therapeutic milieu and, derivatively, from the human potential movement. It is unusual—in fact, Ed speaks of himself as an unusual principal—that a person who is a school principal should articulate these concepts so clearly as guiding principles for himself/herself. But principals are not a lower order of humanity. Rather, the notions of formal role, role prerogatives, role expectations and so forth seem to play a focal influence in influencing the behavior of most people, including principals. But not so with Ed, it appears. First and foremost he is a human being whose theory seems to work, as he engages with his own humanity and that of others in a genuine way; regardless of the position he holds, things will fall into line in a productive fashion.

The notion of genuineness implies two dynamic factors. First is the ability to be aware of both the feelings and ideas that a particular existential experience causes, to be able to identify those feelings and ideas, and own them as part of oneself. This is not an easy task. For example, professionals in human relations training practice will frequently indicate that having to be "in touch" with one's feelings frequently presents a formidable task for many people. Somewhat tragically, it seems, great numbers of people have been taught that the way to get along in life is to suppress their feelings, and if they can't suppress them, at least they don't acknowledge them. For Ed not to acknowledge as his own the feelings that he is experiencing would be a violation of his basic sense of self as a human being.

The second factor associated with genuineness—behaving in a manner that is congruent with a person's feelings, and thinking—is tempered a bit in Ed's comment. Note that he talked about letting people know how he is feeling, positively or negatively "if appropriate." There is a complex issue involved here. A person who is as personally and interpersonally aware and as skillful behaviorally as Ed seems to be, can wield a tremendous amount of power, interpersonally, irrespective of the position that person holds. The power stems from the fact that most people seem to have difficulty dealing with their feelings openly. Correspondingly, they also experience discomfort when others are open. At times they become immobilized, unable to deal with, for example, congruent expressions of anger or love. It is much easier and less threatening to play the games learned in childhood. Ed's "if appropriate" stand, then, is important, for the last thing he wants to do, even though he easily has the ability to do it, is to immobilize another person.

Genuineness, however, is not enough. People must be comfortable with what they are, so that they do not become headstrong with a sense of self that doesn't fit with how they want to behave. Thus, Ed sees himself as having warmth, being comfortable with it, and finding ways to express it on the job. But he applies the idea of comfort not only to himself. Ed applies the idea of being comfortable with self most centrally to his interaction with teachers as he works to help them.

In sum, Ed refuses to define himself as a principal in bureaucratic terms. Instead, he talks about his job in terms of his personal interests.

I'm interested in instruction and curriculum as well as developing a climate where children feel good about being here and teachers feel good about working here. I'm very much interested in human relations, in helping relationships, not only between teachers and children, but also teacher-teacher, administrator-teacher, and most specifically, administrator-child.

And, he elaborated with regard to his concerns about youngsters:

I see kindergarten children coming into the building, very alive, feeling-centered, very bubbly for the most part. And then I see things start to change, maybe after the second or third grade. They seem to become less aware of their feelings, less bubbly, less alive. By the end of the fifth grade when they leave the building—I hate to use the word—they seem deadened. Hopefully, if we can somehow work with their feelings on a daily or weekly basis, throughout the year, I will see the fifth grade kids smiling.

The clues to Ed's view of himself and to his view of what a school should be are congruent and they all seem to be logical follow-ups on his initial statement concerning genuineness and comfort. For example, feeling good about himself and what he does rather naturally leads to his desire for the children and teachers in his school to feel good about themselves. The aim is not only to enjoy school, but also to enjoy each other. Of course, it probably is true that most principals would offer the same opinion. Who wouldn't? What is important here, though, is that Ed was not asked. That is, the comments that he made about children and teachers feeling good about being in school were his first remarks. Indeed, this thrust plays a central function in everything he does. How central that thrust is was revealed in his comments concerning the "bubbliness" of kindergarten youngsters, and how this bubbly pattern seems to dissipate in time. Perhaps it is trained out of them, as they are socialized in the school world, until at the end of the fifth grade—at ten years of age!—they appear to Ed to be deadened.

Ed's interest in developing helping relationships in his school, particularly his focus on the relationship between administrator and child, can be seen in his thinking about the typical perception that school children have of principals:

I think that the administrator has been looked on as an authority to be feared by most children. For example, this really happened: A new group of kindergarten kids came into the building. The teacher introduced me and asked them what they thought the principal did. The response was, "He spanks people."

In *Escape from Freedom*, Erich Fromm (1941) remarked that problems related to the associations that people have with authority constitute the major moral issue of our time. That is, until authority figures let themselves be treated as human beings, and until hierarchical subordinates are freed from their fear of authority, humankind will continue to behave immorally in the sense of relating to a person in a way that denies his/her humanity, focussing instead on issues of power.

Although Ed doesn't frame his concerns about authority in terms of morality, that issue does seem to be present in his thinking. His focus on "treat me as a human being who also happens to have responsibility for this school" puts the problem squarely. Interpretatively, the notion seems to be that the more people focus on his role and de-emphasize his person, the more dehumanizing and thus immoral the situation becomes for him. For Ed, the centrality of the whole education process resides at the point of helping people, particularly students and teachers, to become more aware of their emotionality. And once aware, a person can be more free with himself/herself and others. The person becomes freer to be what he/she is—clearly a moral goal. Ed approached the issue of his own freedom when he talked about the way he allots his time during the school day.

I find that I spend 25 to 30 percent of my time on work such as budget, scheduling, transportation, cafeteria and so forth. That's plenty. That leaves 70 to 75 percent of my time that *really is free*. I guess I could sit in my office and waste the whole day by expanding the managerial aspect of the job to 60 or 70 percent. I *choose* not to do that, most of all because I find it boring as hell.

And at another point, by way of elaboration of his last sentence, he said:

For the most part, the expectations I respond to in my position are my expectations of myself rather than someone else's expectations of me. In other words, because someone expects me to behave in a particular way because I am a principal of the building does not force me to behave that way. There's no reason for me to be the way others want me to be.

Basic to it all, then, is the matter of individual choice, and Ed leaves no doubt about where he stands. Indeed, as will become clear in this chapter and throughout the book, Ed's choice is to be primarily an authentic helper. A principal can choose, for the most part, how he/she wishes to organize his/her work life, that is, choosing what things will have priority. If a principal spends the majority of the day engaged in managerial functions—"administration"—then, according to Ed, that's a matter of individual choice and that principal shouldn't complain about being overburdened with such matters. The wound is self-inflicted. The gospel, according to Ed, is that if you really want to be free, but you aren't, the problem is that you've conceived of your job in a way that mandates your responding more to the demands of others, rather than to those you hold for yourself. There's a large amount of truth in this position. For example, there are many principals who appear to be positively overwhelmed and exhausted by what they see as the necessity of spending their days almost totally in their offices working on "nitty gritty."

Yet, the principals written about in this book seem to tilt the balance quite the other way. It's not that they do not work hard. Indeed, they do. But they spend their time differently. From Ed's point of view, it's a matter of choice, whether the people involved in the former work style are aware that they are, indeed, making the choice or perhaps more importantly, that they have the choice to make. Ed makes the point clearly when he indicated that, if he wished, he could more than double the time he spends on routine administrative matters. Aware of his own needs and responding to them first, he simply chooses freedom. And underlying the notion of choice, though he doesn't articulate it, would appear to be the idea that if Ed can present a satisfactory model of choice-making for freedom to his faculty, then the human values inherent in the process will contage to them.

Being free, of course, is only the start. The critical question is what to do with freedom. The answer to the question rests in a statement of people's interests and the roles that they see themselves playing in order to actualize those interests. We have already seen that Ed's interests are in instruction, curriculum, and in the quality of human relationships that exists between and among principal, teachers, students and parents. Relative to his role, he defined it and his strategy for implementing it in the following terms:

> always as a helper . . . but the most common problem that occurs is a situation of my wanting to help someone and that someone not wanting help. So what I've tried to do is to create a climate within the building such that people see they'd like to change, feel they can change because the atmosphere is conducive to change, and can or will come to me as the potential helper in the building.

Carving out such a role can be a many splendored thing, but as Ed indicates, merely because that is the role he wanted to play was no guarantee that his offers of help would be accepted. This point is pain-fully evident in the schools with regard to supervisor-teacher relation-ships. Historically, for example, the relations between teachers and supervisors have been characterized by mistrust and defensiveness (Blum-berg, 1974). Ed's school, when he became principal, was no exception. He commented on this state of affairs on two separate occasions:

> At the beginning of my tenure, there was no helping base. I was looked upon as a very young, maybe inexperienced person. The feeling seemed to be "Who is that authority coming into my classroom and telling me what I should do?"

and

> I walked into a building that was devoid of trust. It was a very cold climate. The perceptions of administrators were very suspicious and negative. I wanted to have some data to guide me, to help me work with the faculty. So, I used two types of survey instruments. One dealt with "how it feels here" and the other was a leadership profile. I've read-ministered them and things have changed, on the feeling level and with regard to perceptions of me as an administrator.

Ed puts his finger on one of the primary blocks to changing and im-proving the character of the teaching-learning process. Again, historically and systematically, schools seem to have been resistant to change. Ad-ministrators and teachers, perhaps for ample reason, have tended to be protective of the territory they have been willing to grant each other. Encroachments on the territory of the other have been typically greeted with suspicion, distrust and defensiveness.[1] So, in some reiteration, the situation that Ed confronted when he became principal was not an unusual one. It was the rule rather than the exception.

It is interesting to note that Joan (Chapter IV) saw herself dealing with essentially the same situation during her year as principal. She said, "I knew I was going to have to work on plain old human relations." Ed said, "I wanted to build trust on their part." His approach to the trust-building task contained two elements. One was in his organizational role as administrator of the school. The second was his personal style of relating to members of his faculty. Relative to the latter, the problem, as he saw it, was to enable teachers to start to identify with him as a person who was nonthreatening, with whom they could be open, and to whom they could bring problems with the confidence that they would be listened to. So,

1. The counterpart of the teacher's distrust is illustrated by a remark one of the present writers heard an administrator make as he rejected a teacher union's invitation to attend a session on teacher evaluation. He said, "I'll be damned if I'll let them tell me how to evaluate teachers!"

I guess, at first, it was mostly just a type of democratic acceptance of them as people, without any pressure from me. I wanted to feel out what kind of instruction was going on in each classroom. I realized I had my own biases toward instruction, but I tried not to let those biases interfere with my observations and relationships with a teacher. The first year I really didn't attempt to make any changes per se in a particular teacher's classroom style. I guess I wanted to build a feeling of trust on their part.

Ed was caught in a bind that was induced by his own value system. On the one hand he understood that in order to establish the kind of relationship that would let teachers trust him, he had to move slowly, to observe, listen, and be nonevaluative in his interaction with teachers. On the other hand, he observed things going on in classrooms that ran counter to what he valued in teacher-student relationships and the teacher-learning process. Ed realized that if he was ever to be able to play the role he wanted to play, the changes that he would like to see occur would have to wait until he and the teachers could communicate openly with each other. Given the intensity of his feelings about the nature of productive classroom learning climates, he went through that first year with some inner conflicts—seeing some things he really wanted to change, but knowing he had to pull back lest he destroy what he was trying to build.

Was Ed being phony in all this? That is, believing in the necessity of being authentic with people, wasn't he being somewhat dishonest in not letting teachers know that some, perhaps a lot, of what he observed he thought was counterproductive? A "human relations purist" might answer in the affirmative. "Tell them where you are, gently if need be, but be sure to level at all times" might be the motto of the purist. Ed's position was different. Authenticity is a two-way street, and both parties have to own it as a value and a communications skill. Further, the development of the value and accompanying skill is an experiential learning process. And further still, as we infer from Argyris (1976), the majority of people have learned that the way to get along in this world is precisely to be non-authentic—to not let people know what they are thinking and feeling in ways that might reveal themselves. The risks are too high because, as a person reveals himself/herself, he/she becomes more vulnerable to the others.

Again, the question is whether or not Ed was being phony when he observed and listened, but did not reveal himself to the teachers. We think not, given what his goals were during that first year as principal. What he saw and heard became part of his data bank for future use. In a way, there was a parallel between Ed's strategy of working with teachers that first year, and the manner in which he dealt with the school as a human organization. If, for example, his work with teachers is conceptualized as involving nonevaluative information gathering, the same would apply to his work with the school as a social system. Though he undoubtedly did observe and listen to the way teachers behaved and talked with each other, his primary data-collection method was to administer a nonevaluative survey. Interestingly, the data he collected had little to do with the instructional program. It was focused on the emotionality of the school— "How it feels here"—and the behavioral style of the principal. As much as he was interested in the behavior and feeling tone that was present in classrooms, Ed was more generally interested in these same factors as they were present in the school.

The parallelism just noted is indicative of a consistency in Ed as a person and as a principal. Issues of authenticity, emotionality, and behavior seem central to his existence. They not only appear to be present when he describes the ways he works and those things he works for, but they were also present in our interview.[2]

Ed's theory of inducing change in the instructional program and teacher behavior in his school involves, at its heart, illuminating the gaps between what currently transpires and what teachers might want to transpire. But underneath this theory is a philosophical position that highlights the element of free choice. That is, he puts a lot of energy into helping his teachers become aware of the gaps with which they are confronted, but he does not mandate that they do anything to close those gaps. They must make the choice. With the faculty as a whole, the theory became actualized in the following way:

> Early in the first year, I wanted to start developing the school as a community. In our before-school-starts faculty meeting, I started out by reading a statement about myself and about kids. That let them know where I was and I think it made an impact on them. Then I asked them to do two things: First, to write down what they thought was the best thing that could happen to them that year and what was the worst thing. Second, I asked them to write down what resources they had to offer our school community and what resources they wanted from our community. And that was it.
>
> We put it all down on newsprint, examined it, and processed it all together, and then I put all the information on ditto. It's all in the teachers' room now. We have an "I want" board and an "I have" board.

Gaps are deliberately created, and people are free to choose the extent to which they want the gap to be closed. Apparently, from Ed's view, they are now choosing to help each other close some of the gaps, at least to some extent. But the issue is that they voluntarily choose to do so, because implicit in the notion of free choice in a program of change is the idea that unless those involved "own" the change, anything that occurs will leave only a superficial impact of short duration.

2. As an example of this consistency, at one point in the interview as we were trying to understand a position he had taken, he said, "I feel like you're trying to put me in a box." Indeed, he let us know, without anger, what he perceived to be happening.

There is another implicit factor involved in Ed's theory of change that has to do with the change agent's view of the people with whom he/she is working. "Are these people pawns to be manipulated or are they adults who, when confronted with facts pertinent to them, can make intelligent decisions on their own?" Obviously, Ed's strategy views teachers as adults. And this position apparently holds for things occurring in the school that he would prefer to see change.

> I think what I do is to go with the strength that's already in the building. I build on that, and in the process a teacher becomes stronger. Well, the stronger that teacher becomes, the more there is a discrepancy between that teacher, and, for example, the weak teacher who may be across the hall. Then the weak person has a choice: "I see this happening across the hall. It's really going well and I want to get involved in it. Or, I see it happening and I don't want to get involved in it."

We asked Ed if he was content to let the weak teachers make the decision not to become involved in a program that was obviously of help to youngsters. His response was in the affirmative—but there was a hedge because our follow-up question was, "For how long?" His reply was, "I don't know, I haven't set a time limit." We suspect the "how long" question will get answered not by a mandate to change, but by an authentic leveling confrontation between Ed and the teacher, at which time he will share, as nonevaluatively as possible, more data about the situation. This data would include his own awareness of what is going on in him as a person as well as his perception of what is going on in the classroom. And this confrontation would be the start of building a productive relationship. The point is made by Ed, in a somewhat different context:

> I find it very difficult to force a teacher to change. What I will typically do is sit down with that teacher and point out my observations of what's happening in the classroom and sort of check out if the teacher sees the same thing happening. And then I proceed from there and ask the teacher if this is something she is comfortable with. If it's something she *isn't* comfortable with, then we begin to develop a relationship.

The style, then, is consistent from working with the total faculty, down to the individual teachers. Provide information, create gaps, and let people make choices, trusting all through the sequence that their sense of values about education and youngsters will lead teachers to make decisions for change which they as people can feel good about. But there is a limit to the comfort issue.

> I always am concerned about allowing a teacher to feel comfortable with what she's doing as long as it is not detrimental in my eyes to what's happening with the children.

It is at the point of perceiving some undesirable things happening to youngsters as a result of teacher behavior that Ed departs from his general therapeutic model of working with teachers. That is, the therapeutic model to which Ed adheres suggests, by way of some repetition, "collect information, become aware of yourself and others, and examine the gaps between what you are and what you'd like to be. If you are comfortable with where you are after going through this process, well, that's okay." But it's okay only up to a point, the point being a situation where a teacher's comfort with what he/she is doing is having undesirable effects on youngsters. It's at this point that his role emphasis as a helper who happens to have responsibility for a school changes to that of a person who has responsibility for a school and who would also like to be of help. First things come first, and it is the welfare and emotional health of the youngsters in his building that take top priority. Teachers are not allowed to place their own comfort with what they do before the well-being of students.

It is undoubtedly true that few principals would argue with Ed's position; that every principal's working philosophy places the welfare of the youngsters as *the* top priority in their school. For example, if every principal were asked to rank their priorities, the needs of students would come out on top. What makes Ed different, is that he articulates clearly and has a well-thought-out theoretical and pragmatic model to deal with problem situations on a daily basis. The well-being of the students in his school seems to be at the center of Ed's existence as a school principal. It takes precedence over everything else, and not just at times of crisis. Ed seems to be acutely aware of the mostly subtle, but nonetheless damaging, effects on students when, on occasion, a teacher may be comfortable doing what comes naturally—dealing with his/her anger, for example, in a way that may create undesirable, ego-deflating, and win/lose situations for students.

Obviously, then, if a situation reaches a point where Ed cannot allow it to continue, he must behave in ways that cause him some conflict concerning his preferred style of doing things. His remarks illustrate the conflict he experiences at times:

I guess I like the word assertive rather than authoritarian (ed. note: by which he means making unilateral decisions). There are instances when I have to assert myself as an individual, not as a principal, but as an individual either in speaking with parents or working with a teacher. Depending on my relationship with that teacher, I will assert myself and let her know what I find objectionable. In the eyes of many teachers I'm not void of authority, it's still there. But there's another side of me, the assertive side, but assertive in terms of being fair. And, there's the more or less sensitive, warm side of me which gets me a lot farther in terms of relating to people and helping them than does my assertive, authoritarian self.

For Ed, life in school is not one big happy helping relationship, much as he might prefer it to be that way. For one thing, although he dislikes the role of the authority figure, he recognizes that he is sometimes seen that way. In his comments, the use of the word *assertive* seems to be a semantic dodge. That is, he finds it easier to see himself exercising his assertiveness rather than his authority. But the conflict is still there, and curiously, the conflict seems to be induced by his acute sensitivity to himself that enables him to be aware of the different sides of his makeup. Awareness, though, is not all there is to it. Most people are more or less aware of their conflicting needs and values in their relationships with others. The conflict becomes heightened with Ed, it seems, because of his extraordinary commitment to his "sensitive, warm side" as the most productive way to develop his school community. The problem is, of course, that life doesn't permit Ed (or anyone, for that matter) to behave in a sensitive, warm, helping way all the time. Most of us probably handle this conflict without much discomfort. The same can't be said of Ed. Missionaries, and there is clearly a missionary side to him, have never had an easy time of it.

When Ed talked about his relationships with the Central Office (personified by the superintendent) and other building administrators in his district, the impression that was conveyed was that they were matter-of-factly formal and distant, almost to an extreme. Part of this circumstance is influenced by the fact that his building is several miles away from the other four in the district. This separation enables him to feel and be quite autonomous. But more importantly, the formality and distance of the relationships is increased by the absence of shared values and, indeed, what appears to be little basis for communication about the substance and style of education. About his superintendent, for example, he commented:

> The relationship between me and my superintendent isn't poor and it isn't good. I don't think he would take the time to listen and understand what I'm doing. He doesn't listen well and any attempt on my part to describe our program has been completely useless. On the other hand, he's very public minded and he receives a lot of positive feedback from parents about what is going on. But it took him two years before he spoke to me as a human being. He told me he was pleased with what I had done, had a lot of confidence in me, and he talked about wanting to work with me.

Relative to the other principals in the district, Ed said:

> The frequency of my relating to other administrators is not great. What I do and what is comfortable for me seems not to be comfortable for them. So, I sort of backed off and said, "Well, if they feel comfortable doing what they do, that's okay." But I don't want them telling me what I'm doing is not okay. So it's mostly just a "leave each other

alone" attitude. I prefer it that way even though, if given the chance, I'd like to influence them in the direction of dealing with kids' feelings. But that's very difficult for me to do, though I'd be willing to help them if they wanted to.

The structure of the relationship between Ed and his superintendent and the other building principals are different. But the net result seems to be the same—the relationships are characterized by psychological distance and formality. The superintendent's poor listening is probably a result of broader concerns, the public image of the schools, for example. With regard to other principals from whom Ed might receive support and who, in turn, he might help, the problem is one of an absence of shared values. Further, the energy that would be required to change this state of affairs would be too great for Ed to muster.

We have to speculate that these circumstances, much as they may have their rewards, will eventually have their costs. Essentially, Ed is isolated (even though it may be a self-induced isolation) from collegial interaction and support. It may be that he will be able to continue what he is doing and find it exciting for a number of years. But at least the possibility exists that this isolation will become burdensome and a source of discontent. It is even possible that Ed himself will wind down if no emotional sustenance is received from his colleagues over the long run.

The long run, though, is tomorrow, and Ed lives very much in "today." His concern with the affective side of life and with the here-and-now lead him to spend a large amount of time in classrooms, not only observing, but doing. The "doing" involves, at times, taking over the class so that the teacher is freed up for some planning or inservice programs. At other times, and on a more regular basis, it involves working directly with youngsters on the emotional side of their life, or, as Ed puts it, on "the human side of education."

> I'm very interested in Gestalt theory and technique. I have a group of third grade children with whom I meet twice a week to conduct a group session, using the theory and technique of Gestalt as well as the Magic Circle idea which comes from California. I also meet with a kindergarten group once a week and do a similar program with them. I am trying to work the teachers in, trying to build a community.

And on the level of the total building community:

> The whole building community—teachers, kids, cafeteria people, and maintenance people—meets every Friday morning for about twenty minutes. We say the pledge of allegiance, we sing together, we celebrate birthdays—in the gymnasium. We do a variety of things. I play my saxophone. (All my life I wanted to play the saxophone and two years ago I learned.) I also go into my kindergarten and first grades on a weekly basis and play the sax and the kids sing.

It truly seems that when Ed described himself as an unusual principal he was right. But what about the parents? How do they respond to his unusualness, particularly given the fact that the community his school serves would be classified as much more conservative than progressive? From Ed's perception (and that of his superintendent, apparently) the parent community has very positive reactions to the school and what occurs in it. These reactions, however, seem not to be a result of parents simply listening to their children describe their experiences, although that certainly must be part of it. What seems more to the point is that Ed has tried to involve parents directly in some of the educational experiences of the youngsters and in the school as a viable community institution. It's as if he's taking on helping parents understand the school as part of his responsibility. He described several specific activities in which parents have been engaged. First, an activity that was directed at the parents of children who were about to enter kindergarten:

> We have four preschool sessions for parents whose children are coming into the building. I conduct those sessions. What I do is simply to ask parents to write down what they want their children to get out of being in school. Then I read their responses out loud and put them on the board. I put those statements dealing with affect—"I want him to be able to get along with people"—on one side, and those dealing with traditional skills—"I want him to learn reading, writing and arithmetic" —on the other side. At the last sessions, out of forty parents' statements, thirty were on the side of affect and four were on the side of traditional learning skills. Then I talked to them of what I'm trying to do in terms of helping kids with their feelings and relating to each other. The parents say, "Yeah, you know that's really important."

Early on, then, parents are given a sense of the thrust that Ed is trying to develop in the school's program. They are involved and have an opportunity to react to what's going on. They also get a sense of Ed's style and of his value systems. However, Ed does not "put down" the learning of basic skills. To the contrary, he is vitally concerned with them, but he believes they can be learned better in an emotionally healthier environment than he perceives to be current in most schools—thus the emphasis on the affective side of life.

What about the PTA? According to Ed the PTA is strong and also supportive. When we expressed our surprise, for our experience suggests that most PTAs are weak, frequently becoming temporarily strong in opposing something that is occurring in a school, Ed's response was as follows:

> I think they're very interested in their children. I also feel they know they can come to me with ideas and know they'll be listened to. They're very active. Right now there are four or five things going on in which

parents are involved. There's the library-learning center in which parents work, for example.

One thing I know is that the typical turnout at PTA meetings when the kids aren't involved is very low. We had a "get acquainted" night. Usually, this means the parents come in to meet the teachers. But it seemed to make a lot more sense to ask the kids to bring their parents, so that the kids could say, "Hey, Mom, this is my teacher, this is my room, this is where I sit, etc." The night we did that we had 600 people.

And Ed also engages with parents on school improvement projects, the playground, for example:

I just finished working with seven parents, building a real playground. I've never heard of an elementary school without a playground. We went to the state fair, we went to dumps. We got old tires and telephone poles, anything we could lay our hands on that we thought would work and be important to helping kids feel good about being there, and teachers feel good about teaching.

It is clear, then, that Ed departs from the rather puristic helping style that he tries to employ with his teachers when it comes to working with and trying to involve parents in the building of the school community. He initiates, creates, and engages, and most of all he appears to have fun. His eyes fairly lit up, for example, as he told us of the program for parents where a film that was made in and about the school was shown, and they did their "Friday morning program."

More important, however, is the way the themes that were associated with Ed's work with teachers and youngsters became equally vivid in his concern with parents. School has to be a place that is enjoyed, but enjoyed with a purpose. And even though he told us of some pure social activities in which the parents engaged (ice cream socials, dancing, a roller skating party, etc.) the activities that were most important were those in which parents were participants in something that was related to their children. The idea is to reach out to the parents, not in a ritualistic fashion, but in a way that links them to what the school is all about. Thus, the "get acquainted" night is not a situation where uneasy parents meet uneasy teachers because it is something that has to be done. To the contrary, it is seen as an opportunity to assist parents, teachers, and kids to get together to share some of their lives with each other. And the development of the program with the movie had much more than entertainment as its goal. Most centrally it was another effort to reach out, to communicate the sense of the school's mission so that parents could understand, lend support, and perhaps, learn themselves. Even the building of the playground had a purpose that would go beyond merely providing a better facility for recess or other school activities. At its base, as Ed said, it was aimed at "helping kids feel good about being there and teachers feel good about teaching." But the parent involvement in the playground building project went beyond that because it gave the parents a sense of being part of the action, and of knowing that their efforts would contribute to making the school a better place for their youngsters.

The importance of Ed's involvement with parents, however, goes beyond efforts to enable them to become part of the school community, although that in itself is a worthwhile aim. Underneath it all, is that his energy, style, outlook on life in general, and school in particular, serve a modeling function for parents as well as for teachers and students. As Ed invests of himself, his attitudes and his skills, with parents in this case, he also models for them the kind of human relationships and the kinds of attitudes toward school that will best encourage productive linkages between home and school. The school, then, does not become an isolated fortress, forbidding all to enter and be part of it except those who have formal membership in it. To the contrary, the school opens itself up and reaches out to the community and says, in effect, "Be part of us. We all have a stake in what goes on here."

There is a further point of interest concerning the relationship of parents to the school. It focuses on the linking role that Ed plays between parents and teachers, particularly at times when parents may be dissatisfied or upset with a teacher's behavior in the classroom or, in a specific instance, with the behavior of teachers in general during a very tense and conflicting time in collective bargaining. In this latter situation, some of the teachers had engaged in petty, perhaps childish acts of disruption, such as taking fifth grade books and putting them in the first grade classroom. Parents were understandably angry. Their children were being used as pawns. Four parents came in and confronted Ed about the situation, about which he was unaware. Ed's position in these circumstances was an unusual one. He did not become defensive and try to smoke-screen the situation by denying its occurrence, nor did he promise the parents that he, as principal, would take care of the problem—that he wouldn't let teachers get away with that sort of behavior. He agreed with the parents that if there had been the acts of sabotage that they had described they had a right to be angry. Seeing that their anger had been accepted as legitimate, the emotionality that the parents felt subsided. But then, and here the departure in style and attitudes is seen, it was Ed's viewpoint that the teachers had to assume responsibility for their actions. He would not do it for them. His suggestion to the parents was that they either approach the teachers directly or make their views known to the teachers' association. The parents left "happy as they could be" according to Ed. In retrospect, he said:

When the parents walked in the door it was my responsibility to deal with that here-and-now situation. But it is *not* my responsibility to get that teacher off the hook.

The same position holds when a parent comes in to complain about what a teacher is doing in a classroom.

> I feel the same way when a parent calls me and starts to bitch about a teacher. The first thing I suggest is that the problem be taken up with the teacher. I can't answer for twenty-five people. I can only answer for me.

As we interpret Ed's stand on his linking role between parents and teachers, it goes something like this: A central function of education is to help youngsters to learn, over time, what it means to be an adult. Part of being an adult involves assuming responsibility—personal responsibility—for one's actions. If this is so, then when people are chronologically adult, they must indeed be treated as adults and they must assume responsibility for their behavior. They can't have it both ways. They can't pick and choose the times when they will assume responsibility for themselves and the times when they won't. Thus, when Ed refuses to be the "protector" for teachers, when he refuses to take over their problems vis-à-vis parents, he is, in effect, placing his trust in them as adults—even though they, at times, might not like it.

The story of Ed would not be complete without a comment he made toward the close of our interview when he was reflecting on the nature of his relationships with his teachers.

> It's just being myself with them and helping them know it's okay to be angry and it's okay to be positive. And it's okay to be warm. That didn't exist there before. To give you an example, after the negotiations were settled, eight teachers came in throughout the day, embraced me, cried, and thanked me for being so supportive of them. I had to sit back after the first one came in, a sixty-eight-year-old kindergarten teacher, and say to myself, "What the hell did I do?"—I didn't do anything. I was neutral. I was myself. And that was the measure of it all for me, right there. And how does it all come about? What the hell . . . I don't know. There isn't any recipe book for it.

And we can't add anything to that.

7

The Broker: The Low-Key
Service Man Who Confronts

Fred is a man in his early thirties. He has taught in his present school
system for a number of years and was a team leader in an inner-city
school before being selected principal for another building in the same
city. The school is relatively small—300 students and twelve teachers—
and it serves the families of a working class, predominantly white community. At the time we talked with Fred, he had been a principal for two
years.

During our interview, Fred impressed us with his low-key, but rather
persistent style. As he talked, he revealed the wide boundaries within
which he is able to work, taking people as they are, working with them
on their problems, and gradually trying to move them. But it was clear
that he could and did take strong stands on particular issues, most of
which were organizational in nature. He seemed to have no apparent
master plan for what he would like the image of his school to be in the
future. Rather, his whole thrust appears to focus on the improvement of
instruction, no matter what form that might take. To this end he described himself as a "service-oriented person," the services being offered
to teachers, parents, and community organizations that were proximal to
his school. But Fred does not see himself as being service oriented in any
community organization sense. That is, when he engages with groups or
individuals outside his school, it is all with the ultimate purpose of affecting
what goes on in the school, particularly with regard to the learning of
students. For example, a social worker contacted him about the possibility
of conducting an Adult Basic Education program in the school, something
the basic education people were loathe to do, preferring to carry out their
program in their central facility.

> We got two parents to go down and beat on the door at the Adult
> Basic Education Center. I said, "You keep after them from your end
> and I'll keep after them from this end." So, it worked, because the basic
> education people said they would come if we could get ten people,

which we did. It all just happened when I met and started to talk with the social worker from the Adams Community House. I went for it because I thought it would benefit the school. You know, a kid might say, "Hey, Mom's going back to school tonight and that makes some difference to me."

There is more to Fred than meets the eye. When he told the parents that he would "keep after them from this end" he meant just that. There's a sense of persistence in it all, combined with a low level of tolerance for bureaucratic red tape or regulations that stand in the way of getting things done that Fred feels are important. The important thing for him is to get things moving, and once they start to move he backs off, and keeps in contact only to see if he's needed.

Sometimes, though, this style of getting things going and then backing off creates problems, even failures of some programs. Fred related an example of trying to get parents more involved in the school. The teachers, rather reluctantly, it appears, agreed to go along with his idea and formed a committee to implement it. His role, as he saw it, was to let the teachers do it themselves. The idea never really bore fruit. Fred said:

I just never pushed or followed through and I think that's why I fail when I fail. As soon as something is started, I go on to something else. I don't know why I do this, whether it's because I tell myself I have too much work, or whether I'm afraid I might fail, or it's going to bomb out and I would have difficulty accepting failure, or what.

So, we have another side emerging of Fred as principal. He seems to be introspective, even quizzical about himself and what he does. And there appears to be a certain amount of cautiousness in his actions, particularly where new ideas are involved, that may head him into acting, at times, in a self-defeating manner. In a curious way his acknowledged service orientation provides the powder keg on which he occasionally sits. These circumstances apparently occur when the situation demands more direction, forcefulness, and follow-through than he is willing to give, perhaps for the reasons he described above. Failure then, precisely the situation he wanted to avoid, occurs because he has not committed himself. But publicly, at least, it is not his failure. Privately, though, it appears that he internalizes it as his own.

This analysis is not meant to be critical of Fred, but to indicate that he is aware of what is transpiring and that he knows people must be aware of the consequences of their own behavior before any change can take place. Another issue involved here has to do with Fred's newness in the role of principal, and the fact that the principal of the school where he taught prior to assuming his new job did not provide a satisfactory role model for him. He has had to feel his way on his own, through the entire experience. His words are best at this point:

> The nature of the job emphasizes isolation. Unless you have an assistant, which I don't, it's a pretty lonely kind of role. I really felt an overwhelming kind of loneliness.

This is a potent, if somewhat poignant, commentary by Fred about his feelings when he became a principal. Its poignancy comes, of course, from the reactions that feelings of loneliness evoke in most people. Typically they react by wanting to sympathize, recalling perhaps, times of their own loneliness and the frustration that may accompany it. But the impact of the loneliness Fred expressed goes far beyond engendering the ordinary feelings of compassion that one person might have for another. At issue is the effect that feeling lonely can have on the ability of a school principal to get stimulation, to initiate new procedures, to change things, to get feedback on his ideas and behavior. It seems clear that for a principal who wants to do things with his school, feelings of loneliness can act only as a deterrent. There is no support system. But what about Fred's colleagues, the other elementary school principals in the system, particularly those schools in the same area as Fred's?

When we raised this question, his first response was a laugh of derision and cynicism. It was not a smile; it was a laugh. And so we talked at some length about his perceptions of the state of peer relations within the system, and of Central Office personnel and the effects they may have on these relations. Perhaps that's where it all starts, at least from Fred's point of view.

> You know, there are lots of mixed messages. I think they would like, or they say they would like, principals to be instructional leaders. But I have seen some appointments that really surprise me. People have been appointed as principals who neither know an awful lot about instruction, or care about it. It's not that you have to know everything, but you have to care.
>
> So, in a way, Central Office communicates that it's really a maintenance position. They feel that as long as there aren't a lot of phone calls and they don't get a lot of grievances filed by teachers, you are doing okay.

In systemic fashion, then, Fred's feelings of loneliness and the lack of productive peer relations are unintended consequences of personnel decisions made at the Central Office. Public pronouncements speak to the need for instructional leaders, which is what Fred sees as the main responsibility of a principal. The subtle private communication to "keep things cool," adds strength to his perception that what the system is really interested in is a "peace-keeping" operation. If, on top of that, a principal can manage to introduce some new and productive ideas into the curriculum, it's a plus. But don't worry if you don't.

In a rather direct fashion, Fred once raised the issue of the mixed messages with his superintendent.

> As I remember, what I said to him was something like this: "You say you want us to be instructional leaders. But you send out a lot of messages that are different. I get this stuff down the pike all the time. Do this; be here; do this; do that. I have to let a lot of this stuff go by the boards if I'm really going to fulfill the role of an instructional leader. So, maybe you can explain it all to me." His reply was, "Oh yeah, well you've got to do all this other stuff first so that you can then have what you want."

These comments shed some light on another side of Fred, one that is apt to be missed if focus is given only to his description of himself as "service oriented." Fred is also a confronter, and a direct confronter, at that. Note that he did not hedge in his dialogue with the superintendent. He let the superintendent know that the Central Office was issuing conflicting role expectations for principals. Most principals tend not to confront authority directly, if at all. Instead they appear to be silent sufferers, performing a host of imposed routine administrative chores, complaining among themselves, but not likely to try and change things. And rarely do they tell the superintendent that he is running, as it were, a "leaky ship." This is not Fred's style. Rather, to continue the metaphor, his efforts are devoted to finding the leak and plugging it, if possible.

In the situation cited above, Fred's efforts to make the superintendent deal with an incongruity of the system's expectations for principals were clearly not met with a sympathetic ear. Unfortunately, the principal is then left to his own devices and without system support. In Fred's case, he appears to do what comes naturally. He ignores the "Mickey Mouse," as he describes it, lets his secretary, in whom he has a great deal of confidence, deal with most of it as she sees fit, and goes about doing what he sees to be his primary role—trying to improve the quality of instruction.

Recall that this discussion of Fred's confrontation with his superintendent stemmed from his feelings of loneliness which he sees, in large part, to be engendered by the role expectations that Central Office has for principals—primarily the expectation that the role is a maintenance one. If indeed this is the case,[1] then the role of principal as confronter is also a very lonely one because there is little support for this behavior from his/her peers. To confront is to risk, and if the system emphasizes maintenance, then confronting and taking risks are behaviors to be avoided. The principal who decides to confront will, for the most part, be a lonely

---

1. We know of a few districts where the opposite holds, where the superintendents are very much instructionally oriented. Curiously, this orientation has created a great deal of superintendent-principal conflict. Perhaps the issue is that most principals, indeed, are comfortable in and desire the maintenance role.

person. This point, perhaps, accounts for Fred's laugh when we initially raised the question of his relationships with other administrators. Of all our interviewees, Fred devoted the most time to talking about the way he perceived his fellow principals. Several issues were involved.

> I've never developed a good working relationship with the other three principals on the west side. They are all older; one of them is ill. I don't think I could share anything with them. They wouldn't get involved in anything, even when a decision was made to close one of the schools. This one guy's position was "Well, it happened."
>
> They won't become involved politically. They don't mind getting their pictures in the papers with one of their kids who won a prize, or something like that. But the idea of taking a public stand on an educational issue—like picking a new school site—is something they won't do. I can't be like that.

It's a frustrating situation for Fred. Perhaps his frustration led to a bit of sarcasm and anger directed at his colleagues who were physically close to him, but it was also directed at principals as a group. He indicated, for example, that this group, which meets regularly, is not powerful and gives no indication that it wants to become powerful. There are, though, isolated individuals with whom he communicates. For example:

> There's a new guy who was just appointed at Beecher. We talk a lot on the phone because nobody can ever see anyone else. But the principals' group as a group is not a power base. We have very little to say about what happens to us in terms of professional development, for example.

This last point, the lack of any formal professional development program aimed at principals, is a bothersome thing for Fred. He sees it as an important need and one that is totally ignored by the Central Office. The fact that the possibility of developing such a program is given no priority by the school district seems to fit in well with his previous analysis of the district's priorities concerning the role of the principal. The situation goes something like this: The messages sent by the system are that the primary role of the principal is to maintain the status quo. There is no particular educational management expertise needed by a person in order to keep things running smoothly. Principals are appointed because they are presumed to be already competent to do just that—run things. Monthly meetings, which deal mostly with "Mickey Mouse," are designed to keep things as they've always been. No directed, continued, and intensive professional development program is needed to maintain that which seems to be most desired (at least as evidenced by behavior) by the Central Office, which results in at least one talented but frustrated principal and a relatively powerless group of administrators.

An additional comment that Fred made indicated that he is not the only principal who feels frustrated in his role and who yearns for some collegial stimulation and help from the system. At one point he said:

> If we could only have a nonagenda meeting where we could talk about what are our extreme frustrations. No one has ever wanted to deal with them or even listen to them. Perhaps they just feel helpless about it. I don't think principals see themselves as really being able to solve the problems that occur daily. I think they see themselves as just being there, as not being able to change anything. I don't know how to change that perspective. Maybe it takes a few people acting together, but I don't even know how to approach it. And that's frightening 'cause I used to think it could be done.

There is a strong element of tragedy in all this, both for Fred as a person and for our educational enterprise, if what he has said bears any relationship to reality—which we think it does. On the personal side, Fred's enthusiasm and energy regarding his ability to influence what happens in the larger sphere of educational endeavor, beyond the walls of his school, is waning after less than two years as a principal. The system, in which there really are no villians, is taking its toll and the price seems high. What Fred has described is undoubtedly an unintended consequence of the way things operate. That is, the values and procedures by which the system operates are not all designed to sap the enthusiasm principals have for trying to induce change in the system at large. Nonetheless, this appears to have happened in this one case, and probably it is not an isolated case.

Fred, however, is not completely hopeless about the situation. His perceptions are that about one-quarter of the elementary principals in his district feel the way he does, and that if they ever got together they could probably make things happen because the other three-quarters wouldn't oppose any proposals—nor would they strongly support any. There would, of course, be some risks involved, but these are of an ill-defined nature. They have to do with the uncertainty attached to the consequences that might develop if people started to rebel, even softly, against the authority structure of any hierarchical system. Actually, Fred sees the risks as being very low:

> I don't think it's much of a risk because I don't think they'd know what to do if we ever made a demand on them. They'd probably faint on the spot.

So, the reasonable question is, why don't some of the principals get together, formulate a plan, and propose it to Central Office? The answer:

We are just a weak group. And yet we have a number of strong individuals. The problem is that we have never functioned as a group, as a cohesive group, in making demands of any kind. And a good part of the reason for it is that we are by ourselves so much of the time. And the energy required to try and change things just isn't worth it.

Things are thus circular and reinforcing. The nature of the job requires principals to be lone operators most of the time, with the exception of those who have assistants (interestingly, two of the individuals that Fred mentioned as being powerful do have assistant principals working with them). They have complete responsibility for their schools and thus feel constraints against moving out into the wider system. Further, the norms of the system seem not to support reaching out in an effort to establish strong group relationships. It is not so much that anyone has said, "We discourage that kind of behavior." More simply, reaching out to establish the cohesive group Fred spoke of has not been encouraged. The message seems to be, "Stay in your school." And Fred is lonely. In addition, his assessment of the system, at least that part of it to which he was reacting, is that it is relatively immovable. As far as the energy expenditure that would be required to change it, Fred's comment was brief and to the point, "It ain't worth it."

A certain element of sadness and frustration is in Fred's last comment. It is as though the subtleties of the system's operation were forcing him into a constricted role, one that rather effectively prevented him from getting some of the psychic sustenance that he needs as a professional educator. This is no small problem. Indeed, at one point in our discussion, his frustration—not with his work in the school but with his isolation from colleagues—came out forcefully as he indicated that it was a major personal decision of his to stay on as principal for another year.

It would be incorrect to infer from the preceding discussion that Fred is down-in-the-mouth about his work as principal. Quite the opposite seems to be the case. It all seems fun and, as he put it:

You get your jollies at school because you know that as a result of what you do you can see something happen pretty quickly. Particularly this is true if you can help a kid or a teacher.

If the picture of Fred's relations with other administrators is a somewhat forlorn one, the same does not hold true for his behavior and relationship within his school. There are things to be done there, but more importantly, he can have direct influence on the course of events. Things happen, sometimes quickly, and there is much satisfaction in it all for Fred. However, the process of getting things to happen, both structurally and procedurally, was not an easy one. Two major complicating factors were involved. The first had to do with the fact that the role of the administrator in a small school includes all the functions that would normally be performed by several people in a larger school. Thus Fred was the administrator and did the work associated with that function. He was the guidance counselor, the instruction and curriculum specialist, the instructional supervisor charged with evaluation, and the school disciplinarian. He also had responsibility for school-community relations.

This set of circumstances is not unusual. There must be hundreds, if not thousands, of elementary school principals who face similar kinds of multiple role expectations. But the commonplaceness of the situation does not alter the fact that, as Fred said:

> A lot of shotgunning goes on. The whole bit is tremendously frustrating. In addition, I am supposed to help teachers and I'm also supposed to evaluate them. I'd rather have it one way or another, because the way it is now, the situation raises lots of conflicts—for me and for the teachers.

Fred's use of the term "shotgunning," as well as his concerns about the supervising-helping role conflict, provides an important clue to the source of his frustration. The implication is that he must scatter his energies, rarely having the time to devote extended thought and effort to one particular target, even though that may be what he is concerned about doing. Again, these circumstances are not unusual. Furthermore, the hypothesis that schools that are organized the way Fred's is—one principal for the whole ball game—gives subtle reinforcement to the notion advanced earlier: the system is more interested simply in keeping things running than it is in providing instructional leadership through the efforts of the principal.

The second complicating factor that was involved with Fred's efforts to provide leadership for the school was a bit curious, given the fact that the building was classified as "inner city." This factor was that its staff was highly stable. One of the teachers had been on the faculty for twenty-seven years and another, twenty. Patterns concerning how things happened in the school were pretty well established. Working procedures were rather firmly set. How well established and set things were is illustrated by the first major structural problem Fred faced when he became principal. It had to do with class size. More specifically, the problem had to do with the norms that had been established relative to the unevenness of class size. For years the school had operated without any deliberate organizational design to its structure. Teachers were not shifted to take student population into consideration. In the particular case in point, the two fourth grade teachers each had nineteen children in a class while the two first grade teachers each had twenty-eight. The normative attitude that teachers had learned and espoused was that different members of the faculty "lucked out" from year to year. Their attitude was, "This is our year to have fewer kids. Next year somebody else will have it easy."

As much as Fred sees himself as a broker of resources and services in his work with individual teachers, he also has clear notions about what he thinks are effective organizational designs. In this case, he had a rationale that suggested that the first grades should have no more than twenty-one students, and that classes should get progressively larger, by small increments, as the youngsters proceeded through school. This was an important concept to him, and he was not about to buy into the chance pattern that had developed.

How he acted in the situation tells a lot about Fred's style when he is functioning as the *organizational* leader of the school. He took a firm and negative stand on the accepted pattern. He said, in effect, that the system as it stood would have to change, but he did not mandate the substance of the change. Instead:

I said, "Wait a minute. Let's look at some alternatives to what we're doing." We began meeting in October. I generated four of five possible organizational structures. Well, we began to design some things so that by the end of the first year we were able to sit down and manage our structure deliberately, and in a way that I think made sense educationally.

There is a certain firmness about Fred's style, then, that is combined with flexibility and a willingness to engage collaboratively with others in problem solving. He appears to be able to dig his heels in, not let himself be pushed around, and, at the same time, to seek out alternative ways of resolving problems. His "dug in" position in this case was:

There is no way we are going back to our chance pattern of class size. Now let's look at this thing in a different way; see what our options are; what's good about them and what's bad about them.

There are other consequences to this way of working with teachers, and they do not appear to be a deliberate part of Fred's thought processes. Recall that Joan (Chapter 4) viewed and conceptualized most of her interaction with teachers as inservice training. And she went at it with a vengeance. Fred seems not to conceptualize his work with teachers this way, but the same effect seems to hold. By engaging them in an alternative-seeking process, he was also enabling them to move outside of their particular classroom concerns and view the school as more of an integrated social system. This is in juxtaposition to a school's being simply a place where what happens in one part of it bears little relationship to what happens in another part.

There is also a somewhat more abstract way of viewing this part of Fred's style. Implicitly he was trying to get the teachers to raise questions about the "regularities" (Sarason, 1971) by which the school functioned, regularities that have no basis in sound educational practice. He said,

"Now let's look at this thing in a different way . . ." Put differently, he might have said, "Must we always do things without questioning simply because that's the way things have been done?" But what also seems clear is that, as he takes the positions he does, as he raises the questions he raises, there is a sort of softly growling bulldog quality to it all. He hangs on but doesn't make too much noise about it.

This softness or low-key style that appears to typify Fred also becomes apparent in his work with teachers as individuals or in a group. For example, his goals for his first year as principal were modest and were based on his view that the teachers in the school were relative strangers to each other (they rarely communicated about school issues or solved problems together).

> The first year my expectations were that we would meet, talk about instruction, and get to know each other. It was just an opportunity to sit down and let each other know how we felt, the things that bugged us, and so forth. It was really something. For the first time they started to talk about caring what was going on in the school, not just in their own classroom.

Setting up periodic meetings where teachers can just talk with and get to know each other is certainly not a startling innovation. However, it is revealing of him, some of his basic values, and the way he conceives of himself. The values Fred holds seem to be based upon a deep faith that the majority of teachers are wholesomely motivated and have an abiding concern for youngsters. What is required to capitalize on these concerns, on a wider basis than just the classroom, is some kind of structure that enables teachers to talk with each other and to be heard and understood. The problem is to create the appropriate setting. In this case, what was appropriate had to take into consideration the nature of the school, which, as was mentioned earlier, was small and had a very stable faculty. Fred could not afford to be seen as a wild-eyed revolutionary, which he was not. He had to soft pedal things and, in a gentle sort of way, enable things to happen as he felt they would. In no way does Fred's service orientation involve simply being "water boy" to his faculty. Rather, he seems to know what he wants to do, creates a new setting that will enable it to happen, and stays around to assist as required.

On a somewhat different level, Fred was required to legitimize himself in the eyes of the teachers. He was younger than most of them. He could not afford to be seen as a young radical unless, of course, he wanted a rebellion on his hands. He had to move slowly even if he felt impelled to move quickly.

The same pattern is evident as Fred described how he went about working with individual teachers on matters of instruction.

I made a conscious effort to sit down and talk with teachers on a regular basis. Particularly in the beginning of the year, I asked them what goals they were going to set for themselves concerning their performance as a professional person. I didn't use those words. But I did want them to think about where they were going and the ways I could be of help—with getting resources, visiting other schools, getting literature. And I tried to get them to specify something, not a big global thing, but a small thing that would be helpful. Even if it was something like learning how to keep records better.

The message, then, is to go slowly, taking little steps. And speak the language they understand, lest they label you as a theoretician who can't communicate—who knows the words but not the music. But there's more to it than that, as a close reading of Fred's comment reveals. One of the underlying goals of his work with individual teachers was similar to one of his goals of working with the faculty in groups—to get them to start thinking in terms that would take them outside the classroom in order to take advantage of a wider universe of resources for teaching. Thus, he offered himself as a primary resource for them, as a person who could not only bring things to them but who could also enable them to go other places to learn. In a very real sense, he was a broker of educational services and instructional resources. It seems as though he said, "I'll help you create new settings for yourself, if you'll tell me what your needs are."

It is important to take special note of one comment that Fred made concerning his work with teachers. He said, "And I tried to get them to specify something, not a big global thing." The implications of this comment for him, for his teachers, and indeed, for the whole enterprise of schooling, are very large. In the last twenty years or so the schools—administrators, teachers, students, and parents—have been deluged with massive program innovation. The history of these programs has been that few have been smashing successes, for a variety of reasons running from low teacher involvement to the notion that the changes have been too broad to be manageable. It's almost as though the schools tend to reject foreign substances (new ideas) like the human body rejects foreign tissues. Whether or not Fred sensed this predisposition, we don't know. But his focus with teachers was on something small, something they could handle, something they wanted. In a very real way, this is his theory of change, and in the process of making it work he further legitimized himself as a person who could provide helpful services. By working in this manner he also reduces the possibility of failure and frustration at not having been able to deliver on something that was too big to start with. The slogan appears to be "start slowly with little things, and test them out." Additionally, to colloquialize, "half a loaf is better than none." An example of the slogan in action was an anecdote Fred told concerning changing the role of reading aides from one where people took youngsters

out of a class to work with them to one where people worked cooperatively with teachers *in* the classroom. Fred had worked in a school where
aides were integrated in the classroom setting, and he thought it was a
good idea. But he was also aware of the communications and role conflict problems the situation presented. His initial tactic was to visit another
school that was successfully implementing a plan of teachers and aides
working together; the idea of the visit was to collect information from
the vantage point of a principal, not a teacher. He returned to his school
and commenced talking with both teachers and aides. The reactions were
mixed, going from a willingness to try, to "no way." Fred's reaction was:

> Okay. Maybe that's the way it will be. But what I'd like to do is
> try it with the people who are willing, and set up some ways of seeing
> whether it's helpful or not.

Once more, then, a setting was created to test an idea. If it worked, fine.
If not, well, something else would be tried. And this attitude of experi-
mentation reinforces a point made earlier—that Fred appears to have the
kind of faith and trust in teachers that communicates that they are adults
with integrity who know what's good for themselves. But they are
different from each other. When this attitude is communicated to teachers
via behavior and not just words, it can't help being reciprocated. And that
seems to be the direction Fred is going in his interpersonal relationships
with his faculty.

We would be remiss in this discussion of Fred as a principal if we
did not include an issue, which, while related to what he values and how
he behaves, has much wider import. The issue has to do with the quantity
and quality—or more generally, the lack of it—of adult-adult interaction
in the schools. It arose, in our discussion, from the anecdote concerning
the integration of teacher aides into the ongoing instructional life of the
classroom. Fred's analysis of what appears to be a fairly general reluctance
on the part of teachers to engage in task-oriented adult-adult interaction
reads like this:

> There has never been an expectation, first of all, that teachers would
> get along with other teachers. When I was in training to become a
> teacher, I never heard anything said or even intimated that a teacher
> has a role as an adult with other adults. Never ever. And I never came
> in contact with the idea until, by chance, the school I was in started
> a team structure. There seems to be a sacredness about what happens
> once you close the door to your classroom. Or, maybe it's a fear of
> what others will find out about you.

For principals whose goal is to maintain the system, this state of
affairs, which is a fairly accurate picture of reality in most schools,
presents no problem. For Fred, or any other principal who wishes to

develop his/her school into an organic problem-solving system, it obviously does. On the other hand, it is both an opportunity and a challenge to his skill as a principal.

There is one other point concerning the problem of adults working with adults in a school. The fact that Fred is concerned about it is a clue to one of his major thrusts as principal. He sees his major function as improving the curriculum and the quality of instruction. But, he seems to be saying that the avenue to get this done is through enabling his teachers to trust him and each other enough so that their defenses can be lowered to the point where they can be open with each other, thus permitting themselves to work together on problems that really matter. This, too, fits with Fred's sense of himself as a broker of educational services and resources—teachers themselves are a school resource that for many reasons are not used, or are at least underused.

8

The Humanist: The Name of the Game Is "People—Plus Follow Through"

At the time of our interview with John he had just changed jobs. After eight years as principal of an inner-city high school of fifteen hundred students in a medium sized city, he accepted a position as principal of a high school in an affluent suburb. Most people in the area agree that his new position is one of the choice plumbs to be plucked by a school principal. This was the basis for selecting him to be part of this study. If he was selected from a large number of applicants to head the high school of an educationally oriented and highly demanding school district, he obviously had something that a lot of other people didn't.

John doesn't present an imposing physical appearance. Contrary to George, for example, who is a big man, John is of medium build. He is rather soft spoken and gives the impression, again in contrast to George, that his general appearance would not be apt to influence recalcitrant students to knuckle under, if that's what he wanted to have happen.

To an undiscerning ear, John could sound like just another school principal who sees himself as an undifferentiated, nonconceptual "people-oriented" administrator. Indeed, he does describe himself as a people-person, but a people-person with a difference as shown in John's unprompted use of the following metaphor to describe a school:

> I always picture a school as a moving mobile. And on that mobile, hanging out there, you have got the board of education as a group, the District Office, the parents, the faculty, subgroups of the faculty, concerns with discipline (the student), the department chairmen, and teacher union representatives. Each group mobilizes forces to put demands on you. My job is to keep the mobile in balance, and keep it moving in a direction that all these groups really want it to go.

The image is a delightful and tantalizing one, almost begging the listener to give a tug on one or another part of the mobile to see how John would act to bring it back in balance. But beyond whatever artistry may be involved, John's use of the mobile metaphor seems to serve the purpose of providing him with a coherent concept of what he is all about. That is, what we are *not* dealing with here is a soft-hearted human relations person whose aim is simply to keep the peace in a school so that it may drone on and on. Quite the opposite. His thrust was to maintain balance while concurrently maintaining momentum and direction. And this is clearly not an easy task in any high school, let alone an inner city one where conflicting pressures are likely to surface in more unpredictable and, at times, violent ways, than might happen in an upper-middle class suburban school.

The concept that John seems to hold of himself as a school administrator does not appear to include in any salient fashion the classical notion of his being the "educational leader" of his school. That is, he doesn't see himself, for example, as a curriculum expert or, as he put it, a "thing administrator." Rather than derogate that view of school administration, he appears to know what he's good at, and is careful not to put himself into situations where the demands put on him will fall outside his area of competence. This realistic self-appraisal served him well in the two contrasting positions that he held—the inner city high school and the suburban high school. In the former, the community was demanding that stability be created out of a chaotic situation. In the latter, the circumstances were different. The school was stable. Its students, for the most part, would be high achievers almost irrespective of what went on in the school. What the community wanted was not a dynamic innovator (in fact, they turned down precisely that kind of an applicant for the position in favor of John). To the contrary, they were interested in someone whom they thought could keep the mobile in balance and who could ". . . move in with community and parents and get things done with the student body and faculty." John fit the bill, then, precisely because he is not a dynamic innovator.[1]

But John's concept of a people administrator is not a Mr. Milquetoast, be-nice-to-everybody person. Consider the following as illustrative of this point:

> I remember a teacher coming in once with a student in tow and saying, "I want this student suspended." I excused the student and said to the teacher, "Look, don't ever come into the office and tell me to suspend a student. I'll make that decision as the administrator. You certainly should come and tell me you have exhausted all your avenues of dealing with the kid. But when you turn over to me, I will deal with him in my way using *my* best judgment." I don't think the teacher liked that, but we became friends afterward. Incidentally, I did not suspend the student.

1. As an interesting sidelight, we know of two chief school administrators, both of whom are forceful innovators, who accepted positions in stable school communities. Both of them are facing trying problems of mistrust and communications breakdown because, it seems, the moves and demands they made upset the balance.

To reiterate, then, John seems not to fit the stereotype of the "peace-at-any-price" school principal. Although it is clear that the focus of his administrative effort is on the human side of his school as an organization, and not on matters of curriculum and instruction, this focus does not include being anyone's pawn. Further, although John's interpersonal manner seems to be a pleasing one, there is no doubt that he can make hard decisions, nor does he shy away from making them. John is in charge, and people seem to know it.

An interesting question arises at this point concerning the basic strategy used that enables a people-oriented principal, a so-called humanist, to exercise that orientation in a way that has the effect the principal wants it to have. The mythology that is associated with humanistic administration, probably deriving from a misconstrual of the human relations era of industrial management, is that this type of administration is soft-headed, benevolent, accepting, all-forgiving, loving, understanding, and so forth. The myth goes further and suggests that if the administrator simply engages in the behaviors that are associated with these descriptions then the organization will, through some mystical process, automatically run well. In the case of the schools this would mean that the teachers would be happy and productive, and the students would be happy and learn. In short, all would be right with the world.

The point is, of course, that this myth, like most myths, bears little relation to reality. Schools are organizations whose members tend to have incompatible, if not antagonistic, needs. Furthermore, the group constituting the majority in the school organizational population—the students —are there by compulsion. For most students there is simply no alternative. It is hard to imagine, then, with the conflicts that inevitably arise from these circumstances, that an effective strategy for the people-oriented school administrator is simply to evince caring, supportive behavior—and that's all. If that were all, depending on the relative benignness of the student population, the school might come tumbling down around the principal's ears.

It was clear that John understood the nature of the conflicts that are endemic to the schools, particularly high schools. It was also clear that he understood that (1) these conflicts are probably not resolvable in any essential way, (2) these conflicts may need to be sublimated at least for the period of the school day, and (3) in order to make his concern for people operative and effective he needed to provide a stable structure in the school. He said:

Southern High was just racked with chaos when I went there. In order to be successful there it seemed essential to stabilize the situation, to calm it down. Our approach was to tighten down on things in a structural way. We became more strict about student discipline in the sense of strict enforcement of already existing behavioral codes. We let students know pretty well what the limits were and then we followed through to make as sure as we could that the limits weren't violated. Of course, there were some blatant and severe violations, and the students involved had to go for a hearing with the superintendent and they were subsequently removed from school. But people knew about it and why it had happened. An example was set. The result of this is that when the faculty perceived that things were under control we were able to get their support. They put their faith, so to speak, in the administration and things settled down.

The goal of John's structural strategy was to create some stability in the situation so that, as he put it, ". . . we could anticipate things before they happened and be prepared to deal with them." But the sought after stability was not an end in itself. Rather, it was a way station, a very necessary one, between a faculty-administrative relationship that was centrifugal—people spinning off in disparate directions—and one in which there was a coming together of people and interests.

John's analysis of the dynamics of the situation went something like this: During the latter 1960s things started to happen in the schools that had not happened before, certainly not on such a grand scale. Undoubtedly related to the trauma of the Vietnam War, to growing problems of racial inequality, to the development of the drug culture and the concurrent counter culture, and probably to the spread of what has recently been characterized by Marin (1975) as the New Narcissism—"do your own thing"—schools started to experience increasing turbulence that in many cases was severe and marked by physical violence. Both teachers and administrators, for the most part, were ill-equipped to deal with these developments. On the one hand, what teachers had always assumed as a given—their control in the classroom—seemed to be eroding rapidly. On the other hand, principals, whose role was frequently a mixture of routine administration and the conveyance of a benevolent paternalistic/ maternalistic image throughout a school, unexpectedly found themselves confronting incipient or outright rebellion, a situation they were unprepared to handle—and understandably so. The Blackboard Jungle, it seemed, had grown by leaps and bounds far beyond its original confines of the poverty-stricken, inner city, black ghettos.

New administrator behaviors were obviously called for, but they weren't, from John's point of view, unilateral decisions on the part of the principal simply to tighten things up. Whatever decisions were made should have been related to the faculty expectations (demands?) of what was needed. This point may seem so elementary as not to deserve consideration, but this is not the case. The stabilization of a school's student population is not a matter of simply showing the students who's boss, although that may be a first step in some situations. What ultimately appears to be necessary is a mutually supportive administrative-faculty relationship in which each party can count on the other to meet the role expectations they have for each other. John suggests that the process of building that kind of relationship starts with the ability and willingness of the principal to listen to what the teachers are saying, even though there are times when what they say may come across in less than clear ways:

> . . . they made it obvious to me what they expected. They wanted more strict enforcement of student discipline codes. They wanted to be sure kids were not loitering in the halls. They wanted administrators around the building; they wanted you to be visible. They did not want you in your office working on schedules or other such things. As you fulfill their expectations, also taking into consideration your own priorities, you build one hell of an alliance with your faculty. You really get them in your corner, so that when the time comes for you to ask them to do something they would not normally do, they'll do it.

This is an interesting point, then, and one that should not be misconstrued. This passage could be misinterpreted to mean that John paid attention to the expectations of teachers so that he would, after fulfilling these expectations, be in position to demand some sort of reciprocation from the faculty. A better interpretation follows: The school was in chaos. Its structure of stable relationships had broken down. It was a systemic problem that required resolution by system-oriented behavior. In this situation, system-oriented behavior meant paying attention primarily, at first, to the needs and expectations of the most relevant others who had a stake in the system's stability, the teachers. But this did not mean paying attention in a manner that excluded John's own role perceptions and judgments about what action was most appropriate to the situation. For example, in the case that John described, there were some feelings among the faculty and the community that what was called for was the use of higher and external authority—the police. John rejected this demand because, as he put it:

> . . . you can't go after kids head-to-head. You lose, because when you bring in the police, for example, it infuriates them. Force begets counterforce.

If you don't go head-to-head with the kids, what do you do? John's answer is that you demonstrate that you care for them by reaching out, both interpersonally and organizationally. He talks with them as people— about ball games, for instance, or about their families. But more to the point of the problems with the school:

> We used to have a student advisory cabinet where we would meet every two weeks. The kids would talk to me in a very down-to-earth way. We talked about the school and its problems. We would communicate very openly and try to get things worked out.

Thus, the systemic approach to resolving the school's problems seemed to work without threatening the delicate balance that exists among administrators, teachers, and students in every school. The result was the building of an alliance between principal and faculty. But the issue is that John did not engage in this system-oriented behavior for the purpose of building the alliance so that he could manipulate teachers to reciprocate on other issues. To the contrary, the alliance was to be an expected side effect of working systemically. And, not only did it enable John to make reciprocal demands on the teachers, but also it opened the door for them to make further demands on him. This is a good example of both the potential and the risks inherent in administrative behavior whose base is to view the school as an interacting social organism, or in John's words, as a mobile.

Another part of John's image of the school involved the parents. The problems he faced with the parent group seem similar to those faced by most high school principals—one of relative apathy except in times of crisis. The picture is one of frustration:

> We tried to cultivate parent support. We used to send out one thousand letters a month for PTA meetings. After the issues had been resolved, after school settled down and there were no boycotts and no violence, parental concern and community concern settled down, too. We were unable to cultivate a viable group of parents. That was a failure on my part, on the school's part.

Although John was unsuccessful in dealing with the parents on an organizational level, this seems not to be the case on the interpersonal level. He would see and establish contact with them at athletic events and in his office when they came to discuss their youngsters' achievement or behavioral problems. He particularly felt good about his skills with regard to parent conferences. But, rather poignantly, he communicated his sense of sharing the frustration of parents who had problems with their late adolescent—sometimes young adult—children and who could see no way out of the situation, nor could he.

Surely this brief description of an inner city high school principal's relationships and attempts to work with the parents of students is one with which most similarly situated principals can relate and emphathize.

The feelings and perceptions John had about his relationships with the Central Office seem to typify the bureaucratic and interpersonal relationships that are associated with large systems. First, though, John was hesitant to answer questions about these relationships. And then he said:

> My relationships downtown were very positive with most people. You attract more flies with honey than with vinegar. I don't like to make enemies and I don't like to get into conflict with people when I know I

can't win, especially, assistant superintendents. If you alienate that group you can really harm yourself later, both in terms of your school, and possibly, of your career.

The people orientation, then, takes a different turn when John has to deal with upper levels of the bureaucracy that are beyond his direct control. Again, we suspect these circumstances are familiar ones. When the situation is within John's administrative domain—the school—he seems to reach out in order to cultivate (he used that word a number of times) relationships. When he was dealing with the administrative hierarchy beyond his school, his attempts to cultivate support seemed to be characterized by compromise and conflict avoidance. That is, when John had to deal with the Central Office, he saw himself much more in a potential win-lose situation than when he was involved with problems in his school, where he had control, or certainly more control than when he had to communicate and resolve problems with the Central Office. Given that set of circumstances, his relationships with Central Office were distinctly more "political" and not as open as they were within his own school. Although he didn't say it directly, he seems to subscribe to rather basic managerial strategy: "The name of the game changes when you want things from others who have control of scarce resources than when you have control of those resources."

The ethics of that stance in this particular kind of situation is not the issue, or at least not the primary issue. The issue in bureaucracies, particularly when the allocation of scarce resources is at stake, is to behave in ways that will get you what you want. In other words, "Keep your eye on the doughnut and not on the hole" is not a bad rule of thumb, up to a point, of course. That point being when a person cannot live with what may be required of him/her by others in order to get what he/she wants. What was required of John, in terms of his having to compromise and perhaps repress some of his feelings and ideas in order to get what he needed from the Central Office, seemed not to violate any code of ethics he holds concerning his behavior. Most of his fellow administrators probably would take the same stance.

However, some school principals operate differently with upper level administrative personnel. They do not "politic," for example, but are "up front" about almost everything. And they, too, get what they want. It is not merely a matter of personal style, but one of having to develop a very strong power base among their faculty and with their parent community. The message is simple in delivery but elegantly complex at its base, "If the name of the game is power, you have three options: (1) develop counterbalancing power, and use it, (2) play defensively and wait for your opening, or (3) sit on the bench." It seems John took the second one, which appears to have been a wise choice given the circumstances of his school and its constituent parent community.

John's professional relationships with his fellow secondary school administrators seem mostly to have been related to personnel matters. These relationships, similar to those with Central Office, took on a gamelike character, but with an important difference. The game with the Central Office, although possibly sensed by all the players, was played covertly. It was like a stalking contest. By contrast, the game John played with his colleagues was overt. Everyone knew they were involved in it, and it may be likened to duplicate bridge where everyone knows the rules; whether or not you win a hand depends on your skills at bidding and playing your cards.

A substantive problem around which the Central Office game was played involved the selection and transfer of teachers:

> Teacher selection became a problem because more than the building principal was involved. Most often it was a case of when a subject matter supervisor from Central Office and a principal disagreed about transferring a teacher from school X to school Y. School X, when it has to give up a teacher, always gives up a weak one. We (the principals) all know that. We meet once a month and laugh about it. And we think when we get a chance we'll unload on someone else. But that was a source of conflict, because although we accepted the fact that we all had to take our share of problem teachers, we always felt that there were some who took less than their share. They were more successful in wheeling and dealing lemons out of their building.

It seems, then, that a sort of "clubby" atmosphere existed in the administrative peer group with which John associated. But as he indicated, it was not all "hail fellow and well met." There was conflict, and probably some hostility that became cloaked in humor. The most successful players in the games that occurred were those who were able to combine their skills at chess, where the board is open for all to see, with their ability to operate skillfully in the more covert power game of the Central Office.

Considering that this is an imperfect world, it seems that John has presented a rather realistic picture of a school principal's relationships with the bureaucracy of a large city school district. The people orientation that he has described in connection with his role in his school takes second or third place to the political demands on him when he moves into the larger system.

The essence of John's style can be found in his repeated use of three words, which he used in several different contexts. They were *cultivate*, *caring*, and *follow-through*. He used them with respect to teachers, students, parents, and, indirectly when he described his relationships with other administrators in his building.

The concept of cultivation seems to be an appropriate metaphor to describe the focus of John's administrative efforts. As any backyard gardener knows, cultivating a garden involves more than merely putting the seeds in the ground and hoping they will germinate and the resulting plants will be healthy and bear fruit. The ground needs to be watered, fertilized, and weeded; the plants themselves have to be tended, each according to its need. But the gardener also knows that some things are beyond his/her control, such as receiving too much rain or not enough sunshine. However, if he/she has paid attention to those things over which he/she has control, he/she may get a decent crop even if the elements aren't as kind as they might be.

Metaphors, of course, tend to present oversimplified images of behavior, even if they are accurate. But this metaphor can help indicate the complexity of John's concept of himself as a school principal. The thrust of John's cultivating efforts focused mostly on his school and its immediate constituents—the teachers, students, parents, and his administrative staff. The aim of it all seems to have been the development of a stable school organization that could weather unforeseen, fortuitous events and bear fruit at the end of the season.

John's primary cultivating techniques were to demonstrate that he cared about these constituent individuals and groups, and to follow through on his commitments. The ways in which he communicated his caring varied. He listened to his faculty, for example, and not only to the words they spoke but, apparently, to those that were left unspoken. It's a curious commentary, perhaps, on our complex and fast moving organizational society, that the very act of actively listening and communicating one's understanding of others has the side effect of creating the feeling of "He/she cares." For example, on more than one occasion, each of us has dealt with students who, from their point of view, feel they have been "brushed off" by other staff members in the university. We listened to them, and by our listening, and frequently little else, conveyed the impression that we cared—and we did. This is not an unusual example, of course, and undoubtedly most people have shared similar experiences. The issue is raised here only because of the frequency that teachers refer to their principals as nonlisteners.

Sometimes, then, listening to others is sufficient to demonstrate caring. This seems often to be the case, for example, in psychotherapy and counseling. For the school administrator, though, whose job is action oriented, merely listening is an inappropriate stance in most cases. Something has to happen as a result of the listening, even if it is only to express approval or disapproval to the listener. But more often, in John's case, the listening he did was followed by an action decision. However, the cycle is still incomplete because teachers need to know that the decision was, indeed, implemented. There needs to be a following through which in itself is another demonstration of caring. John's words say it all:

Teachers have to see you as caring, as listening to their problems. And after listening, you have to follow through so that teachers know you cared enough to do something and then communicate back to them. You may not follow through the way the teacher thought you should, but at least you did something. You heard the problem and you dealt with it in a way that you saw fit.

Caring is communicated in other ways, by involving teachers and students in decision making, for example. Again, in John's words:

There are decisions that can be made about the whole organization in which the faculty can and should be involved. When you do that the faculty starts to feel an integral part of the school, not just a classroom teacher. It helps develop morale, and it helps bring about a sense of professionalism in the school. The faculty develops the sense that the guy running the place will listen to them and move in directions they feel appropriate.

In a way, then, John appears to reverse the thrust that Argyris (1957) has noted is characteristic of many organizations when they employ adults and treat them like children (by, among other things, denying them responsibility for planning and decision making). It is a truism that if people are treated like children they will behave like children by, for example, displaying a short time perspective, by denying responsibility for their behavior, and by refusing to take responsibility for the larger system of which they are a part.

John carried the same cultivation, caring, and follow-through notions with him in concerns with students and parents, although his sense of failure concerning the parents as a group has already been noted. Particularly with students, it seems that his efforts were aimed at helping them feel less anonymous, less a part of a nameless mass. His strategy was one of interpersonal contact:

If you want to cultivate kids you really have to care about them and convey that caring to them. You've got to be seen as more than just the guy who suspends kids from school. I try to talk to them in the halls, at ball games, in the cafeteria, in classrooms. I try to get to know as many of them by name as I can. In a large school that's tough, but a principal should know four or five hundred kids by name, even in a school of fifteen hundred.

As important as the ability to learn names, though, is John's comment "you really have to care about them." The point is simply this:

If a principal really doesn't care about kids, for example, his concept of his role might be that of routinely administering the school, period— he is probably better off not trying to play the "getting to know you" game.

The youngsters will recognize the game as precisely that, a game. It will be seen as meaningless or, worse than that, as counterproductive, as the principal becomes the butt of jokes among the student body and probably, the faculty. For example, an elementary school principal became the object of hilarious comment because he had a perpetual grin on his face. The grin was there even when he disciplined a student.

Finally, in his relationships with his administrative staff, John cultivated and cared here, too, but his behavior took a different form.

> . . . you've got to get those guys to do things the way you want them done, but they have to want to do it that way. This means you've got to be very supportive, particularly with regard to the decisions they made. I never countermanded a decision that was made by a vice principal for fear that I would have him second-guessing himself out there. If he was wrong, I would live with it, and then we would talk about it at the end of the day.

Thus, it is essential that a school principal cultivate the active support of his/her administrative staff, by caring for them, but that caring is evidenced in ways that are different from those used with teachers or students. In this case, caring takes the form, first, of conceiving of the staff in an adult manner and, second, behaving in a way that communicates this to them. So, they are allowed to make decisions (which is what they are paid to do) and to live with the consequences of those decisions. If they make an inappropriate decision the principal helps them understand why. To do otherwise is to imply that they are not adult, thus committing an act of not caring; the principal will not get nor does he/she deserve their support.

At least, this is what John, The Humanist, seems to be saying.

9

The Catalyst: Stirring the Pot
to Create Action

Almost by definition, a woman who is a high school principal is an unusual species in American education. There are very few of them to be found. Marie is one of that small number,[1] but her unusualness goes beyond her membership in that tiny group of women who have "made it" to the high school principalship. At least, that is the impression she gives when talking about how and why she got into school administration, what she does and how she relates to the people with whom she works, and the values that seem to guide her behavior.

Marie is a rather tall woman, about forty, single, attractive, and lively; she laughs a lot. She can also be rather salty in her conversation. If a group of men took it into their heads to tease her with "men-talk," off-color stories, and so forth, they would soon find themselves on the receiving end of things very quickly. But she is also very female, in that she made no attempt to project any type of "masculine" image. By the same token, she is quite aware of her having been socialized into stereotypical female patterns. She said, at one point:

> I'm female and maybe I tune that out. I think it works better if I do because I don't need to jump up and down, and things like that, when the going gets sticky.

This comment strongly suggested an integral part of the problem that women may have, if they aspire to a high school principalship. The mystique of it all seems to go like this: Women as principals of elementary schools have been accepted for many years. Indeed, the principal of the "grammar" school that one of the authors of this book attended some fifty years ago was a woman. The reasoning behind this acceptance —the mystique—rests in the notion of the mothering function that the

1. We've not been able to get precise figures but Fran, whom we discuss in the next chapter, told us there were about eighteen women high school principals in all of New York State.

public finds acceptable, perhaps necessary, in elementary schools. Elementary schools do indeed have many characteristics that are associated with what Levinson (1972) has described as feminine organizations. There is a major focus, for example, on nurturance, affect, warmth, and kindness in elementary situations. Secondary schools in contrast, are in Levinson's terms, much more masculine in their orientation. The focus is on work, on preparing for work, on learning how to be competitive, on control, and so forth. These foci, the mystique says, suggest that being the principal of a high school is a "man's" job. Men are better fitted by temperament, by their maleness that connotes strength, to manage and control.

Marie "busted the block," so to speak, in the community in which she works. We suspect that one reason why she was able to do so was that she has a lot of the kind of strength that is stereotypically associated primarily with being a man, and she is able to communicate that strength both in words and actions.[2]

Marie's motivation for becoming a principal—the very words that she used—provides key insights into her style as principal and the kinds of behavior and values she encourages in her faculty. She started her career as an art teacher, first on the elementary level and then in a secondary school. Her teaching of art was unconventional—the whole school became the canvas for her students, or at least she wanted to make it that way, which brought her into more than occasional conflict with her administrators. She became somewhat bored with what she was doing, the boredom being strengthened by the constraints under which she had to work. In addition, and in a straightforward way, she knew that the financial prospects were limited if she remained a teacher. But more important than the economics of her situation (she dealt with that in one short sentence), were her needs for excitement, her needs for productively disrupting the system. She said:

> I was getting bored. I needed something else to do that was exciting, new, different, and interesting. I thought about guidance, but it seemed to me the hands of the guidance people were as tied as those of the teacher as far as turning the place upside down for kids. An administrator can do that.

"Turning the place upside down for kids," then, is the theme that runs through Marie's story. She expresses it in a number of different ways. She loves the taste of battle or even the prospect of it. "I just eat that stuff up," she said and followed her comment with:

2. In a way there is a type of tragedy in all this. The tragedy, as we see it, is related to the assumptions, based on stereotypes, that are made about what people can or cannot do. These assumptions and resulting action must lead to an enormous waste of human resources.

When it got calm and quiet in the building, one of my assistants came in and said, "It's really boring. We've got to do something to stir this place up." And I said, "You're right. What shall we do to stir it up?"

In order for Marie to feel satisfied with what she's doing, there needs to be something going on all the time. And, apparently, if there is no bubbling-up process taking place at a moment in time, she is not at all averse to lighting the fire. Critically, though, to continue the metaphor, as a teacher she was able to start numerous small fires that were always in danger of being extinguished quickly by the building fire department—the administration. In her position as principal, the fire laws became much looser. She can start big ones or little ones; confine them to particular pockets of her territory or let them engulf a major part of it. In a way, she seems to be an organizational firebug who does, indeed, like to watch things burn, who gets some intrinsic satisfaction from not only watching, but also being part of the flames and their accompanying heat. But, of course, there's more to it than that. For Marie, starting fires is not just the "thing," period. Beneath it, however, on a level that she doesn't speak of easily, is a very deep concern for youngsters. The cue is in the comment noted previously, "turning the place upside down for kids." Building fires for the sake of building them is not the issue as far as Marie is concerned. There has to be something worthwhile that needs to be heated up, or, on the other side, something that has little utility that needs to be simmered down, or perhaps even extinguished.

Given the history of schools as rather stable, change resistant systems that in the past have reacted mostly to pressures from the external environment, Marie's stance and value orientation as a principal has to be considered a risky one. If, to use an immunological metaphor, she may be considered a foreign body in the system—violating long-standing norms—there is always a chance of rejection. In an interesting way, she seems to have been aware of this possibility as she thought about moving into school administration. By way of illustration:

I like running things. I think it's fun. If I'm working for somebody that I think is sharp, then I don't mind their running things. For a long time I was afraid to accept the responsibility of being out front, but I got to the point where that didn't bother me any more. You see, you can be the power behind the throne and that isn't too tough. You can get the building run the way you want it run and you can do that without anyone going after you directly. I did that as an assistant principal. But then, as I became more self-confident, I thought, "Well, you know, I can handle that out-front stuff."

Marie was clearly aware of her own needs as a person—for action, for excitement, for running things. And she was also aware of school system norms that tend to reject, or at least, not encourage, an administrator's needs to continually stir things up.

Further, although, she does enjoy doing battle—the prospect of being "out front" daily, of bearing direct responsibility for her own fire building, was one that required her to build an image of herself as someone who could "take it." She seemed to have no question that she could do this in a subordinate administrative position, or as a teacher. For a period of time, though, there was a question in her mind about how she would react in a position of top authority in a high school. For Marie the implicit question was, how would she make it as a female firebug? The answer she gave herself was that she could deal with the situation on its own terms. And this she seems to have been able to do. Interestingly, the "terms" of the situation—being principal of a high school—seem nicely fitted to Marie's earlier concerns about getting bored when she was a teacher. Further, she is very much aware of and able to articulate the difference:

> Well, I just like a lot of different things going on, and that's what happens. You never know what's going to happen the next day, who's going to call up, who's going to come into the office, or what they're going to have on their mind. It's the variety and the unpredictability that make it fun.

This comment provides a great deal of insight into Marie as a person and a principal, and it is complementary to her needs to light fires, to keep the pot stirring. Marie, in a very real sense, seemed to see herself as an organizational catalyst. People rather universally strive to make their world less ambiguous and more predictable so that they have a greater sense of control over themselves and their environment; there is security in knowing what is going to happen tomorrow. But for Marie the security that is attached to being able to predict events or from having her environment fairly well structured seems not to be an issue. Thus, she enjoys the unpredictable, the not knowing what's going to happen tomorrow. And she enjoys the unpredictability of "lighting fires," for fires, indeed, can get out of control. Nonetheless, of course, she is human and does need to feel secure, so the natural question arises: If Marie doesn't need the sense of security that comes from being able to predict and thus structure events, from where does her security come? It seems to come from her own confidence that she can handle unpredictable situations, bring them under control, and help create productive learning situations for teachers and for students.

Thus Marie's tolerance for ambiguity seems to be higher than that of most principals. The needs for security are still there, but they show up later in the chain of events. A rather long anecdote illustrates the point:

I found out that seniors didn't have to take exams. When I asked why, people said, "I don't know. It is just because they don't have to take exams." I said, "Well, you know, seniors get kind of zooey at the end of the senior year and without exams it seems to me they might get worse." The teachers said, "Yeah, they really get awful." I said, "A lot of these kids are going to college and don't you think they need the practice at taking exams, reacting to pressure, etc." The response was, "Well, it wouldn't hurt them."

Well, we told the seniors they were going to have to take exams. They got really mad and upset. They were just really furious. As a result of being so furious, they put together a student council. We hadn't been able to get them excited enough about anything before that to develop a student council, so we were able to use their anger as a vehicle to accomplish something that needed to happen. They also did some research on why you should take exams, because I told them that if they felt they shouldn't take them they would have to tell me why and they better have some data. I didn't want to hear their opinions. Well, they were very angry at the whole thing, they wanted to know what my data was. I told them my data was my education, my degree, and the fact that I had this job—"So you come up with your data."

So they did. Several of them did quite a bit of research. The Student-Faculty Senate came out of that as well as some alternatives to taking exams (community projects) but I didn't think too much of them as alternatives. They still took exams.

Well, that's what happened. We didn't know they'd get that angry, but it didn't take as long to figure out what to do with their anger.

This anecdote reveals much about Marie's view of how to induce norm-upsetting change into a school, and her style of dealing with the emotional and behavioral fall-out that may result from such action. Modern organization theory (see Likert, 1967, for example) takes the position that the management style that carries the highest potential for organization productivity is a participative one. That is, a problem is sensed, people who are involved in the problem are brought together and, because people are rational, they work out a solution to which all are committed. Overall, this notion has some utility, under certain organizational conditions. But Marie's behavior indicates that her private theory of change, particularly when long-standing normative structures are involved, doesn't put too much stock in the participative model. Given the present case, for example, what might have taken place had Marie convened a group of administrators, teachers, and students to examine the problems associated with the norm of seniors not taking exams? The administrators would present the problem and give their suggested solutions, some of the teachers would support the administrators, and some would support the students; and the students would undoubtedly take the position of maintaining the status quo. After all, who *wants* to take exams? It is possible in this set of circumstances, of course, for a compromise to be worked that would be more or (probably) less satisfactory, a watering down of each position. It is likely that the administration would mandate the change irrespective of this resistance. If the former decision resulted, things would remain the same and the possibility of a struggle for power in the school in the future would be enhanced. If the administrator's initial position carried the day, the norm would be changed but the resistors—teachers and students—would quite correctly feel that they had "been had." That is, they had been convened to solve a problem collaboratively, but the decision had already been made. This is not an uncommon occurrence in the schools, and the long-term effect upon teacher and student attitudes is usually counterproductive. Few people like to participate in dishonest games.

Whether or not these ideas were in Marie's mind when she made the decision about senior exams, is not clear. What is clear, though, is her behavior and what it tells about the problem of restructuring important school norms. It's almost as if she were saying, (Chapter 11), "If you want to know what to do, do something." Marie's position is that a principal has to have confidence in his/her ability to deal with the flak that results.

Marie's style of dealing with the flak—the anger of the students—varied. On the one hand she was prepared to do battle with them, and she did. Combined with her willingness to engage in a confrontation with them, however, was a corresponding willingness to turn the situation into one that had some learning attached to it (getting the students to research problems associated with taking exams), and to engage with them in building other potentially productive experiences. In addition, of course, one unexpected consequence was the development of the Student-Faculty Senate.

Perhaps the most revealing comment, in the entire story of senior exams, was the last one that Marie made, "We didn't know they'd get that angry, but it didn't take us too long to figure out what to do with their anger." The issue is what strategy and accompanying style a school principal uses when conflict and emotional upset engulfs one or another segment of the school population. There are a number of ways to meet such conditions. A principal, for example, can ignore the whole situation, using the working hypothesis that, in time, what is boiling will simmer down and things will return to normal, however that is defined. In other words, the principal can deal with the conflict by avoidance. Another strategy that might be employed under conditions of emotional conflict would be to engage in a war of attrition. That is, the principal takes a position and fends off attacks under a working hypothesis that suggests that, in time, the opposing forces will become exhausted from the battle, their energies will dissipate, and they will comply in the face of superior and immovable forces. A third strategy is to confront the conflict openly, not in a "heels dug-in" manner but in a manner that acknowledges the conflict, that stands on some basic ideas, and that opens up the system for discussion and problem solving.

Principals, of course, utilize one or the other of these strategies from time to time, depending on their assessment of the situation. Sometimes they avoid, sometimes they fight, and other times they confront openly. But each appears to have his/her predominant or preferred mode of dealing with emotional conflict, which is a product of his/her own idiosyncratic socialization. Our observations of most school principals is that the preferred mode is that of benevolent avoidance, a mode that is supported and reinforced by system norms. That is, it appears that much of the conflict in schools is dealt with in a soothing manner which aims to reassure people that everything will be all right—"Just try and forget about it and go back to work."

Obviously, this is not Marie's style, although there are probably times when she uses it. Conflict for her seems to be the vehicle for change, not to be avoided but to be welcomed for the opportunity it presents to open the system. She is skilled at confronting and she is also skilled at fighting. Most importantly, however, it appears that the idea of a school's being in temporary turmoil does not frighten her. In fact, she seems somewhat exhilarated by it all. There's almost a joyous quality to it, made possible perhaps by her ability to see humor in such situations. It's easy to imagine her saying, after having thrown down the gauntlet to the students, "Wow, that was fun and even funny. Let's see what they can do."

There is a very serious side for Marie to the whole business, that side involving an overall strategy to upgrade the education of youngsters and to help make her faculty a more vibrant, realistic, thinking group. With the faculty, her primary concern seems to focus on their insularity from the environmental scene outside the school. She said:

> What I see in my school is a group of people who are nice and they're interesting, too. I think they have basic intelligence, but I don't think they're terribly aware of what's going in the world today and the implications of what's going on for the schools. For department heads to get angry because their budgets were cut struck me as very unrealistic in view of what's happening in this state, for example. If you read the news, it seems to me, you have to understand the ramifications of it all for the school. For them to sit there and blame me or the superintendent for not getting any money just struck me as naive.

It is apparently difficult for Marie to tolerate adult naivete, particularly when she sees important issues involved. Fairly quick to anger, her tendency seems to be to administer a quick jab. In the situations just described, she asked the department heads if they wanted her to go out and create a school riot so that the community would become convinced and pour more money into the school. Sarcasm, of course, rarely begets a benign response, and this case was no exception; one department head actually suggested that she might well do that—i.e., create a ruckus. The situation was degenerating. It was resolved with Marie saying, with counter sarcasm, that she couldn't think of a riot to create at the moment and that, in any event, "You're just going to have to function on less money."

This incident, not necessarily the most preferred way of dealing with an issue, further illustrates what Marie is all about as a person. She seems well able to tolerate the fact that youngsters may base their attitudes and behaviors on a fairly circumscribed world view, and she is willing to work with them to help them broaden that view. That's why schools exist. On the other hand, her fuse appears to get very short when adults, who themselves are supposed to help youngsters get an understanding of the world, exhibit a narrowness that she describes as naive. Her threshold for this type of frustration is low. The accompanying anger, at least in this situation, was reflected in sarcasm.

Once more, however, despite the fact that many people might turn away from sarcasm as a preferred style, the fire is lit. Her department heads, at the least, are not left with doubts in their minds concerning Marie's position. There's no hedging. Rather, the position is a confrontational one, "Here's the situation. It's real. Deal with it as adults, not children. That's why you get paid."

Marie's frustrations with her department chairpeople, however, have deeper roots than what appears to be either their inability or unwillingness to face up to and deal with the economic facts of life that are confronting public education. What bothers her most are two things: (1) their apparent unwillingness to engage with her in collaborative problem solving on school problems, and (2) their inability to act as educational leaders vis-à-vis their faculty.

I'm used to working with people who will engage in give and take about important things. I think part of the problem is that they were used to having meetings with a principal who sat there and said, "Now this is what you're going to do and this is how you're going to do it." And they said, "Yes sir, no sir, aye aye sir." And if any of them dared to argue with him, they'd get their money taken away. They seem to be a little more open than they used to be. I notice they really don't sit there and just look at me anymore. They do sometimes talk and occasionally they've gotten into some fairly heated discussions. But they're not the innovators. They're not the ones who are doing things. So, when they sat there and told me that the problems they were having were how many plugs were in their rooms and the fact that the boards weren't being erased, I decided for me to get out into the staff and get staff support. I guess I'm just frustrated. I keep looking at them and wondering, you know, what are you doing here?

Marie, then, has little tolerance for dealing with minor problems. The point can be made stronger—she abhors it particularly when she sees people whom she expects to exercise educational leadership consuming their time and energy with such mundane issues—problems they could in all likelihood solve rather easily on their own.

Fortunately for Marie, one of her assistant principals apparently enjoys detail work: "He just loves doing that stuff. He's there till five every day and takes work home every night. He's really into nitty-gritty details."

Basically, it appears that she sees the concerns that department chairpeople have about routine maintenance in the school as their way of avoiding dealing with more fundamental issues of curriculum and learning. And *this* is what is frustrating to her as she sees them, for the most part, as not having a solid conceptual grasp of their program. For example:

Sometimes I just don't understand people. I try to. I spent one entire morning trying to understand that industrial arts guy and his frame of reference, because it obviously wasn't mine. He just flips around and has a good time. I don't think he knows what the hell he's doing, or why, or how. I'm not sure that our kids move out of there with any kind of conceptual skills that are going to do anything for them.

One image that has emerged for Marie as a high school principal, then, is that she finds herself engaging in a number of very frustrating situations with adults in her school. But she has some insight into the situation that helps cushion, minimally, the frustration. The circumstance is, of course, an interactive one, stemming from the conflict between the needs and expectations concerning the attitudes and behaviors of department chairpeople and the way they behave as a group and as individuals:

I know me, and I know I always want things to have happened yesterday. In addition, I have high expectations, and they know that my expectations are high, but they're not really sure what my expectations are. It isn't that I haven't told them, or that I haven't told them why. It's that they haven't hooked them all up. I guess they don't see any rhyme or reason for organization and goal setting. They never had to do it. It's almost as though a lot of people aren't sure what to do with me.

These conditions are similar to those in other school settings, both on the levels of building and system-wide operation. The scenario goes something like this. A new administrator is brought into a school setting, which has been stable over a period of time during which no new or norm-upsetting demands have been made on the staff. The system had been administered with what might be called a maintenance orientation. That is, the primary thrust was to maintain, not change, what was going on.

The faculty and administrative staff were contented and held perceptions of a smoothly running, productive organization. Perhaps most of all, they were let alone to work and teach in a manner to which they had become accustomed, and with which they were comfortable. The new administrator is not satisfied with what has been. The administrative orientation becomes one of change. The resultant impact of this new orientation is two-fold: (1) It is norm upsetting. People have to become socialized to new sets of attitudes, new goals, and new ways of doing things; and (2) by implication, subtle if not direct, the new administrator's concern with change suggests that the way the system and individuals in it have been operating is not as good as they thought it was. What seems to occur then is a sort of pulling away. A distancing effect takes place in which the people involved seek to protect themselves by avoiding confrontations with each other.

These circumstances tend not to be happy for the people involved. The well-meaning administrator becomes frustrated and angry. The staff tends to withdraw, causing the administrator to become more frustrated and angry, which in turn causes more staff withdrawal. A downward spiral of administrator-faculty relationships develops that is buttressed by a trend for one party to attribute negative motivations to another party, regarding behaviors that may have no connection with the operation of the school. An example of such a situation, not in Marie's school, is repeated here to make the point clear:

A new school superintendent was employed in a lovely small town in Pennsylvania. What occurred in his district was pretty much what has been described in Marie's school. The district had been stable and maintenance oriented. The new superintendent wanted things to change. The same kinds of things Marie mentioned that were going on in her school were going on in that district. The staff started to withdraw and the superintendent became frustrated and angry. Part of the staff's verbalized concern was that the superintendent was using his position (thus using them) as a stepping stone toward bigger and better things. Their evidence for this perception was the fact that the superintendent had, on coming to the community, rented a house instead of buying one. The attributed motive was that he did not buy a house so that when bigger things came along he could make a quick getaway. In point of fact, he did not buy a house because he does not like to own houses.

The issue here is not the good guys versus the bad guys. At issue, is that when change-oriented administrators, particularly if they are in a hurry, are employed in stable school settings, it seems reasonable to predict that some unhappy, *but not necessarily unproductive* things will happen. And Marie appears to be in just that kind of situation. She has attempted to stir things up and the results have been predictable.

But Marie is not in a state of deep depression over the circumstances. To the contrary, she almost seems energized by the obstacles that have risen in front of her. The energy seems to derive from the different support systems that she maintains. One is composed of faculty and friends at the university where she received her advanced degree. She maintains continuous contact with them. A second is her network of professional colleagues in the field. She goes to numbers of workshops, for example, for sustenance for herself, or so it seems. A third support system is internal, and is composed of her two assistant principals. Although each of the two assistants has been briefly discussed previously, the focus here is on the relationship that has developed between Marie and her assistants because of its effect on her day-to-day behavior.

Both of the assistant principals are men, one younger and the other older than Marie. She said that they really work well together, but that it took quite a while to develop a good team. Marie's words best describe the situation:

> The older of the two, Charlie, he's about fifty, wanted the job. Not only didn't he get the job, he got me, a woman. As you can imagine, he really wasn't excited about seeing me come in. I knew his feelings weren't directed at me as a person, but at the situation. He's a good kind of person and I knew he'd never take his feelings out on me. In fact, he stands on his head not to take it out on me. The other assistant (Jim) and I just had instant communication. We don't even have to talk and we know what the other is thinking. We really did have to concentrate on making Charlie part of us. In the beginning it was frustrating.

What was frustrating the development of the administrative team was not the male-female issue as Marie sees it. Rather, it was Marie's action-oriented and proactive style. Charlie, on the other hand, is more traditional and conservative and, as Marie put it, "He didn't know at all where I was coming from." It would have been possible, of course, for her to have brushed him aside, avoided him, and simply let him pay attention to the details of running a school. Marie decided this would be dysfunctional not only with regard to their relationship, but also with regard to the relationship of the administrators and the rest of the school, particularly the department heads. That is, if the three administrators couldn't function together, then their nonfunctioning would be obvious to the staff, and would probably split it. Marie understood this situation and decided that the only viable option was to reach out to Charlie and try to involve him in what she wanted to do.

> I knew I was going to have to spend a lot of time talking with him. He had skills and knowledge that I didn't have. So we talked a lot. I listen to him and he listens to me. I think he knows I listen to him and that's important to him. We hash stuff around, the three of us, or the two of us. By the time we're done, we're usually somewhere

between the two poles from which we started. It usually works better. In department meetings, I'll say, "Charlie and I really went round and round before we presented this to you," because I trust his judgment.

So, there is another side to Marie that is different from her impulsive stir-things-up side. This other side is highlighted by a concern with building a cohesive organization, not a short-term affair, and a deep concern for the value of individuals. What apparently triggers her frustration and anger is not the fact that she may differ markedly with the opinions of another person. To the contrary, she appears to welcome a good argument. What does trigger her frustration and anger is the other person's seeming refusal to invest himself/herself in a situation in order to listen to and hear about diverse points of view. Charlie, it seems, was willing to make this investment. The results have been the development of a solid administrative team from which Marie draws a lot of support.

Contrary to most of the other principals interviewed, Marie's relationships with Central Office personnel seem fairly close, though not nearly as close as the one she shares with her assistant principals. If there's a problem, it's with one of the assistant superintendents who, before he went into public education, was in the priesthood. As Marie put it, "I'm not sure he really knows what to do with women." As with Charlie, rather than avoid the assistant superintendent because he, too, has important skills she wishes to use, she alters her style, once more.

I don't avoid him at all. I'm just very, very careful about how I deal with him. I try to be very calm, very logical, very rational. If I'm off on one of my wild kicks, you know, I run it through my assistant before I ever go near Frank with it.

The fact that she is female has also played a role in the community's reactions to her appointment as principal. There was a general curiosity, some humor, and some not unusual male doubts about a woman being the high school principal.

I think they were startled, in the first place, to get a woman and, in the second place, to get a good looking one. Some of the kids, for example, when their parents queried them, said that I had a super pair of legs. And the parents all turned out in force for parents' night to get a look at me. Then there was the time I had to give a speech at the Rotary Club. Fortunately, because it's really a funny group, I didn't get the giggles. Afterwards, I heard one of the men say to a member of the selection committee, "She must have had some set of papers to get this job. I wonder if she's going to mess around with any of her male staff?" I thought to myself, "How naive can they be?"

As was pointed out earlier in this chapter, Marie is very much aware of her femaleness in her role as principal. She also knows that there is a category of reactions to her being a female high school principal over which she has no control, namely her inability to control the reactions of some men to a woman occupying a position that has historically been a male domain. What seems to stand her in good stead when dealing with the problem, are three parts of her make-up: (1) She is not a militant feminist. She reacted to the comments that were passed, not with anger, but with amusement; (2) She appears to have a rather firm hold on herself as a person, knows what her values are, and is not easily threatened on an interpersonal level; and (3) Her sense of humor about life itself enables her to sense life's absurdities and deal with them in a mature way. Thus, she was and is able to brush off unseemly remarks without getting upset or, if need be, play a tough game of give-and-take.

There was, however, one unverbalized issue connected with her femaleness, with which Marie had to deal with as soon as she became principal. The unspoken issue was, would this woman be able to make firm decisions, particularly with regard to discipline? Would she be able to control this school or would the students run rampant over a female principal? Marie was unequivocal about it. She knew she had to establish herself quickly, and that discipline problems were the vehicle by which her position would become most visible.

> They had put a very heavy emphasis on discipline. The fact was that it was rotten. So, the best way to do it, for the first couple of months, was to get the police involved. There was no hesitation on my part because I was used to running a school that way. My feeling is that when the kids break school rules the school will deal with it. When they break the law (stealing, smoking pot, throwing firecrackers) then the law should deal with it.

This strong stand proved helpful to Marie, not only with the community, but with her staff as well, as they gained confidence in her ability to create a more stable environment. As Marie reflected on the situation, although she was aware of issues surrounding her femaleness, she said:

> You know, the problem is not just a female one. It holds for everyone. It's like the "old hand" advice that's given to new teachers: "Don't smile until Christmas." I used the same kind of psychology as an administrator, and it worked. The cops don't have to come in as much anymore because the kids know we won't hesitate to call them. It was partly the kids testing, too, and they found out quickly.

It is true, of course, that being a good teacher is not a predictor of how one will perform as an administrator. However, depending on how one conceives one's role as a teacher, there may be some productive carryover into the administrator's role. In this connection, Marie seems to be saying that if a teacher understands and is able to enact workable principles of classroom management, there is a chance of carryover into at least some aspects of school management. As she said, "I used the same kind of psychology as an administrator, and it worked."

Reactions to Marie's femaleness arose in two other situations. The first had to do with the Board of Education. During the first year of her tenure, the board had voted to include two high school student representatives in their board meetings. They were on the agenda at one meeting to report on how things were going at the school. Part of their report included a reaction to the principal, whom they characterized as cool and aloof. The reaction of the board was, "Good!" On the face of it, this is a somewhat surprising reaction given current educational concern with warm personalities rather than cool impersonalness. Their reaction makes sense in another context, however. If one pictures a Board of Education appointing a woman high school principal, but having some doubts about its decision, particularly with regard to control and discipline, a student report of coolness and aloofness would be reassuring even, if possibly, the reassurance is misguided.

Marie was not terribly upset by being described the way she was, although a colleague at the Central Office was upset. What she did was to talk with the students in order to try to get them to understand how she conceived her role. She told them:

> I was never going to be the "Jolly Green Giant." I didn't have time to run around the building getting to know eleven hundred kids and furthermore, the building wasn't going to run if that's the way I spent my time.

Her style of direct confrontation paid off once more. The youngsters came to learn a bit about the problems of running a school. The relationship between them and Marie now is such that, whenever possible, they meet with her before board meetings to discuss problems that are on the agenda.

The other situation related to Marie's femaleness concerned athletic events. She hates football and basketball, but high school principals are "supposed" to be present at all games on the untested assumption, one suspects, that the principal's presence will be good for morale. The superintendent also thought it would be a good idea for her to attend. She did go to the football games, but not to the basketball games, and for a reason that is both comic and from one point of view, tragic.

> I didn't go to the basketball games because I had gone to the football games with my assistant principal and a rumor started in town that I was having an affair with him. I thought it was hysterically funny,

but he didn't. Anyhow, I called the superintendent and said, "Besides the fact that I hate sports this other thing has come up. Do I have to go to any more of these basketball games?" And he said, "No."

We have probably only scratched the surface of the problems that arise when a woman becomes a high school principal. In Marie's case, it appears that she takes things pretty much in stride although she is very aware that, like it or not, she faces role expectations from the total community that are different from those placed on men, particularly with respect to her personal life. So far, at least, these expectations have not proved more than she can handle—not by a long shot!

There is another point that needs to be raised in order to fill in the sketch that has been drawn here of Marie, the catalyst. In addition to what appears to be her ongoing tendency to stir things up, there is an enduring part of her that can be best described as "up-front openness." It seems clear that she rarely leaves any doubt about where she stands on issues. If she is in doubt about her position, she does not play the "certainty" game. She will tell you she's in doubt. But if she has a clear position, then there is no hedging. She does not like to play organizational games, preferring to put her cards on the table and deal with the consequences rather than engage in intricate manipulative endeavors. Such openness tends to be refreshing. Alternately, unless her colleagues and staff learn to deal with it, it can be the cause of interpersonal and organizational upset. While the results are not yet all in as far as Marie and her school are concerned, she'll continue to conceive of her role as an organizational catalyst for change; she'll continue to "light fires" and "stir things up."

10

The Rationalist: A New Lady
on the Hill

This chapter differs somewhat from previous ones in its overall thrust. The discussions of the school principals interviewed have tended to focus on their world view as a principal and on the recurring themes in their behavior, in an effort to highlight both the stability of that behavior and its idiosyncracies. This chapter also pays attention to behavioral themes. However, a major part of it examines the problems that develop when a woman sets her sights on becoming a high school principal, and then becomes one.

It will be recalled that Marie, discussed in the previous chapter, and who is also a high school principal, tended to brush many of her initial problems aside. Not so with Fran, who ran into obstacles even in her graduate study. Thus this extensive focus on her situation is probably more illustrative than Marie's of the barriers that stand in the way of a woman's becoming a secondary school principal.

Fran is in her early thirties. She is married to a teacher and they have one child. Her aura is one of openness, rationality, and verbal ability. She comes across in a contemplative, but forceful way. She also laughs a lot.

When we encountered Fran she was in the second year of tenure as principal of a high school in a small town in Pennsylvania. She had enrolled in a doctoral program in a large university. She seemed excited about her job, but she had experienced some problems in it that were directly related to being a woman in what had always been, in that town, a "man's" territory. So, this chapter starts with a look at her first thoughts and efforts to move from the teaching ranks as a high school English instructor into administration. She and her husband had recently returned from overseas teaching positions. They were working in the east, a little unusual in itself as their home state was on the west coast, and most teachers settle to work in rather close proximity to their homes. Fran was unable to identify any particular person who first gave her encouragement to set her career sights on administration. There was a series of circumstances and experiences that seemed to push her along. A rather odd one, first:

> There were a few casual remarks by principals that I could have interpreted as meaning that I was too pushy concerning matters of school policy, decision making, and so forth. But if that was the intent I took it differently. That is, I interpreted the remarks to mean that I knew what was going on, that I had some ideas to contribute, and that I should just continue to do that.

Here, then, is some insight into Fran as a person. She is no pushover; she does not scare easily. Furthermore, she has a pretty clear handle on herself and is sure of her motivations. So, while a woman who is unsure of her ground and is somewhat threatened by the school power structure might interpret the remarks that Fran received as advice to back off, for her it was just the opposite. The remarks served as reinforcement for notions that she already had about herself: that she was aware of organizational function and dysfunction, could talk about her awareness in clear terms, and that she was assertive. "Not a bad set of skills," thought Fran. But there was more:

> In my public school teaching experience, which spanned eight years and six different principals, I worked with only one who I thought was an intelligent and dynamic educator. I thought that the batting average couldn't all be that bad and didn't need to be and that I could be better than the average. So, with a little bit of encouragement from a principal, I decided that administration might be an interesting thing to pursue on the master's level.

This anecdote smacks of one that is told about President Jimmy Carter. The story is that during the presidential primary campaigns in 1972 President Carter, who was then Governor of Georgia, served as host for presidential aspirants who were campaigning in Georgia. His reaction to his guests, the story goes, was his feeling that he was as well equipped as any of them to be President, and better than most. Why not me? The rest, of course, is history, as it is with Fran. Beneath the surface, though, there is an important message about her as a person, the same message, in fact, that became evident as she related the comments about the casual remarks that were passed to her by a couple of principals. The message seems to be one of strength, of viewing obstacles not as things from which to back off, but as challenges and opportunities to be seized.

Her decision to study administration was the result of a natural progression—"I decided that administration might be an interesting thing to pursue on the master's level." Fran was not going forth to conquer the educational world. Rather, what appeared to be the case was that she was doing something that was quite natural, following her interests. At the time, as will become clear, she was a bit naive about the whole situation, what it would involve and the problems that would be encountered that were subtly or overtly related to her femaleness.

There was a third set of circumstances that led Fran toward thinking about administration:

> I really liked teaching. When I was teaching, I taught mostly eleventh and twelfth grades. I also had a scattered class or two at the ninth and tenth grade levels. But one summer I taught a class in photography and the kids in there went from the seventh to the twelfth grade. I was really impressed with the wide variety of experience present which led me to think about the fun of dealing with varied aspects of education instead of being confined to teaching English, for example. I guess it really made me think that I didn't want to spend the next fifty years teaching English. So, I thought I'd like to try some other focus in education, and administration seemed an easy and compatible step.

Fran's motivation to move into administration, then, was similar to Marie's (Chapter 9) although it seems to have developed with less emotionality. Recall that Marie pulled no punches when she said she was getting bored with the teacher's role. Fran's tone was of a lower key. She liked what she was doing, enjoyed the variety to which she was exposed, but took the long view, apparently feeling that a continued experience over many years would be dulling for her. Marie was already dulled but, then, she is the older of the two and had been teaching longer by the time she made her decision to go into administration. It's possible that Fran would have been as openly bored as Marie had she stayed in the classroom longer.[1]

In any event, once having made the decision that going into administration would be an easy and compatible step for her, Fran applied for and was admitted to a master's degree program in educational administration.

> I was the only woman there, but I hadn't thought of it too much in that light (i.e., being a woman in what was widely considered the domain of men) before I went into the program. I had an advisor who was extremely cool to me in the first semester, but by the second semester we were working quite well together. Nevertheless, I had to discover a lot of things by myself that probably most men knew long ago. For instance, an internship was required in order to be certified. That's a simple thing for people who know the system, but I didn't know, and nobody told me.

1. It is interesting to note that the issue of boredom or potential boredom did not enter at all in our discussions with the male principals. Although we do not have the data, we do suggest that there may indeed be different factors at work concerning the desires of males and females to assume administrative roles in the schools.

It didn't take long, then, for the subtle prejudices of the system to begin to work. Fran was clearly a minority person in her degree program, and her interests in the high school principalship simply reinforced this status. It's all right for a woman to want to be an elementary school principal because small children need to be mothered. But adolescents in secondary schools need to be managed, and this is a job for men. It makes for a quaint mythology.

The mythology, however, got played out in behavior. For example, when Fran talked with her advisor about an internship, his response was "Well, we'll see what we can do." Fran's interpretation of his comment, which he was later willing to admit was true, was "Dammit, she had to go and bring that up!" Probably if she had not pushed the internship issue he wouldn't have either, being willing to let his "problem" graduate without being certified. For example, after the issue was raised, he suggested that most people did their internships in their own school. In Fran's case this would have created a bit of a hardship as her home was in the state of Oregon, a mere 3,000 miles away from where she was doing her graduate study.

The situation did resolve itself over time. Fran did get her internship and, in addition, it's her perception that she helped her advisor a great deal with his attitudes about women in administration. He helped her, too, but:

> I think he probably gave his men students more help. For sure, he was more concerned about finding jobs for his men students than he was for me. He would say things like "Maybe you can work yourself into a dean of girls position or something like that." The funny thing is it wouldn't really have mattered because I would probably have enjoyed that, too. It was just the reluctant tone of things that bothered me.

Fran finished her internship and started to look for a job, but without much assistance from her advisor. She was considering two positions in student affairs (not general school administration) when she received a phone call from a superintendent she had known previously. Was she certified, and was she interested in the high school principalship? She was indeed, but the selection process wasn't easy and the issues focused, as might be expected, on her being a woman. The primary point in her interviews was student discipline. What else!

> The school board was really concerned about discipline. They wanted to know what I would do about this, that, and the other situation. It was hard for them to envision a woman, really hard, being able to handle an eighteen- or nineteen-year-old boy. They were also concerned about how a woman would handle more serious disciplinary problems because the school had had a lot of disruptive situations—

student sit-ins, student sit-downs, student strikes, teacher pickets. So, it was a real problem.

Despite the concerns of the Board (and probably others in this small community) Fran was hired, but not without conflict. The vote was four to three, and had the superintendent not had strong support from the Board (he had been hired on a 7–0 vote), she probably would not have gotten the position. Why did she take it in view of what she knew to be more than subtle opposition to her appointment? Her answer was straightforward—there were risks involved, but it was a challenge; an opportunity to do something she thought she could do and do well.

The superintendent had communicated to Fran his analysis of the types of political conflicts that he saw both in the community and the school. She was forewarned, then, about what she might expect, particularly with regard to three or four members of the faculty who, it seems, had made an avocation out of making it tough for high school administrators. She was stepping into a hornet's nest and, unwittingly, it seems, she stirred it up very shortly after having arrived on the scene at the start of the school year. The school had developed a pattern that had the entire student body meet at the beginning of every school day to hold, in Fran's words, a "glorified rap session." At this time, students were supposed to be able to talk about their concerns, on the theory that the talk would have a cathartic effect, thus freeing them to concentrate on their studies for the rest of the day. What seemed to be happening, though, was quite different from what was intended:

It turned out to be a sort of sadistic arena. A lot of criticism was leveled at teachers, at individual students, and at the principal who was called a prophylactic for the school board. Prominent students were simply playing to the larger student audience. So, instead of being cathartic for the students, it seemed to me that these daily sessions only generated more controversy.

Fran then made, in her own words, her first mistake—and it was a big one. The mistake was not in her analysis of the situation, but in her action. She decided, because the large session was dysfunctional, to stop it and substitute small group meetings composed of teachers and students with similar interests. It seemed like a rational thing to do, and Fran prides herself on her rational approach to problem solving. Rationality frequently comes in a poor second when opposing forces are mobilized mostly on the basis of emotionality, and this is precisely what occurred. The results of the decision were that "the kids hated it; the teachers hated it; and we had a student sit-in."

Fran was not unprepared. The grapevine had let her know that the sit-in was planned. She scheduled a meeting with the school bus drivers for the morning of the sit-in, so that they would be on hand if it occurred and if, consequently, she decided to close school. The sit-in took place and, indeed, she closed school, sending the youngsters home at about 9:15 in the morning. In addition, eighteen students who could be positively identified received a three-day suspension.

Perhaps Fran's action from the beginning was ill advised, if not a gross administrative error. Indeed, she did say it was her first mistake. But there was more to it than simply suggesting that she was too new in her position, and that she should have waited until her credibility was established before making a decision that would have such a potentially disrupting effect, even though both points are undoubtedly true. Two other factors entered the situation in a prominent way. One had to do with Fran's perspective on and analysis of the total school environment; the other with questions of her decisiveness and ability to handle tough situations.

She saw the school as being on a downhill path. There had been a lot of disruption, and her analysis of it was that not much was happening, in any systematic fashion, that could be called good education. A crisis point had to be reached that would enable her to start turning things around, not only with students, but also with some of the faculty who, it turned out, actively encouraged student resistance, and the sit-in itself. She said:

> It seemed to me, from day one, that it would take this kind of thing to blow something out and get started again. If it hadn't been the big student meetings, it would have been something else like my reactions to too many gym classes too many days a week.

Fran's action, then, was not impulsive, even though it may have been inappropriate for the time. It was a rational, contemplative decision based on her notion that if a program is not producing what it was designed to produce, rational people will want to change it. It was also a decision that Fran knew would shake the structure of the school and thus provide her with the opportunity to demonstrate that she was decisive, and that she could control a disruptive situation. The "New Lady on the Hill" needed to quickly be in a position to indicate to the school and the community that she was no pushover. And this is precisely what happened.

The problems that Fran encountered as a result of being the first woman high school principal in a small town were not confined to the school. In a sense she was being "double-teamed," in the school and in the community. At first she was a little reluctant to talk about the situation; again, the issue was related to being female. She didn't wish to be perceived as a "whiny female." She was having enough trouble establishing her credibility as a legitimate principal so that, in order not to add fuel to the fire, she kept things to herself and tried to ignore what must have been a constant pattern of irritants. Some examples will tell the story.

Six days after the student sit-in, her husband, who also had a teaching position in the school, was driving their car and was stopped by a policeman who issued two tickets: one for driving with invalid license plates and one for an invalid driver's license (they were from another state). When he went to court he was fined $150 when the typical fine for these offenses was $10, according to Fran. It turned out that the judge was the father of two youngsters who had been suspended as a result of the sit-in.

The small town communications and rumor networks also played their part:

> There were a lot disparaging and condescending remarks passed around. They would come back to me and I would kind of bounce them off. Things like, Why doesn't she wear skirts more often? How come she has such long hair? Why does she want that kind of a job? Why don't we see her in the supermarket more often? Why doesn't she join the lady Elks? Who takes care of her kid after school?

Fran's strategy for dealing with the remarks and incidents, as she indicated, was simply to ignore them, to let them bounce off her. It was a deliberate strategy, her feelings being that if she started to react, the community would take the position that she couldn't take it, and that, indeed, women didn't belong in the job of high school principal. And though Fran seemed to be successful with her strategy of ignoring, it took its toll on her. In retrospect, it was as if she were living through a state of siege, particularly in the school, but influenced by the community.

> I guess, in that first year, if I hadn't done anything different, if I hadn't started a teacher evaluation program or tried to upgrade the guidance department or focussed on rounding out kids' school experience, I wouldn't have felt near the pressure. If I'd been smart enough or dumb enough just sort of to maintain things, I wouldn't have felt that I was continually fortifying myself and my programs against attack. The attacks didn't come from all sides, but there were a lot of people involved.
> But some of that seems to have dissipated now and I think the reason is that people have become more familiar with my style. They see my behavior and decisions as consistent with me rather than as inconsistent with the guy who was there before me, or the guy who was there before him, and before him. You know, there were five principals in seven years and five superintendents in seven years.

It is easy to criticize Fran's administrative behavior. The wise old heads, on hearing of the problems that developed in the school and community, would probably shake with an "I could have told her so" attitude. It may well have been more strategically viable for her, in the long run, to have just maintained things in that first year, until people got used to her style and to the fact that there, indeed, was a "New Lady on the Hill." But that isn't the point or, at least, it is not the point of this book. The point is that what Fran is as a person, her perception of herself both as a woman and as a school principal, provide themes that make the situation more understandable. The theme of rationality, and her sense of her own competency, seems to flow throughout. Her decision to become an administrator was a rational one. What was required were knowledge, skills, a desire, and the ability to make decisions, and Fran had these qualifications.

Why the problems, then? Perhaps the answer lies in the very rationality that seems to guide her. That is, people who are guided by a forthright, empirical, rational point of view may wrongly assume that others will see the situation in a light similar to their own. After all, the facts speak for themselves, don't they? Or do they? The facts do indeed speak, but they find their voice through the perceptions of the others, as well. Fran's recounting of the story of the teacher evaluation program provides an illustration.

Even though a program of teacher evaluation had been negotiated in the teachers' contract, for years there had, in fact, been little or no implementation. Tenured teachers, for example, had been observed on the average of once every four years, a clear violation of the contract. Fran, The Rationalist, made the assumptions that (1) the contract should be adhered to, and (2) evaluation of teachers was a healthy thing to do. So, she simply started to implement the contract. After all, if people had agreed they were going to do something, why shouldn't they do it? Predictably, problems arose as teachers resisted the process by becoming defensive about comments that Fran might make about her observations of their teaching. In addition, their resistance took the form of suggesting that she hadn't been in the school long enough to understand the total situation or the teachers themselves. Over a period of two years the situation finally worked itself out as the teachers discovered that the intent of the evaluation was to help, not to punish. As Fran said:

> . . . people are probably a little more secure and accepting now. No tenured teachers were fired and I think they're coming to understand that evaluation has two purposes: to make judgments about continued employment and for professional development. Maybe it's the professional development part that they're a bit more accepting of now.

It is less important, here, to comment on the efficacy of a particular teacher evaluation program than to reinforce the notion that Fran's implementation of it was, once more, indicative of the central theme of rationality that seems to run through her view of the principal's role. But there is another element to it. Fran not only sees herself operating in a very rational way, she also seems to have a very deep faith in the process of rationality. It's as though she were saying, "The intelligent, reasonable thing to do in X situation is Y. People may resist Y initially because it runs counter to established norms. But if I persist they will eventually come to see that Y was the thing to do because it was simply rational, and they will see it that way." Accompanying her view of herself, then, is an implicit position on a technology for integrating the individual's needs with the organization's objectives. That is, her behavior suggests the technology—or mechanism—of socialization. It says, in effect, that "I will present a model, and as you learn to live and work with that model, you will find it is a productive one. It will become part of you."

An additional clue to this part of Fran's make-up was provided earlier when she spoke of the faculty's need to learn that their relationships with her depended less on thinking that what she did was inconsistent with previous principals and more on whether she was internally consistent with herself as a human being. Again, the picture is one of rationality, persistent rationality, that communicates a great deal of faith in the reasonable intelligence of others, and ignores the political consequences of behavior that may be deviant from the accepted normative structure of a school or community. As a matter of fact, Fran seems almost to be apolitical in the way she works. At one point she said, with particular reference to the mayor of the town whose son broke a window in the school during the sit-in:

> I haven't catered to the power structure and, because that was a working policy before I got there, it's created some uncomfortable situations.

It seems clear that her refusal to cater to the community power structure was also reflected in the way she worked in the school. Recall, for example, that Fran didn't mention any consultation efforts on her part when she instituted the evaluation program. She just did it because "what was right, was right." Unfortunately, as she found out, what is right may have little to do with the political or socioemotional realities of a situation. This point is raised not in criticism of the way Fran operated, but to point out that every behavioral style has its costs as well as its benefits. A clear benefit, among others, is that what she did and the way she did it enabled her to maintain her integrity and her view of herself as a person who dealt with facts and objective reality. One of the costs, also a clear one, was that she felt herself under siege.

When it came to curriculum matters, it seems that Fran's strategy, the reliance on reason, remained the same, but her tactics changed. With regard to those matters that she felt were within her administrative prerogatives, she had little hesitation about making a decision and living with the consequences. However, in matters that were essentially faculty prerogatives, she altered her ways of working. Her first concerns with curriculum problems were met in an informal way by attending department meetings, asking a few questions or making a suggestion or two. She also, and again the focus on rationality emerges, provided suggestions for new materials.

. . . because I'm really becoming more and more convinced that the
quickest way to incorporate movement in the curriculum is via materials. You get materials in the teachers' hands and you can work at
changing methodologies. For example, if you get a math teacher some
materials that have differentiated assignments built in, you can start to
work more on grouping with that teacher. To me that's the easiest
way, it really is.

Of course, this position may be debated. But that really isn't the point.
At issue here is that Fran's emphasis on materials reflects, in addition to
her rational perspective, her overriding concern with the use of language—
the right language—that will enable her to reach and communicate with
people in *their* frame of reference. The use of words, the deliberate
phrasing of ideas, then, is Fran's stock in trade as she works with teachers.
She came by this stance naturally:

It was one of those things about growing up. The people around me
were always concerned about their language. My dad, for example,
was in the newspaper business. So it's always been a real natural thing
for me to be concerned about what words I choose and how I use them.

Fran further builds on this concern with language with the following
statement:

The reason I think it's so extremely important is that, through language,
you create reality as well as describe it. For example, I've seen people
create problems for themselves by the way they describe those problems. Perhaps it gets to be a fine line between seeking the right words
and manipulation. But I do think you can change or improve situations
by describing them in ways that are different. The point is not to
sweep things under the rug, but to help people see things differently
through the language they use. So I try to figure out a way to talk
about a problem or a situation in a way so that the other person's understanding and mine are congruent with each other.

Interestingly, the focus that Fran puts on language and its use fits
neatly with the way she spends the bulk of her time on the job. Not surprisingly, she said that the main part of the job has to do with communication; with processing communications, relaying communications, or
getting other people to communicate.

It's sort of putting it all together. If you ask me what I spent most of
my day doing, it would be that, in one form or another. Talking to
people, incorporating data, and giving out data.

In a sense, then, Fran articulates her primary role as principal as an
information processor and communicator. She doesn't see herself as an

innovator in terms of altering the structure of the school (into modular form, for example) or introducing other innovations such as management by objectives or team teaching. Overall, she thinks that the system is a reasonable one, but that the people involved need to make it work better. Her strategy to get it to happen is to collect data, and then to deal with people on the basis of what the data says, not on any preconceived notion about what ought to be. Again, this is a reasonable and rational position, on the face of it, and it should not lead to any particular problems. But reality is frequently different from what appears to be reasonable; this problem resurfaces as Fran talks about the way she sees the demands on a principal whose philosophy and modus operandi resemble hers:

> You have to be a person who doesn't need a whole lot of positive rein-
> forcement, because as I see it, the position is at the vortex of a lot of
> political activity in the school and in the community. You just don't
> get a lot of positive reinforcement. So, you have to be pretty sure
> you're collecting the data accurately and that you don't have tunnel
> vision or tunnel hearing. And you have to be pretty confident in your
> own decisions because a lot of other people won't be.

In a way, it seems that what Fran is saying is that if a principal acts to make a school do a better job and to get teachers to improve the way they work with youngsters and each other, the school becomes politicized, and a battle ensues with the principal on one side and most of the teachers on the other. The principal, in these situations, has to "go it" pretty much alone, according to Fran, and has to be able to move through the day without much positive feedback. This position can be argued, of course. But that's the way she perceives the situation.

The thrust of this chapter has been somewhat different from that of the others in order to consider the problems that may face a female high school principal, particularly in a small, conservative community. The emphasis on these problems should not hide the fact that Fran's concept of the principal's role—above all to be clear and rational in her thought and language—helped her change things. Perhaps she, more than any of the others discussed, tried to insure clarity about her role and her ex-pectations of others. A consequence of this theme in her behavior appears to have been the reduction of ambiguity associated with her role.

The epilogue to this story of Fran is not one of success. The conflict in the school and the community apparently worsened as historical fac-tions grew stronger. The superintendent, her main support, was suspended on what appeared to be trumped-up charges motivated by political conflict in the community and school board. Fran clearly saw the hand-writing on the wall, and knew her survival was closely tied to the superintendent's. Fran and her husband decided they had had enough and they left the community, with few regrets, having learned a lot.

II

The Politician: "It Really Is
a Political Game, You Know?"

Paul is black. He is principal of an inner city elementary school where the student body is primarily black, but in which there is also a sizeable group of other children whose parents were attracted to the school because of some special programs. Listening to Paul talk about his experiences as principal, how he went about learning to survive in the system, and how he clarified his role, was a fascinating experience. It was fascinating for many reasons, but two stand out. First, was his political sensitivity to his faculty, parent community, and Central Office. He projects an image similar to that of a floor manager at a political convention whose primary role was to be aware of where the power rested and whom it was necessary to contact in order to get a crucial vote on his side. Second, Paul conveyed a real sense of having fun through it all. Indeed, there was a gamelike quality to his analysis of his role. But the precise nature of the game was elusive. Mostly it seemed like chess, although the object was not always to win. For example, there were times that Paul made his moves just to "tweek" Central Office Personnel, and he would then sit back and chuckle about it. In point of fact, there was a good bit of chuckling that went on among the three of us during the interview, lending further evidence to the idea that the games Paul sees himself involved in as a principal are fun for him and that, though he appears to win most of the time, others don't necessarily end up losing.

At the time of the interview, Paul had been principal of his school for five years. Prior to that time he had been the assistant principal in the same school for two years. There are unusual circumstances attached to Paul's becoming assistant principal, and then being promoted to principal, which are necessary to understand in order to appreciate his view of himself and his role relations with the various individuals and groups with whom he interacts. First, Paul did not arrive at the principalship through the typical route. That is, he had not been a teacher who, after having taught for a few years, decided on an administrative career, took courses toward certification, waited for an opening, and so forth. Rather, he had been a psychology major in college and had obtained a position with a community mental health organization in a western state. He had applied for the job of assistant principal because he was attracted to the idea of trying to influence the education of black children in an inner city environment.

Second, the fact that he was made assistant principal without the necessary credentials is testimony not only to his skills, but more importantly, to the fact that the principal of the school at the time was a rather unusual sort himself. He was a Wasp college professor who became a principal in order to "go where the action was" and test out some of his ideas about developing a community-oriented inner city school. He was highly charismatic, loved to make speeches at which he stirred people up, and he enjoyed a great deal of community support. Thus, he was able to get a noncertified person appointed as assistant principal, in spite of establishment objections.

Third, the school was organized in a manner that structured and encouraged a high degree of faculty and community participation in problem solving and policy making. This point is important because when the principal resigned to return to university life, both faculty and parents became pressure groups for Paul's appointment as principal, even though he was still without credentials. Thus, in no uncertain way, Paul owes his position to the efforts of those two groups, a fact that he was reminded of from time to time, albeit in subtle ways.

These facts, then—that Paul was promoted to the principalship in his own school, that he was without credentials when he became principal, that he followed in the footsteps of a very dynamic, charismatic person, and that both the faculty, and critically, the parent community played an important part in having his appointment accepted—had a crucial influence on Paul's view of his priorities and his role and the way he developed it. These influences assumed primary importance during his first year as principal, when his primary concern appeared to be job security and survival. He said:

> During the first year, you know, my survival was basically out of my hands. I think the feeling of the staff was, "We're going to support this person because he was our choice, we put him in there." But this was not the same with the parents. Whatever I wanted to do I had to bear in mind the reactions of certain key people who had let me know in no uncertain terms that they had hired me. Two, in particular, were the chairperson of our Community Cabinet and the secretary of the Cabinet. They were two very powerful people.

Two points in Paul's comments need further consideration. First is his concern with survival. Second, and related to the matter of survival, it is of interest to note the way Paul viewed the two groups—the faculty and the parents—without whose support the school board quite probably would not have appointed him. His comments suggest that by lending him their support the faculty had, in a way, limited its ability to reject him or his policies, at least over the short run. That is, once having gone out on a limb to influence his appointment, the faculty indeed had a stake in promoting his success. To reject him after having supported him would cause a severe loss of face in the educational community, and possibly would have had a detrimental effect on the potential of school faculties to influence administrative appointments in that system. This is a particular possibility inasmuch as the school board was not enthusiastic about Paul's appointment to start with. The faculty apparently did not constitute much of a threat to Paul's survival, as he saw it.

The parents were a different matter. The degrees of freedom under which they operated were much greater than those of the faculty. They were not under the same kinds of constraints as were the faculty and, seemingly, felt few compunctions concerning letting Paul know that, in a sense, he held his job at their pleasure. While they might not be able to "make" him, quite possibly they could "break" him.

It was also interesting that Paul's comments about survival as a principal, and his focus on the parents and faculty, occurred at the very start of the interview. These comments provided a theme that ran throughout the interview. They indicated an essential clue to his style as a person and as an administrator—his deep down politicalness. That is, Paul—what he does, his successes and his failures—must be understood from the point of view that he is a most political person whose first impulse, when confronted with a problematic situation, seems to be to analyze it in political terms. In a sense, for Paul, being a principal is a juggling act that takes place as he stands on a teeter board. Not only must he keep things moving in relation to each other, but he must also watch that he doesn't lose his own balance.

Paul's concern with survival was the most forthright we encountered in all our interviews. This point is congruent with his characterization as being highly politically oriented, particularly in view of the fact that he owed much to a nonestablishment constituency. It has been said many times, for example, that the primary job of the politician is to get re-elected—to survive in office. There seem to be two primary strategies by which elected representatives manage to do this. One is to maintain a low profile, keep things running, avoid irritating people, and "don't rock the boat." The other, particularly for those who want to create a high profile, is to develop a strong power base that will lend support in times of stress, thus insuring, as much as possible, re-election. The history of our representative democracy is replete with examples of both strategies. A similar history can be found for school administrators. There are hosts of school principals whose major operational—thus, survival—strategy is, indeed, to maintain things, to try to make sure that no one gets upset, not to "rock the boat." These principals tend to last a long time. There are also a few whose goals are movement and change and who survive, but seemingly not as long as their maintenance-oriented colleagues, by establishing a strong power base in the educational and lay community. Paul seems to belong to this latter group, and the power base he chose to cultivate was a boundary-line one relative to the system—the parents. His thoughts about the group as a power base were analytical and predictive, and also based on hard-nosed political pragmatism. He said, relative to the future:

I think more and more principals are going to have to recognize parent groups as a source of power, and one that they are going to have to deal with. This is already true in many cases. Take Brownsville, for example, where community people, parents and school people, combine to make some decisions or effect some change. It's all coming and principals better believe it.

And, as far as the day-to-day realities of a principal's life and tenure in this job:

You might see your first line of security as being downtown—the Central Office. These are the people who hired you and whom you might expect to support you. Or you might look at your teachers as your primary support group. But I think that anybody who is really aware of what's happening to them on the job as a principal will recognize very quickly that even having your hand in the pocket of somebody downtown will never save you if a parent group comes down there. They can raise so much hell that any superintendent would rather let you go or move you than fight them.

It's important to note that Paul does not speak of the quality of education being enhanced by the power and involvement of parents in school matters. Rather, his concerns are almost totally political. He views school systems as sociopolitical systems and seems to base both his interpersonal and group interactions on that concept. Indeed, as was noted earlier, seeing Paul as a politician is the key to understanding him as a principal.

The circumstances of Paul's appointment as principal—that he was promoted to that position from his previous one as an assistant principal in the same school—is not common practice. These circumstances presented him with problems of role clarification and development that were both political and interpersonal in nature. Somewhat surprisingly, in view of what has been described as his rather acute political awareness, Paul seemed to approach this role change relative to the faculty and staff in a rather naive manner, almost with the view that nothing else would change. But change it did:

When I first started I felt I still wanted to maintain peer status and buddy status, with the faculty. I wanted to be a nonauthoritarian principal, but I think I misunderstood what that meant. What I tried to convey to the staff was: let me be, let me grow, don't push me, leave me alone, and you know you can do whatever the hell you want to do.

This couldn't last because pressures started to mount, particularly from the parents. It was after Christmas and I started to get messages that it was time for me to start producing. But the group I changed with first was with the teachers. The change was in me in that I accepted the fact that I was their leader, whether I liked it or not.

A fascinating process was occurring. Here was a person who wanted to be appointed to a particular position for which, speaking in terms of credentials, he was not eligible. Nonetheless, because of the support and pressure of two district constituent groups, he was appointed. He brought with him the interpersonal baggage from his previous position, and thus the need not to have relationships change; they were comfortable. Paul thought to himself, "If I can swing this, I'll have it made. If they will 'let me be, let me grow, etc.,' I'll be able to be principal, which I really want, and not disturb the relationships I previously had." The naiveté of this thinking is obvious but understandable. Paul wanted his cake and he also wanted to eat it, a difficult task under the best conditions.

That these were not the best conditions for "having and eating" was a result of the previous principal's attempts to build both a powerful faculty group and a powerful parent group. The expectations of both of these groups were that Paul would not simply let things remain status quo. If he was going to grow, he would grow in the process of doing something, a reasonable expectation that escaped Paul, but understandably so. The first crunch came from the parents whose messages communicated "It's time for you to produce." And the first change came, not in action but in Paul's thinking, as he started to reconceptualize his role and accept the fact that he was the leader of the faculty.

Accepting the idea that he was, indeed, the leader of the faculty, was a crucial first step in Paul's development as a principal, but it was only a step and, by itself, implied no leadership. Action has to follow, and this point led to the second crunch in Paul's development—how to deal with the ambiguity of the role of the principal. What is it that he/she is supposed to do? The ambiguity started with Central Office.

This is a fairly good sized city. There is one person who is ultimately in charge of more than forty elementary schools, and he communicates that he doesn't particularly want to know what's going on in those schools. When I was interviewed with five other people, it was made clear that he assumed I knew what the role of the principal was, and his only task was to help me get staffed for August.

For a person like Paul, then, particularly given the circumstances of his appointment, the messages he received from his immediate superior were not helpful. His superior assumed he would know what to do. But, implicit in his message was that Paul should be careful concerning the extent to which he asked for help. Given the tenuousness of his situation and his heavy concerns with survival, it is not hard to conceive that forces came into play that suggested to him that requests to Central Office for help in role clarification might easily be interpreted as a confession of inadequacy for the job. Common wisdom suggested, "Keep your problems to yourself." Adopting this tactic did serve a protective function for Paul, but it did not help in clearing up the role ambiguity of the principalship. In retrospect he had several rather illuminating comments to make concerning the role of the principal, particularly one who is new at the job.

> I think that the role is always ambiguous. The only time you can clarify it is when you take control of it and define it for yourself, or let the most powerful reference group around you define it for you. I haven't talked with a first year principal yet who hasn't said, "Hey, what the hell am I supposed to do?" And this goes even for those who've had an internship as an assistant principal.
>
> When you get to be principal, into the big time, you sit down and wait for someone to tell you what your job is. Nobody from below is going to tell you. And from the people on the top, everything they want from you, you can do by the end of September.
>
> Because of the ambiguity of the role, one thing that I think can happen to a person is that you can produce very little and not get fired. In other words, I think if you ever did a job analysis of what most principals do they would be out of a job. I mean in terms of what they really productively do. You know, you check attendance, you check in at the office to make sure all the teachers are there, you make sure the substitute is in the room to cover the class that needs to be covered, you make sure the janitor is running the boilers. And at ten o'clock you don't have a damn thing to do until lunch time.
>
> The only way you are really going to know what to do, is to do something. And it has to be something outside of routine administration. In effect, you have to step on people's toes, and they will let you know how much it hurts, which means, of course, you'll start to learn your role, what its boundary lines are and whether or not you want to enlarge them. Even if you don't step on their toes, even if you initiate some kind of action that doesn't affect anybody's territory, they'll respond to it. So again I say, "If you want to know what to do, do something."

In a nutshell, these paragraphs speak to school principals and would-be principals in a way they rarely get spoken to, either in university training programs or once they get on the job. There is a certain amount of laughing at the system and the demands it puts on principals, as well as some rather astute advice for the person who may not be satisfied simply with being a routine administrator. Paul reaffirms the notion that the principal's role is an ambiguous one, and there are two general strategies a person can use to clarify it. The principal can step into the situation and control it by asserting and inserting himself into the system, or he/she can become more political and try to decipher the messages that are transmitted by the most powerful reference group with which the principal has to deal. Typically, in elementary schools, this would be either the teachers or the parents.

But Paul says that, as a rule, the teachers won't tell you anything, and then a sort of cat-and-mouse waiting game starts. The teachers wait for the principal to initiate something, and the principal waits for cues from the teachers. When cues are eventually given, if at all, they are very subtle. How to break the game open? Paul's answer has much wisdom in it. "If you want to know what to do, do something." The simplicity of this statement is elegant. In order to reduce role ambiguity and the tension that accompanies it (Kahn et al., 1964) some action needs to take place so that role boundaries can be established. Conceivably there are two general action thrusts. The first is to test out the boundary lines by pressing against established norms, or by initiating action that may not press the norms but, nevertheless, conveys movement. When a principal engages in either of these behaviors the teachers will respond to what is essentially a testing of power. The messages will probably not be long in coming. The principal will find out whether or not toes have been stepped on, and how much it has hurt. Depending on the amount of pain that is felt, and by whom, the principal will start to learn about the role expectations that the faculty has for him/her. Judgments will then have to be made. Did the testing clarify things sufficiently? Is it time to lick his/her wounds? Was the action too fast or too slow? What was learned about the faculty as a group as a result of the principal having "done something"? Are they powerful or are they patsies? Other similar questions can certainly be raised, but the essential point remains the same: "If you want to know what to do, do something."

The second action thrust that a principal can engage in to reduce ambiguity, according to Paul, is to play the system's game by focusing his/her action on the Central Office, rather than on the teachers or the parents, as his/her primary reference group. Undoubtedly there will be many—perhaps most—principals who will disagree with Paul when he says "you can do very little and not get fired"; and, probably with some exaggeration, "everything they want from you can be done by the end of September." And certainly there are school districts that expect principals to do no more than fill their days by engaging in routine administration. This notwithstanding, far too many principals do precisely that; they make a career out of "being busy" and "keeping the peace" (Blumberg, 1974). As they do this, of course, they do reduce their role ambiguity. But as Paul suggests, most of the routine work in a school can be done by 10 o'clock in the morning—and then what?

So much for Paul's analysis. On another level, his comments reinforce the earlier interpretation of his view of himself and of the principalship as, at root, political. In addition, Paul sees the gamelike quality of the situation and the various "game plans" that a principal may adopt. His comments are laced, at times, with a certain humorous cynicism directed less at principals who are overloaded (or overload themselves) with the busy-work of school administration and more at the system for permitting, if not encouraging, that style of school management to prevail. But then, back to an earlier theme, it's necessary to survive; and the route to survival is a matter of personal choice.

Paul's choice of "doing something" was influenced by the parent group's demands for production coupled with his survival needs, as well as his mission to develop a higher quality program for black youngsters. His action took the form of developing a program for the school that emphasized a concern with black culture in the context of a predominantly white society. In a very curious way, this program was a reflection of his own concerns with survival, the thought being that if blacks are to be able to enter and produce in this society they need to have a strong sense of who they are and from whence they came. But the focus here is less on the content of his plan than on his action: he developed the plan, presented it, and in the process assumed a leadership role in the school and the community—all of this not without consequences. The consequences took the nature of radically changed relationships with individuals and groups. For example, with the assistant principal:

> My role with my assistant principal changed first. He was the person I had really keyed in on when we were assistant principals together. When I finally decided that "here's a program" it was the first awakening that there was a difference between the two of us. The difference was accepted but I don't think we ever got good at relating to each other—with me as boss, that is. It wasn't nearly as open as it had been. I got support, but mostly on the basis of my need for it rather than for the ideas.

And with the staff:

> Once I took leadership, after that first year, I never relinquished the fact that I was their principal. I accepted the fact that I wasn't going to be their buddy. I accepted the idea that I was going to take some flack for things I had not done; I accepted the idea that if there were screw-ups I'd take the responsibility for them but that I would also take the role of making final decisions when necessary. And things changed from that point on.

And with the parents:

> Once I had a program in mind which was going to last for two years, I
> went to the parents. I felt like I was principal of their school, I was a
> member of their community to whom they could look to make some
> changes they wanted. It was the kind of role where I was champion of
> educational causes in their community.

And with a subgroup of the staff:

> The black members of the staff had been an important group for me.
> We had become very close. We socialized together, had lunch together,
> and so on. Once I pulled the staff together and told them what I thought
> we should be doing, that I wasn't happy with some things, that it was
> time to get on the stick, the relationship changed. When I walked into
> the lunchroom the conversation stopped. It wasn't disrespectful or that
> I was being responded to negatively. It was just all of a sudden I was
> "the man," you know?

The lesson is a clear one, then. If a principal chooses, as Paul did, to
define and clarify that role as "running the school," that principal marks
out and then crosses a self-made Rubicon. Things will never be the same.
The comment above, that "all of a sudden I was 'the man,' " tells it all,
for it speaks specifically to the issue of power. Responding to the pressure
of the parents by asserting himself and his prerogatives, Paul implicitly
raised issues of power in his school where none had been raised previously.
The effect was to differentiate functions and relationships in the school
and parent community. But as a person gains something he/she loses
something; and he/she risks losing many things. In this case, as Paul gained
a clearer sense of his role and the power he could exercise by initiating
action, he lost some of the warmth that went with previous relationships.
He also risked losing a lot more, in that once he raised people's expectations, he faced the possibility of not meeting those expectations, thus
failing and, perhaps, not surviving.

Recall the teeter-totter, juggling act metaphor that was proposed
earlier. To continue the metaphor, as long as Paul refrained from "doing
something" (reducing his role ambiguity through routine administration)
he remained on the ground, refusing to mount the teeter-totter. Once
he assumed a different role by directly proposing a program, the balancing and the juggling act began. Further, for people who are interested
primarily in movement and change, and not in simply maintaining the
status quo, there is probably no easy turning back once the process has
begun, though there may be occasional rest periods. For Paul, one of
these times was a sabbatical leave, but even then:

> Despite the fact that I am on sabbatical I will never miss a Cabinet
> meeting. I recognized that that can always be a focal point for change,
> and I'm not willing to let the change go on without my being there.

A person in power who wants to create change stakes out territory that's important to him/her and which he/she needs to control. Other people or groups seem to be motivated to chip away at the territory, thus to loosen control. So, although he appears to have much fun playing the game he has started, Paul's life seems not to be a restful one as all parts of the territory need to be continually watched for possible encroachment. The roles that Paul had staked out and clarified for himself —leader of the faculty and educational champion of the parent community—had to be maintained and enhanced.

Paul also had to confront the problem of how to link the role he chose for himself with his faculty with the one he developed with the parent community. In most school situations this link-up presents a minimal problem for the principal because the parent community is not well organized, nor does it become a powerful pressure group except, perhaps, in times of trouble or disruption in the school. In addition, most parent community groups are organized by parents and are treated, for the most part, as a necessary evil by principals, though they make public utterances to the contrary. The situation in Paul's school was radically different. The parent group was very powerful. It had been initially developed by Paul's predecessor, and Paul had deliberately moved in directions that enabled it to exert a lot of decision-making power relative to school programs and policies. It was not a necessary evil, but an integral part of the school's policy-making structure, thus making the linking problem one that demanded attention.

What occurred was the creation of a relationship not unlike that between a superintendent of schools and a board of education. An elected representative group of the parent body became the accepted, if not legal, policy-making board of the school. The principal was the chief operating executive. But policy makers cannot make policy in a vacuum. They must have problems or proposals to consider. Here it was that the link-up occurred. That is, Paul worked with the faculty to develop program proposals, which were then taken to the parents to be enacted, hopefully, into official policy. But it was no rubber-stamp operation. The parents could, indeed, block proposals if they wished. As well, had there been no development of Paul's role as leader of the faculty, there would have been no program proposals forthcoming so that the parents would have some policy decisions to make. As Paul said, "I needed the support of my staff so I could take on a viable role with the parents."

One thing feeds into another, then. But more importantly, this process of reciprocity indicates the character of the school that developed under Paul's principalship, and the demands that the school, in turn, made on him. The political juggling act continued. It was not enough for Paul to deal only with complex faculty relationships, or with equally complex (perhaps more so) parent-school relationships. The two had to interact and contribute to each other. In the process, Paul found that (1) his power to act unilaterally was constrained and (2) his power to induce change was enhanced. This seeming contradiction is not really one at all. What it meant, in this case, was that while Paul became somewhat limited in his personal powers, his organizational power base, and thus his ability to influence a wider range of issues, was enlarged.

Although he had a few close friends who became principals at about the same time he did, Paul's early relationships with the large group of elementary school principals in the system were limited to monthly meetings. In addition, these relationships were colored by the fact that he was new in his role and, as was noted, somewhat insecure. First he describes the meetings, and then his feelings and role in them:

> You have, at least once a month, a principals' meeting where the assistant superintendent stands up and talks for half an hour about nothing. Then there's time for coffee and doughnuts which is followed by some announcement from the personnel department. After that it's talk about the teachers' union and the latest nasty thing they're trying to get away with. And then there's a report from our own union about all the things we're trying not to let the teachers get away with. And that's it.
>
> When I went to my first principals' meeting, I felt like a kid. The first time I walked into that group I thought it was awesome because they all looked to me like principals ought to look. They were old, they were quiet, they wore ties. I sat there very subdued for the first couple of meetings. Then when they started to talk I found out they didn't know anything. And they never should have let me find that out, because after that, oh man, my whole life's happiness would be to go in and disrupt a principals' meeting. I lived for those days. After awhile, though, I stopped going to the meetings. That's when the pressure came on from Central Office. I got some nasty letters telling me that I was a principal and I had to go to principals' meetings. So, I buckled under and decided to go, even though they were worthless. I sent a letter saying I thought they were worthless, and that I would like to go to a principals' meeting where they talked about kids.
>
> So, anyhow, I'd go to the meetings and when they were in the middle of some nonsense I'd raise a point of order and ask if it would be possible now to talk about kids. Or, when they were talking about how they couldn't give in to teachers on some issue, I'd stand up and say that I thought we ought to do it. It was just anything to keep me from going to sleep.

This is a rather sad commentary, albeit one person's, about how school principals in one system spend their time once or twice a month. More importantly, though, is the additional insight into Paul, and his growing security in his role. His comments lend added weight to earlier ones about his concerns for survival when he spoke about the necessity of building support in the parent community. That is, the more powerful his home base became, the less attention he felt he had to pay to the norms of the larger system. There were boundary lines, however, that he could not cross. The norm that principals had to attend meetings was one that he could not violate with impunity. He gave in to pressure from Central Office. The role he chose for himself in those meetings, however—apparently one of a gadfly or devil's advocate—was permissible, if not encouraged. What was required was that he be present, almost regardless of how he behaved, as long as his behavior was civil; another sad commentary.

Other facets of Paul as a principal and as a person come to light as he describes his reactions to the principals' meetings. It may seem, for example, that for a political person he was behaving in an unpolitic way. The principals' group, as far as Paul was concerned, offered no power base through which he could achieve any goals for this school. He could almost ignore it—but not quite. Other forces entered the situation that clearly signalled the extent of deviance that the system would tolerate, and Paul understood these forces well. The penalty for his deviance, as would be expected, was that he became an isolate among his fellow principals. However, this turned out to be not much of a penalty because, as we have seen, Paul devalued the group.

This situation remained stable through the first year of Paul's principalship. Then:

> A year later a lot of new principals were hired and membership in the group became a very different thing. Then I felt I didn't want to be all alone. I wanted to stop playing games, and I wanted to form a reference group of principals that I could relate to and maybe change things.

The situation had changed, and the change meant a potential shift in the power base. Paul's attitudes changed. Perhaps with this new potential for exercising influence the principals' group could shift and deal with issues which, in Paul's eyes, would have impact on what happened to youngsters in the schools. It didn't turn out that way. Paul's efforts failed. Briefly, this is what happened: At a day and a half meeting that was held early in Paul's second year as principal, the school district presented a proposal for evaluating principals. Paul was very upset, not with the idea of evaluation, but with the fact that the proposal contained no reference to problems of urban schools and black children. He cited experiences he had had with other administrators concerning problems they encountered with black children, but he received very little response either from Central Office personnel or the other principals. This lack of response only added to his anger.

At lunch time, Paul gathered the group of new principals together, plus some older ones. They caucused, refused to go to the afternoon session and, instead, drew up a proposal countering the one that had been presented earlier in the day. As can be imagined, the group's actions, particularly when they asked for recognition to present their proposal, were not greeted with enthusiasm by the people running the meeting. A good bit of turmoil ensued, but the counterproposal was finally presented. The upshot of all this was that the group was asked to take responsibility for planning a program for the next Superintendent's Day (system-wide inservice) that would focus on problems of black education.

The group accepted this responsibility and planned a full day's activities with a total black emphasis. The results of the program were both exciting and upsetting. The principals' group, however, became fractionalized. Another result was that the group that had planned the meeting, composed mostly of newer principals, apparently became frightened at the disturbance that had been created, disbanded, and refused to take further responsibility to follow through on the implications of the program for principal evaluation.

What had happened? Paul is not sure, but he has a hypothesis that provides a raison d'être for the story being told here.

I was really excited by the group, but I didn't realize how insecure they were in the system. I wasn't concerned because my support and security was at my school. I could be deviant because back there was the school, the parents, and the teachers.

Just meeting my school's (i.e., parents and teachers) wishes had caused me to get my bell rung enough times so that I was no longer afraid of having it rung again. I began to learn about the impotency of the system.

You know, the only big stick they hold against you is firing you. Well, after a couple of years as principal, you realize they just don't do that. They have to catch you on a morals charge or something like that. Once you've recognized that, if you are willing to risk being alienated, all that can happen is that you get your bell rung.

Things come full circle. Three sets of circumstances seem to have interacted to produce Paul's reactions. First, he had deliberately set out to build a base of support and power among the parent community in his school. As his support and power grew, he was enabled to take positions and behave in ways that were quite deviant, even though these positions and behaviors apparently caused some of his superiors to react with a great deal of anger and distress because he had violated his role as they saw it. Second, temporarily, and as it turned out, mistakenly, he thought he had developed another base of support within the principals' group. He was mistaken about his cohorts for the obverse reason he was sure about himself. That is, he assumed that they were as secure as he and had a support base as strong as his, which was not the case. The politician had made a political error. The votes were not there. Third, Paul had diagnosed the system in political terms. Recall that he characterized it as impotent, i.e., powerless insofar as imposing severe sanctions on the administrators was concerned. Thus his characterization provides yet another clue to his action predispositions and style. He could have described the system in any number of ways. He chose the adjective "impotent," reflecting his concern with power.

It should be said that an effort was made to remobilize the group of principals that had taken part in the earlier action. This, too, failed, and for the same reason—the failure of its members to assume shared responsibility for dealing with and confronting the system on issues that were separate from their own particularistic school needs.

Paul is left a little sadder but wiser for it all. The sadness comes from the fact that he still feels very much alone in his position. The wisdom came from his realization of the basic inertia of the total system and his own impotence with regard to changing it.

In an interesting way, the image presented of Paul as an administrator has changed, but it doesn't change when the focus shifts to his relationships with the youngsters in his school:

> When I became principal I decided I didn't want to become removed from my students. We had developed a close relationship. I was now the "stick," though, and I wanted to break through that. I never relinquished my behavior of touching the kids. But it's a conflict. You are an image for them; the kids will psyche you out. They will know if you're a person they can respect and depend on. They'll know whether or not you're a "bad ass" principal, which is good, or whether you are just a principal to play with. And you can get involved in their lives, which really blows their minds.
>
> When I had lunch duty I used to get a group of kids during lunch time, because I was not about to walk up and down the halls, and go outside and play with them. The older kids, as soon as they knew I was going to play, like in a snowball fight, would gang up on me to see if I would get mad. I figured that one out, but I got mad anyway. The younger kids—well, you're like a Messiah to them. If you come out and touch them they just think this is the most wonderful thing in the world. Here is the person who comes out of the loud speaker, which is right next to God because the loud speaker is "up there." That's really the way they treat you.

The beginning of this discussion of Paul mentioned the funlike quality that he communicates, as well as his gamelike style, and the balancing and juggling acts he performs. All of this comes through clearly as he talks about his relationships with "the kids." The fun is there; it is easy to visualize him in a snowball fight. But the political game is there, too, particularly with the youngsters who are older. They test him "in combat," so to speak, and he is aware of their testing. "Is he really one of us, or, when the chips are down, when we challenge his authority, is he 'the Man?'"

Once more, then, the question is how to keep the power balance, a question that becomes difficult to answer given what appear to be Paul's needs to be close to the students in his school. In a sense he creates his own problem, but he probably wouldn't have it any other way. Relative to the students, if he chose his role as "principal," there would be no issue. He could do what principals tend to do, maintain his distance and no one would question his stance. His needs for warmth seem to lead him down other paths, thus creating situations that he must balance. It gets untidy, at times, but the untidiness also contains some beauty and elegance.

12

Complementary Perspectives on the Principalship: The Job and Relations with Others

As was mentioned in the introduction, the aim in interviewing these eight principals was to develop some basic understanding of the manner in which these men and women described and dealt with the problems they confront in the principalship. This chapter thus begins an integration and analysis of some of the observations collected in the eight preceding sketches. The first portion of the chapter draws on some of the interview excerpts mentioned in previous chapters, for two reasons: (1) to provide a brief review of the differing perspectives these men and women have toward the principalship, and (2) to illustrate phenomena other than their individualistic approaches to the job.

As expected from the outset, these principals reported both similarities and differences vis-à-vis their work world. The description and discussion that follow here are offered as a framework for understanding some of the similarities and differences in their lives. They were not, for example, as functionally idiosyncratic as they might seem from the thumbnail sketches.

The chapter is organized in the following way: First, the general viewpoints of each of the principals will be briefly reiterated, focusing on several of their most distinguishing characteristics. Second, their relations with peers, superiors, teachers, students, and parents will be described. This chapter will conclude with some general observations and speculations regarding some of the factors that have influenced, and continue to affect, the daily on-the-job behavior of these eight elementary and secondary principals.

VIEWS OF THE PRINCIPALSHIP

Although we began this study with a number of preconceptions regarding the results we would get to our rather simple invitation to some principals to talk with us, we were nevertheless surprised to find that our hunches were not as accurate as we had anticipated. Perhaps the most startling discovery was that while we had expected to find among these out-of-the-ordinary principals some common approach to the problems they encountered, we found that they held rather idiosyncratic perspectives regarding their work worlds. While the general types of problems they reported were fairly similar from one school situation to another, their reference points for action were individualistic. Each of the principals interviewed held a particular view of himself/herself in his/her role which served to guide his/her day-to-day behavior on the job. Paul, The Politician, suggests his viewpoint in the following comments:

> I think the role is always ambiguous. I think that the only time you can clarify it is when you take control of it and define it for yourself, or you let the most powerful reference group around you define it for you . . . you can produce very little and stay in the role. In other words, I think that if they ever did a time job analysis of a principal, we would be out of a job. You know, in terms of what (principals) productively do . . . check attendance, you check in at the office to make sure that all the teachers are there . . . that the substitute is in the room to cover the class . . . make sure the janitor is running the boilers. And at 10:00, you don't have a damn thing to do until lunch time . . . we don't really know what people expect of us . . . there's nobody below you who is going to tell you. And everybody above you is going to tell you what they want from you, you can do in September . . . it was clearly understood that you know the role of principal and that the only task for him (assistant superintendent) was to help you get staffed in August . . . and then give you a list of reports that he was going to need from you—most of which I could do in September. . . . Once that's done you will not hear from downtown again. . . .
>
> The only way you are really going to know what to do, is to do something. And it has to be something outside of routine administration. In effect, you have to step on people's toes and they will let you know how much it hurts, which means, of course, you'll start to learn your role, what its boundary lines are, and whether or not you want to enlarge them. Even if you don't step on their toes, even if you initiate some kind of action that doesn't affect anybody's territory, they'll respond to it. So again I say, "If you want to know what to do, do something."

The sort of limits-testing behavior implicit in these remarks characterizes Paul's approach to problems of the elementary principalship. George, whom we've called the Value-Based Juggler, takes a somewhat different approach to the demands of his high school work world. For example, he stated:

If I get an idea in my head, right or wrong, I tend to pursue it and convince other people or groups regardless of whether or not it's the faculty, parents, kids, central administration, or what have you. Let me give you an example. It's been my worst experience ever as a principal. Graduation has traditionally been held outside on the football field which is a beautiful setting. (The school is nestled in a beautiful valley.) Four out of the last seven years it has been rained out. A year ago I attempted to switch graduation indoors. The students said "NO!" and against my better judgment I gave in. Not only were we rained out, we were flooded out! We regrouped two hours later in the gymnasium and that area of the building was hit by lightning. It was a bad scene.

My judgment on it was that *that* was not the way to conclude thirteen years of education. If graduation was at all meaningful—then let's do it right. The following year I made a dictum—come hell or high water it's going to be inside. I told the superintendent and the president of the Board of Education, "Next year you are going to have to get another principal if you want to hold it outside. It's going to be indoors." And they both concurred.

One of the things that was so striking, as the interview with George progressed, was the continual and strong reference he made to his value system when it came to making decisions affecting both the substantive education of youngsters, the quality of their life in the school, and the quality of his relationships with the faculty. The problem that concerned George in the foregoing example is not that the weather fouled up the outdoor graduation and necessitated a move inside to the gymnasium, but rather that graduating under these less than idyllic conditions was just "not the way to conclude thirteen years of education." In other words, it was disturbing to George's personal sense of values to have it end this way. As he said, "if graduation is at all meaningful, let's do it right."

In contrast to, although not incompatible with the preceding perspective, is that of John, another high school principal, whom we referred to as The Humanist:

I always picture school as a moving mobile. And on that mobile, hanging out there, you have got the Board of Education as a group, the District Office, the parents, the faculty, subgroups of the faculty, concerns with discipline (the student), the department chairmen, and teacher union representatives. Each group mobilizes forces to put demands on you. My job is to keep the mobile in balance and keep it moving in a direction that all these groups really want it to go.

John's sense of himself as balancing the competing demands of individuals and groups implies a view of the high school work world that is quite different from George's. John's frame of reference doesn't suggest that he is guided in his work by a strong sense of values about education per se, or that he is a change-agent bent on making his impact in the schools. Rather, John sees himself as a "people man" concerned that all the school machinery is well oiled and that nothing gets in the way of his staff's efforts to be successful at their work. He knows he's best at working with and through people; that he's not a "thing administrator," as he put it.

A more proactive view is taken by Joan, an elementary school principal, whom we called The Organizer. Joan's approach seems to be to keep "the big picture" continuously before all the participants in her school:

> . . . I see myself as an organizer; a person who puts ideas together and presents them . . . because I don't think teachers are organizing their classrooms and their instructional program, and they don't have time to see the huge scope of everybody's involvement . . . so I see me putting all those ideas together. I gather the information from them and I put the ideas together . . .

And again:

> See, for me personally, we are going awfully slowly. In fact, I would like to go ten times faster, but I knew I had to control myself . . . I knew when I talked that the first words out of my mouth, for instance, people didn't even understand the difference between "cognitive" and "affective." It was just appalling to me when I first talked with the staff and used those words and I looked across a whole room of blank faces and I understood that I had to back up twenty paces . . . and so, I think, while the change has been very slow for me, for some people the pace has still been pretty rapid.

In a very real sense, then, Joan is more of a promulgator of change and innovation than any of the others interviewed. She recognized that she was aggressive, always on the initiative, and that she had to guard against becoming too frustrated over her staff's not getting "the habit," not getting hooked on her ideas as hard and as fast as she'd like. She clearly assumed an openly proactive style as her approach to the day-to-day problems evolving out of the elementary school work world.

The viewpoint of another elementary principal contrasted sharply with the rather aggressive, change-oriented perspective just mentioned. Fred's view of himself as delivering necessary services to school participants, as being at the center of many of the exchanges and bargains which occur in school, led us to call him The Broker:

> . . . I spend probably the greatest portion of my time with teachers, in a couple of different roles, one in a direct supervisory role and another in a less formal but . . . still sort of a quasi-supervisory role just talking about directions in the school and things like that, where

we are going, how we are going to get there, and trying to get them to commit themselves more to the organization . . .

I see myself as giving direct service to the teachers in a sense of getting them involved and helping them in areas that I have expertise in, or finding resources for them, trying to work with them in solving problems, again, just seeing myself as a service person.

Fred's service orientation extends not only to his faculty and the children in his school, but to the parents and other members of the school community as well. For example, he states:

I guess that a lot of my work with parents has been in terms of problem solving. It is often in a negative situation, although we have gotten down to the point where we did a little needs survey in the community and said, you know, "What are the things parents need and want?" One of the things that came out was they wanted an adult basic education class and we got them to set it up in the school; and they also got some recreation services going for kids in the evenings, again, branching out into the community. I have gotten involved with groups like the Rescue Mission and some of the local neighborhood groups . . .

While some of the other principals interviewed touched upon the "brokerage" and service aspects of their role and of the school, none seemed to make it as much of an anchor for their behavior as Fred did.

Ed, another elementary principal, may most vividly be referred to as The Authentic Helper. It was clear in our discussions with Ed that helping teachers help themselves was his major reference point in his role as principal. Above all else, Ed sees himself as a human being first, a principal second. Ed has a desire to help improve the quality of life in his building, and he clearly wants his staff and the children in his charge to view him as more than merely an authority figure. He reflected on his orientation.

I'm interested in instruction and curriculum as well as developing a climate where children feel good about being here and teachers feel good about working here . . . I'm very much interested in human relations, in helping relationships, not only between teachers and children, but also teacher-teacher, administrator-teacher, and more specifically, administrator-child.

Marie, whom we refer to as The Catalyst, noted early in her discussion that she liked to get things going in her school. As was mentioned earlier, Marie's prime orientation to her work world environment was to "stir things up." It was important to her that things were happening, that people were alive, in her school. Part of the basis for Marie's orientation as a "catalyst" seemed to stem from the difference between her personal perspective on school and society, and that held by her staff:

What I see in my school is a group of people who are nice people, and they're interesting people, and I think they have basic intelligence, but I don't think they're terribly aware of what's going on today . . . they're isolated; here is the building and this is what I do all day; this is the community and this is what I do at night; and here's the world—and it doesn't really have too much to do with me.

The Catalyst spent much of her time as principal stirring up people's awareness of what they were doing, why it was important (or silly), and the relation between what was occurring in their school and the larger society.

Another high school principal, Fran, The Rationalist, seems to be distinguished from others primarily by her deliberate and calculated approach to the problems of the principalship. Fran was a stickler for clarity of language, and went to great lengths to reduce ambiguity in terms of her role relations with others. She was viewed with suspicion as the "new lady on the hill"—in light of this she took great pains to ensure that others did not misunderstand her actions, her intentions, or her motivations. Fran observed:

The reason I think it's so extremely important is that, through language, you create reality as well as describe it. For example, I've seen people create problems for themselves by the way they describe those problems. Perhaps it gets to be a fine line between seeking the right words and manipulation. But I do think you can change or improve situations by describing them in ways that are different. The point is not to sweep things under the rug but to help people see things differently through the language they use. So I try to figure out a way to talk about a problem or a situation in a way so that the other person's understanding and mine are congruent with each other.

For The Rationalist, then, it was critical to introduce change and encourage diversity, but to do it in a careful and deliberately calculated manner. As Fran noted toward the end of her interview, one of the biggest problems she confronted was "misinformation or misinterpretation of actions."

PEERS AND SUPERIORS

These principals reported that they spent little time with their administrative peers. With some exceptions, these men and women didn't talk to, observe, consult, or otherwise interact with their fellow administrators except to the extent required by their presence at meetings called by superiors. When asked directly about how principals relate to principals, a typical response was "They don't." While their assessment of the situation is not surprising, their comments on the consequences of this relative isolation from one another shed important light on understanding the principal's work environment. Fred noted that "the nature of the job certainly almost emphasizes isolation . . . it's a pretty lonely kind of role." He continued and pointed out the source of the problem as he saw it:

> . . . I don't know how you break down the isolation and develop . . . relationships with other principals. . . . It is a lot easier for me to have a good relationship with a teacher than it is with another principal. . . . I mean, just the time that you expend with other principals is minimal. You see them for meetings, and generally what happens at a meeting is there is an agenda . . . and we have never planned to sit down and just, you know, have a nonagenda meeting where we could talk about what our extreme frustrations are at this point. No one has ever wanted to deal with our frustrations. . . .

Fred went on to say that:

> . . . principals don't see themselves as being able to solve any of the problems they face on a daily basis. . . . They have existed all their lives and they don't see themselves as being any kind of agent that could ever change the situation.

In Fred's school district a special effort had apparently been made to facilitate interaction. "Intervisitation teams" of principals had been established but, in Fred's view, he "never developed a working relationship with the other three principals. One guy used to be the principal in the building I am in, and another guy is physically ill. . . . They are all older principals . . . I don't think I could share anything with them."

Joan, The Organizer, in commenting on her situation, suggested other factors that may be related to the lack of interaction and support among principals. She said:

> Maybe it's because they feel that they are not skilled in it, or maybe they feel they don't have enough time to assess you, or maybe it's because they are frightened, or maybe it's because you haven't built a relationship.

Joan was even more emphatic when she confided that she thought:

> . . . there isn't much of a relationship. . . . I think administrators are really frightened to tell other administrators about their behavior. . . .

Paul, The Politician, when asked how principals related to each other matter-of-factly stated "They don't!" He went on to comment about his first year on the job:

I felt so all alone my first year. The first time I walked into the principals' group I thought it was awesome because they all looked to me like principals ought to look. They were old, they were quiet, they had on ties, and I would sit there very subdued for the first couple of meetings. Then when they opened their mouths, I found out they didn't know anything. And they should have never let me find that out, because after that, oh man, my whole life's happiness would be to disrupt a principals' meeting.

The Helper also seemed to see himself as rather distant from other principals. Ed commented that the frequency of his relations with other principals was "not great." He stated that he:

. . . never really looked at his relationship with other principals. What I do and what is comfortable for me may not be what they do or is comfortable for them . . . so I sort of backed off. . . .

He continued to talk about his situation.

The school district that I'm in has only four buildings, so there are only four administrators plus a vice principal in the high school. . . . three of the buildings are close to each other in proximity . . . my building is six miles away from the rest. So in a sense, I feel very autonomous. The frequency of my relating to other building administrators is not great . . . what I do and what is comfortable for me may not be what they do or what is comfortable for them . . . so I sort of backed off and said "Well, if they feel comfortable in doing what they do, then that's okay." On the other hand, I don't want them saying to me "What you're doing within your building is not okay." So it's almost like a just "leave each other alone" type attitude.

While this is representative of the general thrust of how these eight principals perceived their relations with other principals, several of them were more pointed in their remarks. The Humanist noted:

. . . a lot of infighting among building principals, but we all learn to accept it. . . . a school having to give up a teacher always gives up a weak teacher. We know that and when you are—there are thirteen or fourteen other colleagues—all principals . . . you meet once a month and you laugh about it and think about it, and when you get your chance you unload a lot onto somebody else. That was a source of conflict.

The Juggler observed.

. . . in groups, I find it very difficult to relate to other administrators on how they act or behave, or the way they feel. . . . I don't respect the way they operate. . . . They are different than I am . . . dull, dumb, noncreative, authoritarian, not open. . . . I view myself as . . . a unique school administrator—in terms of experience and background. I feel I'm different from most school administrators. I got into it at a very early age and so I don't have the background of classroom experience and the classroom teacher feelings that other administrators have. In groups I find it very difficult to relate to other administrators on how they act or behave, or the way they feel. I don't respect the way they operate.

When Fran was asked about her relationships with other principals, she said "There are none." The Rationalist went on to clarify her comment by adding: "Well, there are two but . . . there are no other junior-senior high schools in town. There is no one, sort of, that would be a colleague." When pressed to consider the possibility of relating to assistants within her school, she said: "Somewhat. They've been there for years, and there they are, all settled in and mostly they're just—you know—nothing too exciting, nothing too terribly wrong either, but they're just kind of there."

Marie's circumstance was similar to Fran's in terms of other principals, but she did seem to have established a somewhat more productive relationship with the two assistant administrators in her building. In speaking of her relationship with them, The Catalyst stated:

The older assistant, he's fifty, wanted the job—so he not only didn't get the job but he got a woman. But, I'm finding that older men have sort of made their peace with men and women and the difference in sexes. And even though they may be raving, screaming chauvinists, they still accept you for what you are and never mind what sex you are. But he wasn't really excited about seeing me come in; and it wasn't directed at me—it was just directed at the situation. But he's the kind of person who would never take it out on me; he stands on his head not to take it out on me, which he accomplished. The other assistant and I had just "instant" communication—and we don't even have to talk and we know what the other's thinking about; and so we really did have to concentrate on bringing the older assistant in as part of the group. . . . We bat stuff around, the three of us or the two of us, and by the time we get done, we're somewhere between the two ends of the poles, and it usually works better. . . . It isn't a fighting kind of situation—I present my side and he presents his.

While a variety of views are expressed in these remarks by principals regarding their relations with other administrators, they appear as a group to be somewhat dissatisfied with this situation. Although some were clearly more emphatic than others in detailing the inadequacies they perceived in the quality of their relationship to other principals, each of them directly or indirectly observed that there was just not sufficient opportunity for them to interact with other principals. In those cases where opportunity was not a problem, these principals suggested that they did not view the peers with whom they could interact as particularly worthy of their attention—they were not seen as good models, or as having special skills or insights. Clearly, they did not seem to value or rely upon other administrators for help or advice regarding job-related problems.

Although these principals didn't interact much with their administrative peers, they did seem to have more frequent contact with their superiors. It should be noted that in most cases the quality of the interactions reported seemed to be of a relatively low level. In other words, the inadequacies in peer relations were in no way made up for or compensated for by relations with superiors. Usually those contacts reported were a function of either a specific problem, which the principal felt the superintendent could help solve, or an initiative on the part of the superintendent. Again, while interaction between principal and superintendent seemed to occur more often than between principal and principal, it was not frequent.

The excerpts noted below suggest the character of these principals' encounters with their respective superintendent and Central Office staffs. Marie observed:

> They're in and out of our building quite a bit, which is fine. The superintendent—I like very much; and we have an assistant superintendent . . . and he's not real sure what to do with women. . . . I don't avoid him at all, I'm just very very careful about how I deal with him. I try to be very calm, very logical, very rational. . . .

Marie interacted relatively frequently with her district superintendent and seemed to pride herself on the fact that he and members of his Central Office staff felt free to come and go as they pleased at her high school. She saw them as resources she could use, and she mentioned that, even though they were her evaluators, she would go and sit down with one or another of them and discuss what she had in mind for her school.

> I go do that and then they know what's going on in the building and how I'm thinking—so that they don't perceive me as pulling a fast one—the superintendent said the only thing he cares about is "no fast ones". . . . No one is going to tell you you can't do it—or that you can do it. That's not the issue, the issue is no surprises!

In fact, in her circumstance, the superintendent was one of the few people she felt she could rely upon for expert advice:

> I like the superintendent. . . . He has skills . . . on perceiving groups, and he's about the only one in there I can call on and say "Okay, give me a reading on that group." And we'll go back and forth on it, and so, he's of extreme value. . . .

She went on to point out that the assistant superintendent in charge of special services had been a big help to her with developing her guidance department. Marie concluded her comments on the superintendent and his two assistants by noting that "all three of them feel a lot more comfortable about coming into the building now that I'm there—rather than the former principal—like then they were fighting."

In a similar vein, Fran also made a point of commenting on her relationship with her superintendent. In fact, the historical relation of the former high school principal to the superintendent had been somewhat problematic, so that she now prided herself on the positive character of that relationship. The Rationalist elaborated:

> . . . there's some historical business here, too. The superintendent and principal have never been able to work together . . . and it's distracting, I think, for the faculty, because they know that fifty people aren't going to agree on everything—and these fifty people always had an audience somewhere. They've always either had a school board audience . . . or superintendent, or the principal. The superintendent and I have no public disagreements, and that's worked to my benefit, to his benefit, and the school district's benefit.

Part of the basis for her good relations with the superintendent seems to stem from the general political environment of the small community in which she worked. In discussing the general base of her support in the face of criticism, Fran commented that:

> . . . support comes forth in critical times with people, but I don't think it's strong enough that if the superintendent were fired, that support for a local person wouldn't be overpowering . . . to be really realistic about the situation, politically, I'm very much aligned with the superintendent, and that's inescapable in this town . . .

However, in addition to this reason for interacting with and maintaining good relations with her superior, Fran also viewed him as the one fellow professional in town with whom she could talk in a nitty-gritty way about problems on the job:

> . . . we're able to sit down at the table and bang our fists, and say "You stupid fool—you shouldn't be doing this" and "This is why." You know—that kind of thing. I mean it's, who else—you know, on a day-to-day basis—would I have to do that with? There isn't anybody. . . .

For Fran, then, her relationship with the superintendent was both politically necessary and a source of professional feedback and criticism that she valued and felt was otherwise unavailable from her administrative peers. While she was aware of the disadvantages of her alignment with the superintentent, she placed a high premium on having someone she could really talk to about job-related problems.

In contrast to the situations of Fran and Marie, John's relationship with his superintendent and Central Office staff was much more distant and infrequent. The Humanist's high school was one of four in a large city school district. His remarks contrast somewhat with those of Fran and Marie:

> . . . in dealings with Central Office . . . my relationships with most of the people down there were very positive. I'm of the opinion that you attract more flies to honey—I don't like to make enemies. I don't like to get into real kinds of conflict situations with guys I can't beat, particularly with assistant superintendents. And in alienating that group you could really harm yourself later, in terms of the school and even in terms of your own career, if you're thinking of that. So, if you get into situations with those folks you just try to work them out as best you can. I always realize that I cannot win them all and I accept that.

John has recognized his need to maintain good rapport with the Central Office staff, but he did not view the superintendent or any of his assistants as a real source of political support or as any sort of professional confidant. Further, he did not interact very often with either the superintendent or members of his staff.

George's relation with his superior seems to be somewhat of a blend of the situations of Marie, Fran, and John. Although George's high school was smaller than John's but larger than either Fran's or Marie's, The Juggler's situation seemed similar to theirs in at least two respects. One is that the town in which his school was located was fairly small—the high school was a visible entity in the town's social and political life. In this respect his situation was more like Fran's and Marie's than John's. Another is that his relation to the superintendent and the Central Office staff was relatively infrequent and fairly distant. Unlike Fran and Marie, George did not have a very close relationship to the superintendent, so in this respect his situation was similar to John's. When asked about the superintendent, George stated "The new superintendent—I don't know him. The old one—I ignored him." We asked George to explain the reason why he ignored the former superintendent:

> . . . the only reason I was beginning to go to him . . . was because another building, another principal was beginning to really interfere with our act and I couldn't fight that battle—two principals, two schools.

George was unable to work out his difficulty with the other principal and thus went to the superintendent, even though George viewed him as relatively unimportant. He explained that he did this largely because of his relation with the "interfering" principal:

> . . . as two equals we had gone through all discussion. "Let's look at the problem and talk things out." We had gone through all of that and it came down to either the situation remaining the same or one of us shouting the other dead. And so I was going to the superintendent to get power.

Even though George viewed the superintendent as a relatively powerless individual, he believed he'd be able to gain some leverage as one principal in relation to another, if he were able to gain the superintendent's support. He explained a bit further that "It was the only place to find it—except if I wanted to go to the Board. But at that point I wanted to try the superintendent first . . . there wasn't any harm in it."

While George viewed himself as a fairly independent operator, vis-à-vis the old superintendent, he was somewhat unsure of his standing with the new one:

> I'm not clear about how this new fellow is going to operate. One of the first things I'm going to do is to sit down and explain some things about myself, and let him explain some things about himself. In fact, when I wrote up my year-end report, almost the whole thing was aimed at the new superintendent. . . . It was to serve him as recommendations as to what I saw as necessary.

Even though George had not had much to do with his former superintendent, he seemed pleased at the prospect that things might be different with his new boss. When we asked him to talk about what sort of relationship he'd like to have with the new superintendent, George said:

> I'd like it to be very open. I'd like him to have a sharing type of relationship with me as the high school principal. I view that as a great opportunity to learn from a guy who ran a two-thousand student school. And I feel I might have some things to offer him in how to work with groups of people.

What he seemed to be saying, then, is that working with his superintendent hadn't been very fulfilling or helpful in the past, but that he saw the possibility of much better things in the future. George clearly wanted more out of his superintendent than he'd been able to get previously. He evidently attaches great value to establishing contact with someone with whom he can interact and have a dialogue regarding the problems of administering a large high school serving a rural community.

These four high school principals' relations with their respective superintendents and Central Office staffs were not particularly extensive or fulfilling. However, when compared with the elementary principals, the high school principals seemed to have closer and more continuous contact with their superintendents and Central Office staffs. The elementary principals reported having very little to do, either directly or indirectly, with either their superintendent or the Central Office staff.

For example, Ed, in reflecting upon his relationship with his superintendent, had these observations to make:

> I don't feel I have a poor relationship with my superintendent, but I don't feel I have a good relationship either. I don't think he would take the time to listen and understand what I'm doing. He is, in my estimation, a very poor listener, and any attempt on my part to describe for him a program that I have going on in my building has been completely useless. On the other hand, he's a very public-minded person, and I'm sure he's received a lot of feedback from parents, because I get letters from parents all the time about things that are happening in the building, and I know he received phone calls about this also. It took him two years, and the end of last year was the first time he ever spoke to me, I think, as a human being. He said to me that he was very pleased with what I had done, that he had a lot of confidence in my ability as an administrator, and talked about working with me.

While Ed, The Helper, seemed reasonably sure that his superintendent thought highly of him and of the programs in his school, there seemed to be a certain pleading in his comments for more frequent and more meaningful contact with him. Ed felt it was important that the superintendent be sincerely interested in and actually understand the focus and the substance of the programs Ed had developed with his teachers and students—but that this really was not the case, and was unlikely to occur given the low level of interaction and understanding between the two of them.

Paul, The Politician, seemed somewhat more jaundiced than Ed in speaking of his relation to the superintendent and Central Office staff. Paul's elementary school was in a larger system and because of this his formal contact was with the assistant superintendent in charge of elementary education. Paul suggests the nature of this relationship in the remarks below:

> When he interviewed me . . . it was clear that the only task for him was to help you get staffed in August—to help you in the selection process . . . and then to give you a list of reports that he was going to need from you, most of which I could do in September. These have to do with attendance . . . with supplies . . . and with finalizing the staffing ratio. Once that's done, you will not hear from downtown again.

Paul went on to explain the other sort of contact he had with the Central Office staff:

. . . the other thing they had you do from downtown was to come to meetings. You have, at least once a month, a principals' meeting where the assistant superintendent stands up and talks for a half-hour about nothing. Then they allow time in there for the chairman or the person who held the meeting to give you doughnuts and cookies, and then you have a few minutes when you hear from the personnel department about whatever is new in terms of monitoring attendance . . . teacher contracts, and all the nasty things they are trying to get away with. Then you will hear from your own union about all the things we are trying not to let them get away with . . . and that's it.

Paul viewed the Central Office staff as more of a necessary evil than as a resource for him or his school staff. Indeed, if Paul had his way entirely he would not even go to the monthly principals' meetings. The only other occasions for Paul to interact with the assistant superintendent and the Central Office staff were either the need to account for or explain the basis of a parent complaint, to discuss a severe discipline problem, or to take care of certain routine matters such as a mandated state-wide immunization plan. All in all, then, Paul, The Politician, seems not to place much stock in trade with either the assistant superintendent or his Central Office staff.

Joan expressed laments similar to Paul's. The Organizer had virtually no contact with the superintendent, and her interaction with the assistant superintendent and Central Office staff was minimal:

. . . we have no contact. We meet once a month . . . and we get lecture 902 from somebody—or the assistant superintendent lecturing about something ridiculous—we get lectured to instead of becoming a problem-solving interacting group . . . A policy decision will come out and, you know, it will be something that is just absolutely ridiculous. We have to decide—do we ignore the policy and go on?—because probably nine chances out of ten they are not going to know you are ignoring it anyway. . . .

Joan and Paul were both in charge of large elementary schools in different sections of a large school district. While they both faced fairly similar sets of problems, and while they both seemed to have equally limited contact with superiors in the Central Office, Joan seemed to think there was some possibility that principals and the Central Office staff could in fact work together and develop into a viable problem-solving team. Paul clearly differed from Joan in this respect.

Fred, the most recently appointed among the eight principals, had the following commentary to offer regarding his superiors:

. . . they feel that as long as there are not a lot of phone calls . . . and they don't get a lot of grievances filed by teachers, you're doing okay.

Fred, The Broker, had been on the job only two years, and while he indicated that he read a lot on his own, he felt it was unfortunate that he hadn't really had much of a chance to bounce ideas around with peers or his superiors, or to reflect on his situation. He noted that:

> For the first time, this year, the difference between this year and last year, is that the assistant superintendent and the director of elementary schools came into my building twice—which was a whole different pattern of behavior. Once to sit down and say "Hey, how's it going, what's happening?" You know, "What are some goals you want to set for yourself? What are some problems?" You know, they did ask if there was any way they could help. I didn't have confidence that they could, but the fact that they asked was at least something.

For us, Fred seemed to represent the epitome of the character of the typical relation between principals and their superiors—there just wasn't much of a relationship. The extent of interpersonal interaction between principals and superiors at all levels was infrequent, and practically non-existent at the elementary level. While there did seem to be somewhat more productive relations between superiors and principals in the smaller school systems, in larger systems the interaction was sporadic and usually impersonal at best.

While Fran and Marie seemed to come closer than the other principals to having what might be termed a healthy, productive, and mutual-benefit relation with their superiors, all of these men and women seemed to put a high value on the possibilities extant in a relationship with administrative peers which permitted reflection, feedback, criticism, and exchange. Their message is clearly that they sorely missed what might best be termed a "sounding board" for their ideas and problems. They all seemed troubled somewhat by the risk and the burden of performing their administrative and leadership functions with so little contact with other members of the administrative reference group. While most seemed able to cope adequately with this circumstance, they all seemed to feel that it detracted from their productivity and general feeling of belonging-ness, and that in many instances it resulted in frustration and stress that might otherwise have been energy devoted to developing themselves, their peers, or aspects of their school program.

PARENTS

As a group, parents seemed more involved in school affairs at the elementary level than in the high school. All four elementary principals viewed parents, and indeed, subgroups within the larger parent community, as having an important influence upon their behavior in the principal-ship. For example, The Politician stated:

. . . the parent groups influence me in the sense that any time I would like to make a major decision, I have to find a way to present it to parent groups. It is not one group; it is not one concise group, but it is several groups . . . and there are several different ways of presentation; there are several different key words that each of these groups are going to respond to, which usually causes a hassle. For instance, if you are talking about report cards, there is going to be one segment of the population that wants to see skills reported. . . . There is going to be another group that is going to be very much into traditional reporting, in terms of grades, so that they have some references to where the child is and how they should react and respond to the child. So, if I wanted a new plan in reporting, somehow I would have to endear myself in that program to both sets of parents. And, of course, if they are both in the audience at the same time, we really have a juggling act. . . .

And again:

. . . anybody who is really aware of what happens to them on the job as a principal will recognize very quickly that even having your hand in the pocket of somebody downtown will never save you if a parent group goes down there. . . . If you want to make some changes, you have got to have somebody to support you, and you can't count on the teacher group to support you because the change you want to make may be exactly what they are fighting against. They may be the group you want to change or motivate. You can't count on the district to support you because, again, they are affected by a greater body— maybe politically or by other factions of parent groups that may be stronger or have their ear. So, in a sense, if you want to make a change, it seems to me that (parents) have to be your key group to get together; and once you have cohesiveness with them, they reflect some kinds of power that you don't.

While Paul clearly viewed parents as a power source relative to the principalship, Joan, The Organizer, held a somewhat different perspective. For her, parents were viewed more as an ingredient in the education of children than in the survival of the principal. For example, in explaining a special Monday morning program she and her staff inaugurated to help students make the transition from a weekend at home to the demands of school, she said:

. . . we realized that a lot of things happened on weekends that we did not know anything about, and that the kids brought problems to school on Monday—whether they were family versus family or just kid and kid, something that happened on the playground at their apartment building, or whatever. . . . We instituted what we called "Drop-In" to try to get feedback from parents; and that happens two days a week at different times, where parents can just drop in and talk about anybody, doesn't necessarily have to be the kids that go to our school, but any kinds of problems. . . . We asked the parents if there were problems over the weekend, if they would communicate to us problems that might have occurred that would affect their kid's behavior in school on Monday morning, or at least cause them some frustrations during the day. . . . So the first hour of every Monday morning, what we do is we check down those things. . . . If we didn't take care of those problems, the teacher would have to keep taking care of the individual problems and disrupt the whole instructional atmosphere.

For Joan, then, the parent reference group was viewed not as a direct influence on the behavior of the principal per se, but was instead seen as a possible source of help about problems affecting the instructional environment of the school.

The Broker viewed parents in a manner similar to The Organizer's, although Fred had not been as successful as Joan at developing a way to involve parents in the education of their children. In relation to an adult education program he helped start, Fred stated:

. . . I saw that as benefiting the school because our kids saw their parents going to school at night in our school . . . motivations for a lot of kids, then, to say "Hey, Mom's going back to school tonight and that makes some difference for me." So I saw it in that light . . . what effect it would have on the kids.

While he viewed parent involvement in school affairs as a positive influence upon the education of their children, Fred lamented that he had not been as successful in gaining their participation as he would have liked:

. . . this year in particular I had said I am going to set aside some time, we are going to sit down with some parents and try to get some input from parents about what they see as problems in the school and, you know, how we could possibly improve any kind of parental commitment, or whatever. Just, you know, even the numbers of parents coming through that door to sit in on classrooms, to do a number of things in the building and possibly even leading to some types of educational programs—if they so wanted. Other than the adult education thing that we talked about . . . we began this fall with a goal-setting workshop where we took the time to call the parents, we had like ten participants in our school of three hundred kids; that's, you know, ten parents is a fairly insignificant number. . . .

Fred was clearly disappointed that he had not been able to secure more input from parents, particularly so because of the added influence such involvement might have on the educational program.

As was mentioned earlier, Ed's major orientation to his work world was his authentic "helper" thrust. He said that his PTA was extremely strong. We asked him to account for what we viewed as an uncommon view for a principal—to have a strong PTA:

> I think they're very much interested in their children. I also feel that they feel that they can come to me with ideas and will be listened to. . . .

Ed was as concerned about helping parents as he was in helping children and teachers.

While these elementary principals appeared to expend considerable time and energy working with or trying to involve parents in school affairs, the four high school principals seemed less inclined to involve themselves directly in such activities, although all acknowledged that parents could have considerable impact on what occurs in schools. The Humanist indicated:

> We tried cultivating parent support. We used to send out one thousand letters a month for PTA meetings. . . . We were unable to cultivate a viable group of parents that represented our school. That was really a failure, I guess, on my part, the school's part. I was just unable to do that. As a result our PTA group fell away and was not viable any longer. The only contact with parents I would have after that would be at ball games, or in parent conferences when parents would come to school to discuss their student's achievement or any problems we are having. Most of the parents, I felt, were very nice people, were concerned about what was going on with their child, were frequently so caught up in the economics of making a living that they didn't know what to do. And frequently the child was eighteen, nineteen, even twenty years old, and they felt that their child was an adult at this point and there was nothing further they could do as parents; and if the school couldn't do anything they didn't know where to go. Frustrating sometimes! But most of the people were good people and did care about their kids; and were positive in their dealings with the school. I wouldn't have very many parents at all come in angry. . . . If we did have parents come angry, I was always able to turn them around so that when they left they felt good.

The Juggler expressed similar sentiments:

> I want them involved and I can't get them involved. We started two years ago what we called a PTSA—Parent, Teacher, Student Association; and our hope was to . . . form a PTSA which was outside the formal organization of the school, which would meet to discuss the same things that involve parents, teachers, and students, and it was used as a sounding board for faculty meetings, department chairmen; . . . so I think parents can be a great help.

When George was asked to explain why he wanted parents involved, he indicated ". . . we can then use the parent group as a sign of approval. . . ." When pressed to explain their reason for not becoming more involved, he said "They are satisfied."

The Catalyst's relations with parents did not consume much of her attention, although Marie did note that some were "curious" about a female high school principal. She said:

> . . . one of the first things I did was pull together a philosophy committee, and I included parents on it, and they were really pleased to be included—I had no problem in getting parents and they all turned out in force for the parents' night, because they wanted to see what the new female principal looked like, but they're getting kind of used to the fact that they've got one of those.

For Marie, then, parents did not seem to be as critical a reference group for her as they were for some of the other principals.

The Rationalist's relations with parents were, again, somewhat limited, and mediated more by parent special interests than by deliberate initiatives on the part of the principal. Fran indicated that, as a group, parents did not have much direct influence on the high school:

> . . . although individual parents and their concerns certainly have an influence—but not as a particular advisory group. There is a pressure group in town . . . and I would say they do exert some influence in political kinds of ways, maybe more at the superintendent's level than at my level.

While parents were involved as participants on various committees, and while Fran did indicate that she dealt occasionally with individual parents concerned over particular child-related issues, she did not interact with or relate to parents as a group in any systematic or frequent way. They were not, for example, viewed as a potential power source that the principal could draw upon, as was the case with Paul, The Politician.

All eight of the principals were involved in varying degrees with parents. While two viewed the parent group as a power source relative to influencing policy decisions in the school, four felt that parent involvement in school affairs would contribute to the educational program for children. Of the eight, only The Politician and The Organizer were able to turn this desire for parent input into operational programs.

STUDENTS

Students, like parents, also had some impact on the daily lives of these principals. In contrast to their relations with parents, the high school principals seemed more involved with student affairs than were the elementary principals. Further, while all eight seemed concerned with the behavior of students, the magnitude of concern was greatest among the four high school principals. Conversely, the magnitude of principal concern over academic achievement of students appeared strongest among the four elementary principals.

The Humanist spoke of his relations with students in the following way:

My relationships with students, I think, were very good. I think kids saw me as not an authority figure. I am speaking now for those kids in the inner city and I suspect that those kids in the suburbs are going to behave quite the same way. Might begets might. In other words, you can't go after kids head to head, you lose—an authority figure just infuriates them, police, and things like that, and so do school principals for the most part. So, I think in cultivating kids, I think you have really got to care about kids and you have got to somehow convey this to kids—that you do care and that you are more than just a guy who suspends kids from school. If you get a chance, meet them in the hallways and talk to them about the ball game the night before; or in the cafeteria or in the classrooms. You try to get around as much as you can, to get to know the kids by name. Now that's a big thing. A principal should know as many kids by name as he can possibly get to know. Now, in large schools, that's tough. But he should know four or five hundred kids by name, even in a school of fifteen hundred kids or more. It is so much better when you can walk down the hall, or in the cafeteria and you say, "Hi, John; Hi, Bill; Hi, Tom;" and they know that you know them. That means a lot to them.

And another thing I have noticed particularly, is after kids have graduated—two, three, or four years—and they are now young adults and you are walking down Main Street, or you are in a store and they bump into you, you call them by name, they are delighted that you still remember them and they convey a lot of happiness that, you know, that they are happy that you remember them. And I think that means a lot to the kids. You know, they are from large families; they are still living in the neighborhoods. They talk to their brothers and sisters and that came to be a help in years to come because I have worked in the inner city around fourteen years. I got to know families, and brothers and sisters, and I could ask the younger brother how's the older brother doing, and where is he working, and how is he doing in school. And they saw me as someone not transitory, not passing through, but someone who had been on the scene quite awhile and who knew their family. And this helped. It helped with their parents, it helped with the kids. But I think, too, there are certain groups you can set up. We used to have a principal's cabinet, or a student advisory cabinet, where we would meet every two weeks and the kids would talk to me on a very down to earth plane and discuss the school, the problems in the school. And we would communicate very openly and we would try to get things worked out, and I think this helped.

It seems from the comments of The Humanist that he spent a good deal of time with students; indeed, *cultivating* a good, healthy relationship that carried beyond the immediate work environ of the school. It was important for students to know that John really "cared" about them, and that he was more than ". . . just a guy who suspends kids from school."

The Juggler, in contrast to The Humanist, was much less intimately involved with the students in his high school. George stated that he paid most attention to students, as a group, ". . . when organized. When they have power. When they are going to be sitting up on that hill across from that school if you don't do something." He seemed to view students less as individuals and more as members of an intermittently influential group within the school. For example, George says:

> . . . one of the things I do is, you know, put the knife in the ground and see which way the herd is running, and either build a stone wall or a bridge depending on which way I want them to go. . . . It seems as though it comes from all around you. You try to find out from what direction it is coming and then you begin to deal with it before it gets to that stage. And I think it is a more effective way too—it gives you a little more time to plan and look rather than reacting.

This tendency of George's to think of school participants as members of groups becomes even more evident in the following remarks:

> If you stay on that knife edge, it is an extremely difficult job—where the students don't view you as being wishy-washy. And so you find that—and I think it is very narrow—the zone of acceptance between the view that the students tolerate and think is necessary and the one which the faculty tolerates and thinks is necessary. That's just in discipline.

The Catalyst, on the other hand, did not seem to have close contact with students as individuals, although as a group they were important to her. In addition to her concern for their academic development, Marie made it clear what the standards for their behavior were going to be:

> . . . my feeling is that when the kids break school rules, the school will deal with it; and when the kids break the law, the law will deal with it. . . . The cops don't have to come up so much anymore because the kids know we'll call them—it was partly the kids testing, too, and it made the staff feel comfortable that the halls are clear and things are quiet . . .

Marie's contact with kids, then, was sporadic, and usually occurred in relation to some discipline issue. In her view she was "never gonna be the Jolly Green Giant . . . and didn't have time to run around the building and get to know eleven hundred kids." As she saw it, "the building wasn't gonna run if that's where I spent my time."

The Rationalist's relations with students were similar to those of the other high school principals. While students were indirectly of concern as the eventual focus of particular curriculum development efforts by the principal, they did not get directly attended to as a group, or as individuals, except as particular discipline problems arose. Again, as was the case with other high school principals, the issue for Fran was one of control and maintaining school behavior standards that would facilitate, not impede, the educational program she was trying to build.

While their styles differed somewhat, two of the high school principals felt it was especially important to know students. It was important for George to "know" the "zone of acceptance" of what students would tolerate in terms of controls imposed by teachers and administrators. The Humanist felt it was important for the students to know that the principal really cared about them as individuals, that he was more than "just a guy who suspends students from school." The Catalyst and The Rationalist were both somewhat more removed from students than The Humanist, but like George, The Juggler, Fran and Marie felt it was important to "know" what was happening vis-à-vis the education and behavior of students in their schools. They were not "close" to students, but certainly did make a deliberate effort to keep themselves informed. In each case it seemed clear that these four high school principals viewed students as a group of important school participants whom they needed to understand and be attuned to if they were to be effective on the job.

The four elementary principals, in contrast to the high school principals, seemed to us to be able to exercise much more choice over the nature and extent of their involvement with students. Unlike the high school situation, where there seemed to be a tendency to exercise control over student behavior in terms of their adherence to school-wide norms, the focus of the elementary principals seemed more concerned with the behavior of individual students in relation to their academic performance, and the quality of their relations with the teacher and the students in their classroom. While there was *some* concern with adherence to school-wide behavior norms at the elementary level, this group seemed to be primarily interested in assuring that students experienced success in school-related activities, particularly in academic aspects of the curriculum.

The focus upon school-wide behavior norms is evident in these comments by Joan, The Organizer, about the results of a three-year effort by her staff to socialize students in a particular direction:

. . . we have really helped kids learn . . . that there are acceptable ways in school to solve a problem, and we have told them "We can't control your behavior outside on the street—that is like swearing or fighting. If that's what you do when you are home, and that's acceptable to your parents and it is acceptable to you, then we can't do anything about that. But it is unacceptable in the school situation and really stops you from learning, and so what we'll ask you to do, is instead of engaging in physical battle, to see if we can work out the problem, and problem-solve."

Even here, however, in contrast to the situation described by the high school principals, there is an implicit attempt to integrate these norms within the school curricula—in a word, to teach students how to behave in an acceptable way, and not merely to sanction them negatively for misbehaving. The Organizer in describing how this was accomplished, stated:

We listed all the kinds of problems that stopped kids from working in a really acceptable learning environment. After that we brainstormed all the different kinds of ways that we could alleviate those kinds of problems . . . and decided that problem solving was a really important part of the instructional program. If we didn't help kids learn that, there were lots of things they couldn't do.

In a similar vein, Fred, The Broker, reported that:

I spend some time with kids in class meetings, and direct contact with kids. I don't know if that is for my own ego or just for fun and relaxation. But my purpose there is more or less to get kids involved in problem solving with teachers and with themselves. And we do role playing and things like that. . . .

Although Joan was not as explicit as Fred, her sentiments about the relation between principals and students were similar to his comment that he "will make a fuss over kids . . . being an advocate for kids." In further clarification, The Broker stated:

I sometimes get into that role (advocacy) dealing with some teachers in our building. In other words, if teachers are, for instance, demeaning a kid in any kind of way, you get into that. I find myself advocating for kids a lot of times, and I have been accused of being on the side of kids at times. I don't feel uncomfortable doing that. But I also talk with teachers from the point of view of "Hey, look, there are other alternatives in dealing with kids' behavior. Let's explore what they are . . ."

In his role as student advocate, Fred had chosen to extend his service orientation. In a sense, he "served" students as an arbiter with teachers. That the elementary principal seems to have more degrees of freedom in choosing the nature of his/her relations with students contrasts sharply with the almost "given" expectation in the high school that the principal is the disciplinarian. The high school principals did not appear to have as much "choice" over the character of their relations with students. This is probably in part due to the increased size and complexity of the high school situation, as well as a function of the organizational culture extant in schools regarding "appropriate" student behavior.

Ed saw himself as very involved with the children in his elementary school. For example, in addition to becoming involved in a large group activity with all of the children each morning, The Helper held special "therapy" sessions with smaller groups. All of these efforts were, in Ed's view, part of his goal of making schools more humane and helping children develop their emotional and feeling capabilities along with their cognitive development.

The Politician described a wide range of possible student-principal relations in elementary schools. When asked what students did that required the principal to attend to them, Paul replied "Not much, not much; I think that's by choice." He elaborated:

> I think it's the choice of the principal as to whether, for instance, if you get bored with the two hours worth of work that you do in an eight-hour day, you know, some people could then expect you would take over the problems and discipline with kids. Therefore, you might get to know the kids as a disciplinarian, which could keep you busy all day if you did it right, you know? If you had people sent to your office, six or seven of them in a row, and you talked to each one of them for fifteen minutes, and took a cigarette between them and the next group that came in, you could keep yourself busy all day with kids.

Paul then went on to suggest the nature of his relationship with the students in his school:

> You are an image for them. You can set yourself up as a person whom they respect and look for, and they really always know who their principal is. And they always are going to decide whether you are a bad-ass principal, which is good, or whether you are just a principal to play with—you know, you are a principal who will give a kid a piece of candy if he cries long enough or kicks you in the shins long enough and often. Or, you can get involved in their—really—in their lives, which then blows their mind. They are just like teachers. When you go out on the playground and play with them, the kids who are fifth and sixth graders, who have been involved with principals before you, that blows their minds. You know, I used to do that. I'd go out; if I had lunch-time duty I was not about to walk up and down the halls. I got me a group of kids to do that and I went outside and played with the kids, you know. Then, you know, the older kids kind of look at you like "What's your plan, sucker?" You know, or "How much will you take?" For instance, when we had snow I would go out and have snowball fights with them. Well, as soon as they would see I was really going to come out there and play, their first thing was to gang up on me and see whether I was going to get mad and use my authority role.

Well, I kind of figured that out so I, you know, I got mad anyway. You know, I could tell what their game was. The younger kids, you know, you can be a Messiah to them. If you come out and touch them, they just think this is the most wonderful thing in the world, because for the most thing, you will never see them discipline-wise, the little kids, and here is a person who comes on the loudspeaker, which is right next to God, because the loudspeaker is up there and you see, now, that's really the way they treat you—"Oh, wow, and this person will touch me?" Then you can, really, a few years later it'll pay off. But the older kids look at you—"What are you, some kind of kid?"

From Paul's perspective, then, elementary principals have many alternatives regarding the sort of relationship they establish with students in their school. In his own case he distinguished between the views that older and younger students have of the principal, and noted that fostering a little "hero worship" among the younger students will have positive results relative to the relationship they have with the principal as they grow older and become more experienced in the ways of schools and principals. We felt that, in some respects, Paul's view was similar to Ed's in his belief that principals need to be seen as more than just a disciplinarian if they are to be effective with students; they must be seen as human, caring, credible, and trustworthy individuals. Beyond this, and establishing oneself as a good model for children is certainly not the easiest task to accomplish, Paul, The Politician, felt that principals really don't have much to do with kids as a group. He contrasted sharply with Ed on this point.

In summary, it seemed from our interviews with these principals that at the elementary level two conditions appeared to obtain: (1) the principal had a great deal of choice in defining the character of his/her relations with students, and (2) there seemed to be a tendency for principals to conceive of their relationship with students more as an extension of the school's instructional program than as an organizational phenomenon related to issues of control and coordination of school participants. The nature of the principal-student relationship in the high school seemed to be more a consequence of the structure of the school situation than of the principal's personality. However, even in the high school, as The Humanist maintained, some felt it was important for the students to know the principals as more than "just a guy who suspends kids from school."

TEACHERS

Unlike their relations with parents and students, all of the principals seemed to have much more in common relative to their relationship with teachers. As will become evident from the excerpts to follow, they put a high premium on the necessity to establish and maintain an open and trusting relationship with their faculty toward the ends of securing commitment to school programs, and involving participants in the decisions affecting the teachers' work world.

These principals tended to speak of their relationship with teachers in terms of either organizational maintenance activities or program change. For example, relative to faculty expectations, The Juggler observed that:

> An awful lot of people look at the school as a maintenance type function. You know—being sure the supplies are there on time, the machines are operable, master schedule isn't screwed up, the change of schedule done neatly so everybody knows where the hell they are going, and that duty rosters are balanced out with fairness and equality for all, and that teachers' time isn't impinged upon to any great extent, too, you might balance, you know, teacher's time versus the job, the administrative jobs to be done. And you find that we can't get everything we want done but we can get this much done, and we better get secretarial help for the rosters. . . . I think in the area of leadership, real leadership, the principal has a free hand and makes his own decisions— nobody's pushing the principal to a new curriculum, nobody's pushing somebody to make a new schedule or new program for students. There is no push for that, there is no push for new budgeting techniques . . . you take the school budget and just let it be and nobody would care about it. Even though one department had 50 percent of the budget, and could be that way for ten years, and there would be very little pressure to change it from other departments because it is too big a task for them. . . .

In clarifying the different relations he had with teachers, George indicated that on issues of change "you have to be a salesman," and that "on issues of maintenance . . . there is more debate on how it's divided up or how it's done rather than what is done." In trying to clarify these differences in his relations with teachers, George said, regarding changes:

> . . . you trade. You know, like, "All right, if I do that, what do I get for it?" You might get an extra period of planning time to get this thing set up, you might get four weeks' summer work for it. You don't do that for the maintenance.

For The Juggler, then, his relations with the faculty group varied according to the types of issues at hand. Maintenance issues required a sort of "balancing act" on his part to ensure that these activities, the demands on teachers, were fairly and equitably distributed. On the change-related issues he assumed a "salesman" orientation wherein his relations with teachers assumed more of a "bargain/exchange" quality.

The Catalyst related most directly with the department chairmen in her school, and Marie was especially sensitive to the historical pattern of poor relations between the faculty and past principals. She commented:

. . . a lot of people aren't sure what to do with me. I don't think people perceive me as threatening as they used to, and usually when I sense that, that's where they're coming from, I back off. And I'm very cautious with them because that isn't going to accomplish a whole lot if they're scared to death. Sometimes it's appropriate for them to be scared to death, but not these people in this situation.

In contrast to Marie, Fran interacted more directly with her faculty. While her faculty was organized by departments, there were no department chairpeople. Fran indicated that she worked most closely with faculty on curriculum matters, usually effecting change by making new materials available and helping faculty learn how to use them. In terms of department meetings, Fran, The Rationalist, would call the meetings and sometimes attend—sometimes not attend. She was generally perceived by the faculty, in her view at least, as competent relative to instructional matters. While they were generally supportive of her as a principal, she did not view them as particularly helpful given her needs for feedback and reinforcement:

. . . you have to be a person who doesn't need a whole lot of positive reinforcement. . . . You have to be pretty sure in your own mind that you're collecting data accurately and, you know, not having tunnel vision or tunnel hearing. . . . You have to have a lot of confidence in yourself because you just don't have a whole lot of support from a large group of people.

There was contact with teachers, then, but it seemed more of a crisis intervention or initiation of change variety than the sort associated with a collegial or collaborative relationship.

Another high school principal, The Humanist, raised similar issues, but couched them in different terms. On the issue of maintaining an orderly environment and good student discipline, John reported:

. . . teachers made it obvious to me that . . . they wanted more strict enforcement of student discipline codes, they wanted to be sure that kids were not in hallways loitering. They wanted administrators around the building and not working on scheduling things or, you know, they did not want you in the office; they wanted you around and visible. So that teachers made their needs known in various ways. In faculty meetings in the halls, issues would come up. I think as an administrator, you have to sense what they are saying to you. You know, you do think through what they are saying, where are your priorities, how should you be behaving, what should you be doing, and then you tried to fulfill those expectations that that group of people had for you. . . . Now, in fulfilling their expectations you build one hell of an alliance and, with those people, they really get in your corner, so that when the time comes for you to ask them to do things that they normally would not do, they will do it for you—plus it establishes tremendous morale. An administrator always has to cultivate faculty support. If you lose faculty, you have lost—you can't exist without that faculty. . . . Teachers have to see you are caring; teachers have to see you as listening to their problems and really caring about their problems. If teachers bring problems to you, I think it demands follow-through. . . . You involve faculty, too, in decisions in the organization that affect them, like "Should we go to computer report cards or do you like the hand grading system?" Now that should be a faculty decision and they do appreciate a guy who will involve them in the decision. And then, as an administrator, it is always your task to get people, if you can, to do the things that you would have done anyway. If you can. Now sometimes, that will backfire, but I think here is where you sharpen your skills a little bit in forms of dealing with people, and see if you can maneuver a group into doing what you really wanted to have them do. And there are decisions that can be made about the organization that you can involve the faculty in so that they really feel an integral part of the school. And it helps. It helps in morale; it helps them in feeling that they are professionals and that they have something to say, and that there is a guy running the place that will listen to them and move in the directions that they feel appropriate. . . .

John went on to elaborate on how he cultivated the faculty support he felt was so necessary, and what some of the results of his relations with faculty yielded:

. . . we used to meet once a month with representatives from the teachers' union, and this would be to go over mutual concerns. And when the teachers would lay their concerns out, you know, I would respond to them and we would follow through. We would take action if the concerns were legitimate—and they usually were legitimate concerns. And this helped cultivate that kind of faculty support. It even got so that some of the teacher representatives would come in and see me confidentially and say, you know, "So and so's bitching today about something and I was not going to bring it to you, but, you know, I am a teacher rep; but I am just telling you and what they are saying is—I'm telling you, but I don't expect you to do anything about it." I say "Okay, fellow; gee, thanks." And you would get that kind of report. And it's not that teachers would come in and be stool pigeons; they didn't do that. But when they did get complaints from different people in the organization, a lot of times they would slough them off, which helped me. And it even came to a point . . . where we didn't have these monthly meetings anymore, which I was grateful for.

Thus the bulk of The Humanist's activities with teachers was concerned with organizational maintenance issues, although at times it was clear that change, some new direction, was at stake. John more specifically addressed his style as a change-agent in suggesting his part in curriculum development:

> . . . I can develop curriculum if what I do is . . . do it from the grass roots level, and they will come to me with situations, and I will perceive whether or not it is a direction we want to go, or that it is educationally sound. I can make those kinds of decisions, but I see myself as facilitating the kinds of directions they want to go. That's my function as an administrator—to pull everything together and make it go. And that's the way I see myself. I am not a curriculum leader. I think I can get people to do things I want them to do. And it might be a function of personality; I think it is. I like people, I'm very sensitive to facial expressions, I can tell, I can usually read people pretty well as I'm talking to them. But, what they may be thinking about—I can detect if somebody's nervous. Very suddenly you can usually tell if somebody's got a hidden agenda. I think this ability to read people and to be able to work with them is probably my forte.

Although John was perhaps a bit more indirect regarding the focus on his relations with faculty, he and the other high school principals seemed to us to put a high premium upon establishing and keeping a healthy and supportive relationship with teachers. While most of the issues at the base of their relations seemed maintenance oriented, each of them felt it was very important to be a sensitive listener and observer and to involve his/her faculty in making and implementing decisions. None of the four high school principals indicated that there was any strong teacher pressure for change. When demands were made, they usually were related to maintenance issues, which faculty perceived to fall primarily within the principal's domain of responsibility.

The four elementary principals' observations of their relations with teachers were similar to those of the high school principals, although the focus was more diffuse in some areas. The Politician was the clearest of the three regarding his relations with teachers. Paul stated:

> If I wanted to maintain the status quo, I think I would deal with my staff first. I think teachers, your staff, would be your cohesive group that would maintain; that's what keeps the machinery going. . . . I guess I don't see myself as a principal as having the answers to a lot of the ongoing machinery type things. I think that I can sit down on Sunday mornings, before the football games, and analyze what it is that needs to maintain the school without ever having to do it, you know, in such a sense. The key thing for me would be to pick out four or five people whom I could count on, who are upwardly mobile or for some other reason are very much attached to the same idea of maintaining the school; maintaining whatever it is—short-sighted but

very consistent every day. You know, and pick them out in different areas, for instance, and make sure that these kinds of maintenance things are going on. . . . I would have another reference group in terms of people who would make changes, or who would be looking for improvement. In other words, an improvement committee would be very different from your maintenance people.

He differentiated, though, his use of upwardly mobile teachers:

I would look for some people who are upwardly mobile, within the organization, that I could count on. You could depend on them. . . . You know—"I'll make you a unit leader" or "I will train you to be an assistant principal." Or, "You are an administrative intern and you want to get into administration. Here are some tasks—and they are really 'Mickey Mouse' everyday tasks that have to be done. . . . They have to be done, but if you delegate them, you are the one whose head will roll if they don't get done." So, it is very important to you to know that this person's going to take almost as strong a look at it as you would, and probably do a better job.

For The Politician, then, it was important for him to identify dependable teachers who could be counted upon to carry out many of the organizational maintenance tasks the principal does not want to do himself. Regarding the clarity of his role relations with faculty, Paul made it clear that the quickest way to reduce ambiguity was for him to do something:

. . . if you don't do anything, you remain ambiguous . . . as soon as you begin to initiate some structures, as soon as you begin to make some decisions, the effect of that is going to be to reduce the ambiguity because you sure as hell are going to have a clear understanding where your problems lie, where people are coming from, which reference group you should have paid attention to. . . . Even if you don't step on their toes, even if you just initiate some kind of action that doesn't step on their toes, they will let you know—they will respond to it.

The Organizer, in describing her relations with teachers, echoed many of the observations made by other principals. Joan elaborated on her feelings about the importance of touching base with her staff before making decisions affecting them:

. . . I always do it, because if they don't support the idea, then it does not get going no matter what I do. If they don't believe in it, they're the people that for the most part have to implement it; and I can't do that by myself. . . .

In analyzing their involvement in the decision process, she stated:

I don't think they do any of the organization. The ideas don't usually originate with any one person, meaning classroom teachers, but they are clarifiers, they are—they have their input . . . they feel very much a part of the decision.

The Organizer described her relations with teachers as:

Positive. Trusting. It's a pretty warm relationship. They still—I'm sure—see me as their administrator. There is no way you can take that away, because I do make judgments, I do make evaluations, I do make recommendations to them, so they still have to see me in that light somewhat. But they are a lot freer now to bring their—not personal problems, we don't even deal with that, there is no way I even want to deal with people's personal problems unless it is affecting what they are doing in the classroom—but they are very free to say, come in and say, "Hey, I tried something today and it didn't work. Do you have any ideas?"

It was clear that Joan's work to establish an open and trusting relationship with her faculty had paid off.

It is also important to note here that each of the principals interviewed made it clear that it is a misconception to think of teachers as a *single* group sharing sentiments. Rather, these principals' perspectives indicated that teaching staffs are composed of various factions and special-interest groups adhering to different and sometimes conflicting views and priorities. As The Organizer indicated when commenting upon the introduction of a change at her school:

. . . you never put anything out unless you go to each group and find out how they feel about it. . . . I never take anything to a large staff meeting. It would be ridiculous of me to go to a staff meeting with a brand new idea and try to sell it to everybody at one time. I just never do it.

Joan, like the four high school principals and her elementary peers, felt that if changes were to be made, they would likely be directly or indirectly initiated by the principal. In either case, they perceived that it was important to test their ideas with a few teachers before attempting to convince the entire faculty. Of the principals interviewed, the one with the least experience commented repeatedly upon the difficulty of introducing change in his school. In trying to explain the difficulty as he perceived it, Fred, The Broker, stated:

Adults don't spend very much time together—there has never been an expectation first of all, that teachers would ever get along with other teachers. Never ever. That was never raised, until we began to get into some teaming. I think there is a whole area of sacredness here about, you know, not discussing really what goes on once your door closes; that's some of it. I don't know whether that's because there is some fear that somebody may be doing something that may not be in agreement with someone else, or nobody ever thinks to share what's going on in a classroom. I think time pressures are some of it—that keep people from communicating. I think people may be afraid to communicate with other people; I don't know. I don't know why. I think sometimes they think it is easier just to close the door and get away from me—take this number of kids and just deal with them and maybe the problems will go away.

Indeed, The Organizer reflected a similar frustration when she made it a point to mention that, after three years, her staff had finally grown comfortable enough in their interactions that they could begin to rely upon and consult each other: "They are very quick to say (to other teachers) 'Look, I have a really tough home visit today. I don't think I can make it alone. Is there anybody who can go with me?'"

The foregoing is not to suggest, however, that everything is "peaches 'n cream" in terms of principal relations with teachers. The Organizer, for example, made it clear that one of her most persistent problems was getting individual teachers to solve their own problems rather than bringing them to her:

> . . . one thing that I have instituted is "I will not do it for you, but I will help you learn it." And that's when I got in a bind. When I started doing things for people, then I became dissatisfied with me as a person. . . . Every time a teacher had a problem—and you know just before vacations teachers have a lot of problems, okay—they're tired, they're exhausted and they (see the trend coming?), they start sending kids down, one right after the other. And I kept doing that—I kept taking the kids instead of doing what I would normally do. I fell back into the trap. And I knew the reason for it. But instead of trying to help the teacher by relieving her for ten minutes, or taking her out of the classroom to help her solve the problem with the kid, I was taking on the problem again and trying to solve the problem. I was not liking myself. I wasn't helping the teacher because the problems kept recurring.

Joan indicated that she'd been working on this problem for three years, since first coming to that school, and that it had affected her relations with teachers:

> I would sit and confront a teacher about a problem, for instance, and say "Could it possibly be your problem?" and watch the teacher get very offended; and instead of dealing with me on a factual level, deal on an emotional level and say things that were very cutting and hurt. I would sit there and I would grind my teeth so as not to, say, play

the same game which I tried to help them learn that they were always losing with kids, if you play it on that kind of level. And so I would sit there and grind my teeth. But it still hurt. And you know, when they went out, the door closed, and I cried a lot, and I got it out of my system, and I started over again. And it took a long time. It just didn't take overnight. And, I'm sure, I'm sure I can safely say that there are probably two or three people that I probably don't have a good relationship with right now. I'm sure there are.

In commenting on his relations with teachers, The Broker echoed The Organizer's feelings and also suggested that interpersonal relations among teachers themselves were at times problematic:

. . . in a small school, you can't let people get upset; there is a real need to keep a balance of personalities. I mean, you get two people going at each other in a small building, it seems that it can really raise hell as far as staff relations can be. I have one person that cannot get along with anybody and it's raising hell, you know, everybody is all upset all of the time because of the one person.

The Helper's relations with teachers reflected his response to the general condition noted by The Broker, and were aimed primarily at setting a climate conducive to growth—establishing a trustworthy relationship with teachers was a major priority for Ed. He observed:

. . . as far as teachers—it's just being myself with them and developing a sense in them—that it's okay for them to be themselves. It's okay to be angry, and it's okay to be positive; it's okay to be warm. That just didn't exist before.

Good relations with their teaching staffs was a primary concern of all these principals. While the focus of their interactions could roughly be categorized into issues related to maintenance or change, they all felt that success in both spheres was necessary if they were to be effective principals.

CONCLUSION

While The Juggler, Rationalist, Catalyst, Humanist, Politician, Organizer, Broker, and Helper each brought a different perspective to bear upon the daily work world demands of the principalship, they each felt they were perceived as effective principals by relevant others. Even though they did not have extensive relations with either other administrators or their immediate superiors, all of them were actively involved, on an interpersonal level, with parents, students, and teachers. While the demands of these three reference groups varied somewhat across different school and community circumstances, and the strategies and behavior of the eight principals differed according to the particular viewpoints they held toward the principalship, their responses to the demands of the school work world had many elements in common, probably, in part, because of similarities in the conditions of their work environment.

The principalship portrayed in the observations reported here is of a highly ambiguous and normative character, mediated primarily through face-to-face interpersonal interaction between the principal and other participants in the school situation. These principals were "people administrators" in the sense that effective interpersonal skills were a critical ingredient of successful on-the-job behavior. They also were inquiring individuals in the sense that, although their perspectives were different, it was crucial to their effectiveness to keep themselves informed of and responsive to the work world demands characterizing their particular school situation. Also, they may have felt isolated from other principals and supervisors, but they were certainly not alone in terms of the amount of time and energy they expended in interpersonal interaction with students, parents, and teachers. The quality of their relations with members of these three groups was perceived by them to be closely tied to their success as principals.

One of the most striking observations is that while each appeared to have evolved a rather individualistic and idiosyncratic ideology toward his/her job, the types of problems he/she experienced were similar from one school to another. The "commonality" of problems encountered generally reflects the evidence reported in other studies of school organizations. However, the strikingly different yet similarly effective conceptions guiding these principals' orientations toward their work world run counter to what seems an implicit, if not explicit, notion abounding in the literature that effective administrators hold some common viewpoint regarding their role and the nature of their work situation. While it is true that these principals experienced a number of similar problems in their relations with others (individual and organizational change, and "keeping the peace" in their respective school systems), each held a rather unique perspective toward his/her role. Some of the behavioral results of these seemingly idiosyncratic viewpoints have been highlighted by reporting a few of the more obvious differences in their role orientations and administrative style characteristics. Although the distinctions that have been drawn may at times seem fuzzy, such gross categories do begin to capture much of the essence of these individuals and the nature of their on-the-job behavior.

While these principals definitely have a "framework" for understanding their work world, it only remotely resembles the sort of highly abstract and rational conceptual frame one would find in the usual textbook on school administration. It is, instead, highly idiosyncratic to the needs and dispositions of the particular principal and the context of the particular work situation. This individualized view of the role serves as a reference point for action for these people—problems and solutions are shaped by the nature of the individual's personal perspective.

All of these principals spent a great deal of their work day in direct interpersonal interaction with students, teachers, and parents. While each of them perceived few opportunities for interaction and dialogue with their administrative peers, all felt that this would be highly beneficial. Students appeared to be a more potent reference group for the high school principals than for the elementary principals. In each of these cases, success seemed to depend largely upon their ability to listen to and dialogue with members of these reference groups. The degree of the principal's interpersonal competence, particularly those skills related to establishing and maintaining desired identities, both for the principal and for others, serves to mediate much of the principal's work world activity, and as a consequence is probably pivotal in differentiating the more effective from the less effective principal. These principals reflected a low conceptual/technical, high human relations orientation to their work world.

The principal's general work situation is ambiguous and as such is likely to produce much psychological stress for the individual and, in some instances, may severely impair the principal's ability to perform to the level of his/her expectations. The performance/expectations discrepancy created by these circumstances seemed to be managed effectively by these eight principals—they seemed to be able to cope well with their circumstances.

The particular coping strategy adopted by each of them seems to be a critical variable intervening between the potentially impairing aspects of their situation and the actual level of their on-the-job performance. Each believed he/she could influence the situation. In this regard, it appears that they maintain a *proactive confrontation*, rather than a *reactive avoidance* strategy toward the problems they encounter.

Further, the proactive coping strategy employed also seems related, in part, to the character of the organizational situation and, additionally, to the level of interpersonal competence of these principals. It is reasonable to speculate that proactive coping strategies are most likely to be used if a principal has a high degree of interpersonal competence and if the character of the organizational situation is sufficiently ambiguous to permit reinterpretation and channeling of role demands. Principals who are able to employ such a strategy will probably experience a lower performance/expectations discrepancy in their on-the-job behavior than will principals using an avoidance or reactive strategy. These data suggest that principals who cope in a proactive manner will be perceived as more effective than those employing an avoidance strategy. The character of the coping behavior of these eight principals has much to do with their success on the job.

Two themes underlying this discussion need to be emphasized. First, while each principal held a tacit and almost unconscious understanding of factors related to his/her on-the-job behavior (Polanyi, 1967), each had an extremely difficult time explaining specifically why they did what they did on the job. In other words, they could perform, but could not clearly explain or otherwise systematically articulate the why and wherefore of their behavior; they just knew that it "worked." Their theories of action (Argyris and Schön, 1974) were effective, yet they were unable to explain them. Second, the socializing influence of the school situation itself appears to have had an informal and unobtrusive impact on the development of the interpersonal skills, the work-world perspectives, and the coping strategies guiding these principals. While the data are unclear on these two issues, the relations among these phenomena will be explored further in the closing chapter in the discussion of the implications of these data for school systems and university training programs.

13

Three Elements of Effectiveness:
Vision, Initiative, Resourcefulness

In coming to an understanding of the many similarities and differences among these eight principals, we identified three factors that offer a partial explanation for their on-the-job success. While they seem to hold fairly idiosyncratic perspectives toward their work world, and while these viewpoints appeared to condition their manner and style of behavior as principals, all eight were also (1) desiring and eager to make their schools over in "their" image, (2) proactive and quick to assume the initiative, and (3) resourceful in being able to structure their roles and the demands on their time in a manner that permitted them to pursue what might be termed their personal objectives as principals.

First, it is important to understand that they had definite ideas regarding what they wanted their schools to be like. Fran, whom we described as The Rationalist, said:

> What I don't want it to be is a single-minded approach. I don't want it to be an open school or a traditional school, or a school without walls, or a math school or a science school. . . . I want to be able to accommodate the different learning styles of different kids and teachers, the different strengths of different teachers. I think if we have that rare person who is an excellent lecturer, I say let that person lecture, and in fact, encourage that person to lecture . . . capitalize on those strengths.

While Fran talked in terms of creating a set of school-wide norms to facilitate diversity of learning and teaching styles for students and teachers, Fred, The Broker, had a vision that was less broad in scope and centered on his being able to establish enough good rapport with teachers, children, and parents to make it easy for members of those groups to use him as a resource. He stated:

> I see myself as giving direct service to the teachers in the sense of getting them involved and helping them in areas where I have expertise,

or finding resources for them, or trying to work with them in solving problems . . .

In a more direct statement he noted that he "created an atmosphere in the school where people feel comfortable coming in and talking about problems . . ." For Fred, this "service" image pervaded what he and teachers did within the school as well as the close relations the school had with community members and social agencies in the school's neighborhood.

Ed's image of himself and his school was similar to Fred's. Ed's primary concern was "developing a climate in the building where children feel good about being there and teachers feel good about working there." While Ed, The Helper, was concerned that all the children in his school acquire needed skills in reading, writing, and arithmetic, he was especially interested in creating conditions where children and teachers can express their feelings and learn about the affective/emotional aspects of their lives as human beings. For Ed this is a sorely neglected aspect of the schooling experience, for teachers and principals as well as children. A comment noted earlier bears repeating for it vividly captures the vision Ed has for himself and his school:

> I see kindergarten children coming into the building, very alive, very much feeling-centered, very bubbly for the most part—I'd say 95 percent of them are this way. And then I see that at about the second or third grade, change has started. Kids become very unaware of their feelings, less bubbly, less alive, and by fifth grade when they leave the building, most of those children, I hate to use the word, but they seem to be deadened. So my feeling is if we can somehow work with their feelings on a daily basis, or a weekly basis throughout the year, each year, that hopefully I don't have to see that happen in the fifth grade. I will see kids smiling.

Paul, The Politician, differed from Ed, Fred, and Fran in that he wanted a school situation wherein teachers and members of the parent community were integrally involved in developing educational and administrative policy for the school. Paul saw this cooperative activity as the best way to secure the kind of educational program needed to serve a poor, urban, and predominantly black school clientele. For example:

> I think you have got to look at the parent group as the key group that's going to keep you on the job. . . . If you want to make a change, it seems to me that has to be your key group to get together.

For Paul, then, the image he held for his school could only be realized with the help of teachers and parents together. Paul recognized that he was in a politically and organizationally vulnerable position and that the primary way to achieve his educational objectives was to build an alliance of teachers and parents, putting the parents themselves on the front line, so to speak.

John, The Humanist, held an image of his school which was somewhat complementary to Paul's, except that it was a high school rather than an elementary school. Unlike Paul, John was never able to secure the parent support he saw as vital to program development. John's image of an inner city high school with few student behavior problems and high academic achievement was never quite realized in his view:

> . . . when I went in there . . . I think the essential thing was to make calm out of chaos. . . . For the most part we were successful in doing that. . . . I don't think I was successful in turning around the education program . . . in terms of scholastic achievement. Each year we took an increasingly larger number of students who were already academically troubled in reading and basic skills . . . and we instituted programs to deal with this clientele but I always felt that we were not getting the kids to achieve like I felt we should be getting them to achieve. . . . We had too many kids graduating with "D" averages, just barely minimum, and that was the failure that I saw from my standpoint.

George, The Juggler, faced a different situation from John and Paul, and he held different objectives for himself and his high school. For George it was vital to develop a school situation that actively involved students, and ideally, parents. In his words, he "was interested in getting students into the working of the school." In reference to parents, he said "I want them involved and I can't get them involved." George's aim was to create an educational environment that would facilitate the intellectual and social growth of the children in his charge. If he saw events occurring that he felt would be detrimental to students' interests, he'd intervene. In trying to explain the basis for his action, he said "If you want to, you can trace it all the way back to concern for the C student in high school." That is, much of what he did was premised on a concern for the "just average" student.

It seemed that the guideline for George was something like the maxim —the more you put in, the more you get out. His aim was to foster active involvement of all students in the school program—the more involved they became, the more they'd benefit as a result. This seemed evident in his effort to involve students in the Parent-Teacher-Student Association, special college level curricula, an alternative senior year, and a family life program.

Marie, The Catalyst, was much different from the other principals in her vision of developing a more worldly and enlightened faculty. She was concerned that faculty in her high school had become insulated from the outside world, and frequently from each other, and that students ended up engaging an academic program that not only lacked internal integrity but also bore little relevance to the world outside the school. Marie expressed her frustration this way:

> I figure if the staff gets educated, and gets exposed to new ideas, they'll transmit them to kids . . . and I found it very frustrating in the beginning to realize where they were, because I kept thinking they were here, and I'd get more data and find out they were even further back than that. . . . They're flying by the seat of their pants. They don't know what they're doing, they don't know why they're doing it. They're doing the wrong thing up in their own classroom, and I don't think that's okay. I think they need to know why they're doing what they're doing. Maybe they won't change a thing . . . but at least if they know . . . what purpose it has to the total picture, then that's okay.

Joan, The Organizer, had a concern similar to Marie's regarding the school faculty, but her vision seemed more encompassing because it extended to helping both faculty and children build more positive images of themselves, their school, and each other. While Marie seemed concerned about a general complacency among her high school students and teachers, Joan's situation in an elementary school setting seemed more volatile:

> I came in on the heels of turmoil. The parents were revolting, the kids were revolting, and the teachers were all upset. . . . Teachers did not like other teachers—they never came out of their rooms . . . they didn't know what anybody else was doing and they were so threatened by parents coming in that it was just an unbelievable situation! The parents were so threatened by teachers it was incredible. And the kids hated the school . . . they just came in with a terribly negative attitude . . .

In describing some of the programs she developed to deal with this situation, Joan noted that:

> . . . it all stems from the fact that what we're really trying to work with at school, all of us, is trying to build a positive atmosphere— schools for a long time have been built on very negative kinds of things.

And reflecting upon the situation:

> I spent the whole first year knowing that what I was going to do was work on just plain old human relations. . . . The second year I knew what direction I was going in, continuing the human relations and then going to work on the instructional program. The first year I touched the instructional program indirectly; like teaching with teachers. But

really, my big focus was on human relations—trusting kids, being a model for the kinds of behavior I expected from adults. The second year I really zeroed in on the instructional program—really individualizing the instructional program.

She went on to note how much the situation had changed in two years:

. . . the realization has come to me that I have different kinds of responsibilities now than I had either of the other two years. The first year I walked in, the first month, in September, in my office I had 127 kids referred to me for discipline—this September I had nine total, the whole month of September. My role has changed entirely—mostly because of the inservice training we have given teachers; saying if you really want to be in control of the situation, or you really want to build a relationship with kids, then you can't send them to me because there isn't anything I can do about it that way—but I will help you learn techniques in dealing with the kids themselves.

Joan, like each of the other seven principals studied, had an idealized image in mind regarding what she wanted her school to become.

In some cases the focus was primarily upon students, sometimes parents, and frequently the vision held by these principals involved teachers and the school curriculum in some major way. Regardless of the particular emphasis, it is important to observe that each of these principals had a job-related goal that went well beyond merely continuing the status quo. While each attached importance to the need for maintaining and stabilizing the organization, they all held personal educational visions which went beyond the bureaucratic dimensions of their job. In our view, it was this personal commitment to a particular educational or organizational ideal, and their willingness to articulate and work for what they believed in and felt was vital to the success of the students and teachers in their schools, that distinguish them from many of their administrative peers.

A second factor related to their personal effectiveness was their propensity to initiate activity and to assume a proactive stance toward their job situation. They did not allow themselves to become bogged down in "administrivia." These points are addressed next.

Excerpted below are a variety of comments made by each of these men and women which we believe reflect their general work-world orientation:

I see myself as an organizer. . . . I gather the information . . . and I put the ideas together. I like the word "initiator," but "pusher" may be the idea. Yeah, am I aggressive—yes, I am! (Joan)

I like running things. . . . I know me and I know I always wanted everything to happen yesterday. . . . I have high expectations . . . you can get the building run the way you want . . . and you can do what you want without anybody's going after you directly. . . . (Marie)

If I get an idea in my head, right or wrong I try to pursue it, and convince other people. . . . I get involved. . . . (George)

. . . you have got to involve people. . . . I see myself as facilitating . . . that's my function as an administrator—to pull everything together and make it go. . . . I can get people to do the things I want them to do. . . . I can usually read people pretty well. . . . I don't like conflict, but a leader has to deal with conflict, or potentially hostile situations, or uncomfortable situations, and you've got to deal with it and resolve it and win; and in winning you gain leadership momentum. If you don't deal with the problem, you lose. . . . (John)

. . . I try to coordinate things and I try to identify those things that I need to get involved with . . . and those I don't need to get involved in. . . . I try to check out perceptions. . . . (Fred)

. . . I keep hoping that I'm going to be the savior, or that I'm going to make the breakthrough with people who happen to be resisters. . . . I will take pains *not* to involve the board in the administration of the school. . . . I think you can improve situations by describing them in certain ways. I kind of try to search for the language that will be best for whatever group I am talking with. . . . (Fran)

. . . I am not willing to let the change go on without my being there . . . with the staff I took leadership and I don't think after that first year that I ever relinquished the fact that I was their principal. . . . The most important thing to do is to define your own role. (Paul)

. . . For the most part, the expectations I respond to in my position are my expectations of myself rather than someone else's expectations of me. . . . I'm interested in instruction and curriculum as well as developing a climate where children feel good about being here and teachers feel good about working here. . . . (Ed)

Each of them was sensitive to the need to be proactive and structure their role, the school situation, and the expectations others held for them. All eight principals were careful observers and listeners and seemed to us to have a very keen ability to determine what was necessary to adjust successfully to the requirements of particular situations—when to sit back, when to push, how to secure the involvement of others, to search for and to evaluate alternatives. By actively and continuously initiating structure in interaction with others, they were able to keep their respective organizational systems moving in productive directions, not so much in leaps and bounds as by a shove here and a nudge there. They were sensitive to the changing character of their school environments and consistent and persistent in their on-the-job performance as principals.[1]

The third factor that seems related to their success in the principalship is reflected in their ability not to become consumed by the organizational maintenance requirements of the job. They did not ignore these demands,

---

1. For an excellent review of the literature on leadership and organizational climate read Chapters 7 and 8 in Hoy and Miskel, 1978.

but rather seemed to be able to satisfy them by using either a *small* portion of their personal time and energy or capitalizing on the capability of other personnel to meet these organizational demands. The following excerpts from our interviews with these eight principals are instructive:

> . . . the key thing for me would be to pick out four or five people whom I could count on, who are upwardly mobile . . . short-sighted, but very consistent every day . . . they are going to be there every day; they are going to do the job every day ; . . (Paul)
>
> I would say the majority of my time is spent in the instructional and climate developing areas, as opposed to say, management. . . . I feel I'm an unusual administrator. . . . I find that spending maybe 25 to 30 percent of my time on work such as budget, scheduling, transportation, cafeteria, and so forth, is plenty. And that leaves 70 to 75 percent of my time that is really free. (Ed)
>
> I think ultimately the principal is responsible . . . even though somebody else might do it. I think in the area of leadership . . . the principal has a free hand . . . nobody's pushing the principal to a new curriculum, nobody's pushing to make a new schedule or new program for students. (George)
>
> I think your vice principals are crucial. They are your arms and legs. In a large high school you can't do it all . . . you need a vice principal who is a good detail man, who is good for the organization, who is good on scheduling, who is good on doing the things that schools have to have—bus schedules, all the paperwork that gets shuffled through a school office . . . someone who is good on students. (John)
>
> I never got any strong messages from upper levels of administration about what I'm supposed to do. . . . I often let the "Mickey Mouse" stuff go by and try to develop the instructional aspects of the school. . . . I've got a fantastic secretary . . . she saves me. I never have to get anything done, reportwise—I give it to her . . . so I've got a lot of other time. (Fred)
>
> I think we are unskilled in lateral thinking. . . . It amazes me how little thinking administrators do in terms of solving problems. . . . Maybe they solve problems for teachers by taking on the problems themselves—but that doesn't help the principal. . . . And I think that's what gets people so overwhelmed with their jobs—they take on so many other kinds of responsibilities that might not necessarily be their own. . . . (Joan)
>
> I have one assistant who just loves dealing with plant maintenance. He's just super with numbers, and he's dead accurate. He just loves that stuff and he's there till 5:00 every night—and takes it home . . . as far as the nitty-gritty details, he just loves doing it. (Marie)
>
> I try to shove the paperwork to the periphery of the day. I get there at 7:15, so I do paperwork from 7:15 until 8:00. . . . I try to relegate those kinds of tasks to times of the day when I don't have a lot of people around. (Fran)

While some spoke more directly than others to the problem of becoming consumed by organizational maintenance activities, each of them shares an implicit assumption that he/she, and not the demands of the job per se, determine his/her on-the-job behavior. The four high school principals were in a somewhat more advantageous position in having available administrative assistants or vice principals to whom many nitty-gritty, routine administrative and clerical tasks could be delegated. However, the four elementary principals also found ways to avoid becoming bogged down by the day-to-day maintenance demands of the job. In the final analysis, if some of this work couldn't be handled by secretaries, volunteer parents, or upwardly mobile teachers, it either didn't get done or, if it was important enough in the eyes of the principal, he/she would come to work very early, stay late, catch up on Saturdays, or take it home in the evenings—practically anything but letting it interfere with what he/she considered the leadership dimensions of his/her role. They do this not because of any organizational mandate or guidance from superiors, but because they do not want these routine maintenance activities to interfere with what they individually consider their top priority—the realization of their personal vision. Thus, their on-the-job "time" is left "free"—free in the sense that they can use this time for the exercise of personal initiatives related to the realization of their particular educational or organizational goals. Stated quite clearly, their success in approaching realization of these goals seems related to the following:

1. Their individual commitment to the realization of a particular educational or organizational vision,
2. Their propensity to assume the initiative and to take a proactive stance in relation to the demands of their work-world environment, and
3. Their ability to satisfy the routine organizational maintenance demands in a manner that permits them to spend most of their on-the-job time in activities directly related to the realization of their personal vision. They do not allow themselves to become consumed by second-order priorities.

14

All That Glitters Is Not . . .

Part of the design for this study of some out-of-the-ordinary school principals called for their reactions to what we had written about them. We wanted to know how they would feel about how they were seen by others, and how accurate we were in our portrayal of them. In addition, and more important for our purposes, we wanted to know what this group of intelligent and skillful administrators would talk about together. What would be their concerns? How did they feel about their jobs? What was the job doing to them as people? How did they perceive their futures?

Six of the eight people interviewed and written about were able to meet with us for about a four-hour, rather free-floating, discussion. Some of them knew each other, others were strangers to the group. Each had been provided with a copy of our sketch of him/her so that they were not coming in cold to the situation. The meeting started with our asking the individuals to talk about the reactions they had as they read about themselves. We sat back and listened.

For the most part, what had been written, the descriptions of their behavior and the interpretations we had made, was seen to be accurate. The reactions they had ranged from one person's being somewhat uncomfortable and embarrassed at being pictured in too heroic a fashion (his interpretation), to another's being frankly pleased and flattered. Mostly though, each individual said, in effect, "Yes, that's the way I am. The picture you painted tells the story." More important for our purposes, however, was that sharing their perceptions and reactions to our sketches of them led to a wide-ranging discussion of what life in general was like for a school principal. The discussion was problem oriented in the sense that it focused on some issues that these people had to live with, on a day-to-day basis, that were emotionally and intellectually draining. It was also problem oriented in that the principals were saying, in effect, "Here are some things that stand in the way of our doing the job better, of creating a better setting for the education of youngsters."

Our interest in this discussion was not a casual one. Indeed, the case was quite the opposite. While we were not interested in conducting a "bitch" session, we were most attracted to the idea of engaging the principals in a thoughtful analysis of some of the factors in their work life that had the effect of inducing a long-term negative emotional impact on them. Our attraction to this type of discussion stemmed from several sources. It first started conceptually, with our reading and discussing between ourselves and with several of our students the notion of the "emotional toxicity" (Levinson, 1972) of work environments. Levinson is a clinical psychologist who has devoted much of his career to inquiring into the psychology of person-work dynamics. He suggests that there are four major feelings with which every individual has to deal throughout his/her life: ". . . love, hate, feelings about dependency, and feelings about one's self image" (p. 36). The work situation—the problems that arise, the pressures that exist, the interactions that take place—create conditions that confront an individual with the necessity of dealing with these feelings as they arise. To the extent that a person is able to cope successfully with these feelings on the job, work and the demands of work become less emotionally toxic for the person and he/she can devote optimum energy to the tasks at hand. By contrast, if the individual is unaware of these feelings or aware but unable to cope well with them, the work environment becomes more emotionally toxic, with results that may be observed in psychosomatic illness, lessened ability or desire to do the job well, or a physical disengagement from the job, perhaps through resignation.

Second, it had become increasingly apparent that the conflict occurring in the field of public education was inducing larger and larger amounts of stress into the lives of practicing school administrators. The data came from a number of sources. For example, we had only to talk with some of our students who were principals to note their weariness and frustration, not merely from working long hours, but from continually confronting situations—with parents, teachers, students—that were charged with high emotionality and, thus, extremely draining. It was almost a relief for many of these students to come to the University for conferences or classes so that they could, for a brief span of time, withdraw from the action they encountered all day long. In close connection with this point, we have in recent months held numerous talks with chief school officers concerning problems they faced, and how we at the University could bring our resources to bear to help resolve those problems. Their suggestions have unanimously and consistently been, "Help us learn better how to cope with the increasing stress that is attached to our job." The pressures from the community and teachers' unions are putting these people squarely in the middle of a no-win situation. They are damned if they do, and damned if they don't.

The phenomenon of emotional toxicity that accompanies the work of school people is not confined to isolated pockets around the country. That it is a widespread concern is evidenced in the announcement of the 1977 Suburban Superintendents Conference, organized by the American Association of School Administrators. A featured highlight in the conference was an all-day program entitled "Learning to Deal with Stress: How to Cope." The program was conducted by The Menninger Foundation, the same organization that sponsored Levinson's (1962) early research concerning problems surrounding individual-organizational relationships. The present study, of course, deals with school principals and not superintendents. The substance of the problem, however, remains the same.

The third source of our interest in getting our group of principals to talk about the emotional toxicity of their job stemmed from a seminar we conducted with several of our graduate students in the Fall of 1976. The seminar focused on a phenomenon we called "administrative impairment," a term that was difficult to define precisely. Despite its imprecision, and thanks to some informal data that our students collected in the field, it appeared that things were indeed happening to school principals that were having deleterious effects on their morale, their energy, their motivation, and their perspectives on the future. What was occurring seemed to have little to do with the technical competence of the individual to do the job. Rather, and probably symptomatic of our society in the last quarter of this century, school administrators like other public officials seem to be becoming "emotionally battered" adults. Indeed, as the tremendous turnover of school superintendents shows, and as more and more school administrators apply for early retirement, there is a strong suggestion that they are "burning out," and that they want relief from a difficult situation. It appears for many that the only relief in sight is to get out of it as quickly as they can. "Getting out" is probably the extreme example of burning out, according to the findings of Maslach (1976). In her study of people involved in social services of a broad nature, Maslach reported that the primary symptom of being "burned out" was the tendency of people to distance themselves, psychologically, from those they were serving. For example, a nurse, instead of referring to "Mrs. Jones, in 419, the person with the heart condition" might say "the coronary in 419." By objectifying, by removing the humanity from the problem, the nurse is able to insulate herself from the human trauma that accompanies the job. Our concerns, of course, are not as dramatic, but when a school administrator is "burning out," that person is putting both physical and psychological distance between himself/herself and a situation that is at least emotionally, if not physically, debilitating.

The stories told in this book indicate clearly that these eight principals are vital people and that they have or were in the process of making an impact on their schools. Nevertheless, it is important to learn—indeed, it is striking—that all but one of these principals has either left the school in which they were working at the time of our interview, or is now thinking about leaving, despite what appears to be the ever tightening job market in public education. Their reasons differ, of course, but behind most there is some factor which has, once more, to do with the frustration that accompanies the negative emotionality that is part of their everyday work life. Thus our interest in inquiring into these situations that drained them and caused them to distance themselves, at times, from people and situations that were ultimately important to them.

THREE MAJOR PROBLEMS

There were three major problems that seemed to emerge from the discussion that our principals had that seemed to have a negative emotional impact on them relative to their jobs. They were:

1. The problem of the exceeding difficulty and accompanying frustration that is attached to the process of terminating a tenured teacher.
2. The problem of power and/or powerlessness that they felt relative to their prerogatives inside and outside the school.
3. The problem of the behavioral constraints that are put on the person of the principal by reason of the role expectations that are held for him/her by others.

The Problem of Tenure

While problems that school principals encounter with tenure ultimately involve issues of power, they seem to be in a class by themselves and so are here considered separately from a more generalized discussion of power, which will follow. Concern with the effects and complexities of school tenure laws in the various states is not a new phenomenon. In recent years, however, particularly in the light of the economic difficulties schools find themselves in, declining enrollments, and increasingly concerned and vocal parent groups, tenure as a global construct and as a specific fact of life in the schools has come under heightened criticism from a variety of sources. Parents ask, "How come, if a teacher is not doing a competent job, that teacher can't be released?" It is a good question. The answer is that a teacher can be released, but the problems associated with the legal procedures involved frequently become overwhelming for the school principal and the superintendent who, of necessity, become central figures. There must be an iron-clad, well-documented case that has been built over a period of time before school administrators will risk the trauma associated with bringing action to terminate a tenured teacher's contract. Evidence for this statement can be easily had by querying any school superintendent about the number of tenured teachers who have been released while he/she was in office. The chances are excellent that there will have been very few, and that the superintendent will be able to recall vividly the circumstances surrounding specific cases—inferential testimony that when these situations occur they are most unusual. Even so, superintendents and principals will talk freely of teachers they feel are less than adequate—but not so inadequate that a solid case could be built, one that would "stand up in court," figuratively, but sometimes literally.

On a level somewhat removed from the building principals who are the concern in this book, but important nevertheless in any discussion of tenure, is the problem faced by school boards as they try to balance budgets. Their question is, "How come, if we think a particular teaching job is unnecessary in order to accomplish our system's goals, we can't release a tenured person?" Again, this is a good question, and again the answer is that it can be done. The outcomes of the decision to take such action, however, may be even more in doubt than in the case of the incompetent teacher, because the school board must then deal with the power of the teachers' union and their concern with job security. Just such a set of circumstances developed recently in a nearby school district. The case involved a board decision to eliminate the position of nurse teachers in an effort to cut costs. The union reacted strongly, and the case ended up in binding arbitration where a decision was rendered in favor of the teachers. The board was not permitted to terminate them. The long term result of this situation was that the board decided its management power had been eroded and, in its next bargaining round with the teachers, it endeavored to develop a major revision of the contract. What eventuated was a damaging teacher strike. The cycle seems to degenerate.

The message that comes from teachers, then, loud and clear, is "Don't tamper with tenure!" This view seems to be silently reinforced by school boards, under the notion that the cost of revising tenure regulations is too high compared to whatever benefits might be gained. The maintenance of the system is a clear priority for teachers, taking precedence, or so it seems, over the potential positive effects that such changes might make in the quality of teaching in the schools.

Our task here, though, is not to make a brief for the abolishment of tenure laws. Rather, we are concerned about what happens to these eight principals as they confront the constraints that these laws impose on them. Several comments that were made during the meeting illustrate the problem.

Ed, an elementary school principal, has an overriding concern for the emotional health of youngsters while they are in his school. Perhaps more than the others, because of his therapeutic training, he is more acutely aware of some of the behaviors of teachers that are punishing to children, and that these behaviors may cause children to see school as an environment not to be enjoyed, but to be psychologically, and perhaps physically, avoided. He said:

> I've had lots of confrontations with teachers when I saw children being harmed to a degree that is uncomfortable to me. I used to think that I could help any teacher but I've learned that I can't. I've learned that positive relationships don't necessarily develop no matter what. Teachers do not always change. And that's the frustration that I have to deal with.
>
> Legally, I really am not sure what recourse I have. We're talking about tenured teachers, some of whom have been in the district for twenty-eight years. And I'm stuck.

It's not hard to imagine Ed's concern about the situation. Two factors seem to stand out that have emotionally debilitating effects on him. The first has to do with his frustration at not being able to apply his skills—and he is skillful. The school situation is clearly light years away from the therapeutic situation when it comes to intervening in teachers' lives. In the latter, a person recognizes a problem and seeks out help voluntarily. In the former, the need for help and change is seen by the intervener, the principal, while the teacher may, probably is, perfectly satisfied with his/her performance. Understanding this, of course, does not at all relieve the frustration. Indeed, it may not only increase it but also transfer it— the second factor—to the system. For what Ed is really saying in his comment about having little recourse, is that the system unintentionally supports mediocrity and practically gives an implicit license for school people to damage youngsters For a person like Ed, whose aim is to combine authenticity in the classroom with effective subject matter, confronting this circumstance becomes, at times, extremely aggravating.

Ed went on to say that the problem doesn't rest at the point of his being nonconfrontive, for he sees himself being quite the opposite. Nor is the issue that of there being only one teacher in his school who creates a problem for him. Rather:

> I'm not just talking about one teacher. I'm talking about a staff of twenty of whom 25 percent I could easily be rid of tomorrow and be very comfortable with not having them there.

The fact, then, that there is a sizable percentage of his faculty whom Ed judges to be incompetent teachers—teachers who harm children—and about whom he can do nothing, creates a situation that borders on being hopeless as far as he is concerned. If it were only one teacher, Ed might be able to collect the necessary data to institute termination proceedings, or simply to ignore that person as best as he could. But to collect data and institute dismissal proceedings against five teachers out of a staff of twenty would be too disruptive for the system and, in all likelihood, for the community to take. The political fall-out would be intolerable. And Ed is left essentially in a situation in which he is helpless to do what he sees to be necessary.

The result of feeling helpless in these situations has a powerful impact on Ed, more so perhaps than on others because of one part of his make-up that was not shared by the other principals. It is that he sees clearly that there is a part of him that can be described only as missionary:

> I'm trying to understand the missionary side of me. I'm beginning to see that my wanting to rescue teachers, ultimately rescue children, is coming from my own needs to rescue myself.

These are powerful words, and there are people who might take the position that this type of motivation is inappropriate for a school administrator. But a principal's reasons for wanting to develop a healthy learning climate in a school should be unimportant. What is important is that the effort be made. Where motivations and needs do become important is when consideration is given to the consequences of failure. In Ed's case, unless he is able to downplay, perhaps soften or put in perspective, the missionary self-rescue side of himself, his failures will probably tend to increase the toxicity of the school environment for him to the extent that he may no longer be able to function as he wishes. If this happens, he will probably seek another position, quite possibly outside the field of education. In fact, when another principal asked him how long he'd been at the school, Ed said, "Four years, but this one could be my last."

As George joined in the discussion, he seemed concerned about the manner in which the tenure laws limited his prerogatives, but he was not emotionally tied up in the situation. This is understandable both from the point of view of personality differences and differences in school environments. Although there seems to be a bit of the missionary in George, it was of a much lower key than in Ed. He appears to be better able to say "the hell with it—I can't take care of everyone" and not let it eat at him, as it does with Ed. But perhaps the nature of their respective schools makes a bigger difference, at least as far as the emotionality of the situation is concerned. Ed is principal of a relatively small elementary school. Everyone, teachers and principal, is visible most of the time, particularly for a person like Ed who spends a great deal of time outside his office. The problems are there for him to see daily. George, on the other hand, is principal of a high school which while not huge, is spread out physically, and has a faculty of about fifty. It is somewhat easier to put things aside in this situation, or at least not have to confront them on a daily basis, thus lessening the tension the principal might feel. Nonetheless, George does have a concern, and a deep one. He first reacted to Ed's situation by

agreeing it was a difficult one, and then by talking about some things that
had occurred in his school:

> When I first took over the school, we got rid of one teacher through a
> superintendent's hearing. And that was a bad scene. One left last year
> as a result of a job change. He was forty years old, had seniority and
> everything else, but he left. We put him in a different position and he
> left.
>   I'm not really strong at the kind of conflict and confrontation that
> Ed faces. I was fortunate to hire an assistant principal who just loves
> that kind of eyeball-to-eyeball conflict. I hired him, not deliberately
> for that purpose, but to balance me. He is keeping tabs on one or two
> teachers that we think are at the point where they're harming kids.
> Either they're going to change or they're going to be out. It's a long
> process.

The terms "got rid of" or wishing to "get rid of" characterized much
of the talk about problems associated with inadequate teachers who are
tenured. It is strong wording connoting being relieved of something rather
noxious, not merely a passing annoyance. And that may, indeed, characterize the tenure problem. It is noxious for school principals both to
have to confront the problem and to have to go through the long and
arduous task of preparing a case for termination. George recognized both
of these issues. He referred to the "bad scene" that developed as they
were finally able to terminate a teacher, and to the "long process" that
will be involved in present and future cases, to say nothing of the interpersonal and organizational trauma that accompanies the process. No
wonder principals will avoid, if they can, starting down the road to
termination. It is wearying and painful for all parties concerned.

Yet George seemed rather confident of his ability to do what he
thought might have to be done. He also seemed happy that he has an
assistant principal who does not shy away from the kinds of interpersonal
confrontations that will inevitably take place if and when the prescribed
procedures are started. As he said, "I'm not strong on that kind of conflict
and confrontation."

Marie, another high school principal, agreed with George concerning
the trauma that would accompany the whole process:

> We're coming up on a teacher now about whom we know something
> needs to happen. He's bad for kids. He only changes when we exert
> enormous pressure, which means we're constantly in his classroom, and
> constantly doing conferences with him. It takes a tremendous amount
> of time and energy. I don't mind confronting him and telling him, "I
> think you're a crappy teacher. What are you doing here?" But when
> you talk about firing him—Wow! I sat down with our lawyer the
> other day and talked about what I would have to deal with. The

lawyer talked about the fall-out, the ramifications, the Board meetings—about keeping the thing under control so it doesn't disrupt the whole community. As you know, I like action in my school. I do stir it up, but it's controllable. This other thing is uncontrollable, and I don't know whether or not I want to go to bat on that issue. There's got to be another way. I don't want that kind of conflict. I'm getting tired, really tired. And I'm not sure that if that's part of being a principal I want it. I'm strong enough and I know my assistant is, too, to deal with it. But you almost have to destroy the community.

It's interesting that Ed, George, and Marie all echoed similar themes. They were not talking about teachers who were merely not the best of all possible teachers. They used the words "children being harmed," "harming kids," "bad for kids." Obviously, they are not dealing with situations that can be ameliorated by a good inservice program. To the contrary, they were involved with people who, according to their best judgment, ought not be, perhaps never should have been, in the classroom in the first place. So the circumstances are serious, at least from their perspective. Further, each of them talked about the emotional trauma, for them and others, that would inevitably be a partner to any legal proceedings they might institute. This inevitability was seconded by other members of the group. Thus they see themselves caught between "a rock and a hard place," feeling damned by others if they do, and damning themselves if they don't.

Recall that the aim of this discussion was not to debate the issue of tenure, but to inquire into some of the circumstances in the lives of school principals that had the effect of making their environment emotionally toxic for them. Having to confront the prospect of a tenured teacher who is damaging to youngsters, and who ought to be removed, is one of those circumstances. Conflicting values are involved. How does a principal balance the benefits that might accrue to a school by terminating a tenured teacher against the possibility of severe disruption of the school community? What does he/she do with his/her feelings of guilt if he/she does nothing in the face of a situation that is obviously wrong, that should never have existed? How does a principal weigh the costs in time and energy that would be needed to institute termination proceedings, against the way that same time and energy might be spent in working with other teachers and other parts of the school program? Further, and more specific to Levinson's points about emotional toxicity, what does the principal do with his/her frustration and anger at not being able to remedy a bad situation quickly when the answer is obvious—get rid of the teacher?

Clearly, the circumstances described put an emotional burden on some school principals, but not necessarily on all of them. For those principals whose concept of running a school keeps them mostly in their office, and there are many of them, probably the burden is light. For those like the people who were part of this study, who are activists, who are of the school as well as in it, the burden is probably much heavier.

Conditions of Powerlessness

The concerns and frustrations that these principals felt, their relative helplessness to deal quickly and effectively with tenured teachers whom they judged to be incompetent, can be subsumed under a more general heading of feelings of growing powerlessness, an increasing loss of potency. However, in addition to problems associated with tenure, they spoke most directly of their concerns about loss of power in general, and their frustrations at not having as much as they wished in a variety of situations. They were concerned with both personal and group power.

Fred, who was an elementary school principal when we first interviewed him but has since been promoted to the Central Office, started the discussion:

> As you know, I had a strong feeling that there was very little power in the elementary principals' group, and there was very little of a support system other than with isolated individuals. But with these individuals, it was a random kind of thing, not a planned support system in any kind of way. We've just come through a period when the superintendent has talked about decentralization and giving more power to the principal. I got into a confrontation with him about the role of the principal as an instructional leader. I said, "We've got to talk about what it means to be an instructional leader." He said, "Okay." I said, "If you're telling me that in buildings where we've got more than 500 kids, we've got breakfast programs, we've got kids with a lot of problems, with learning disabilities, and we're also giving all sorts of messages out to principals that they're now king of the castle but we're not giving them more resources, then why bother? We're cutting supervision back to nothing."
>
> I got to the point where I called some principals and said, "I think you've got to get a proposal together and make some demands. You need additional building personnel if they're cutting back on supervisors." I got some receptivity and the superintendent was at least willing to listen. But nothing happened and I still feel that elementary principals are powerless. And I don't know how to help them be more powerful.

It is an interesting and conflicting scene. Not only are double messages being sent—"Be more powerful, but we are not giving you any help"—but they are being sent during a time of financial crunch, when administrative positions and salaries are facing closer scrutiny than ever before. Principals seem to be increasingly insecure about their jobs. It is not surprising, though still aggravating for some, that as a group they wish to maintain a low profile. Paul, an elementary principal in the same district as Fred, provided a specific case in point:

I think Fred is right about principals being powerless in the sense that they see themselves as being powerless. I know that, in reaction to the superintendent's reorganization plan, about four or five of us tried to get together. We picked a few key people and said, "We're going to come together and we're going to make some demands. We're going to tell them they're not going to reorganize the district without involving the people who are supposed to pull it off." I spent two days going around to half the principals—about fifteen buildings. At least seven of those fifteen principals were actually afraid for us to come together and demand of the superintendent that we be listened to, even though we were going to have to carry it out. And of these seven a couple of them are definitely going to be cut. They have no idea what their job is going to be next year.

Another illustration of the same phenomenon—school principals being a frightened group, leery of asserting themselves—was provided by George. When the right to bargain collectively was granted to school personnel in New York in 1966, he took the lead in organizing the thirteen administrators in his district. But George realized that though they negotiated a strong contract, the group itself was not strong. As he said, "I got tired of holding the ball. A lot of administrators would just sit there and then I'd have to do it myself." The problem was compounded when a new superintendent arrived on the scene, took a dim view of the administrators' bargaining unit, and wished to dissolve it. The principals were upset and there was talk about going to court. George responded with:

> And who's going to take him to court? Me? For you? Not on your life! The problem is that principals are scared. I just sit there now and when the issue comes up I'll tell them that I have my own problems in my building.

If these anecdotes are at all representative of the wider picture in education today, and our casual observations and discussions indicate that they are, an interesting and vexing development seems to be in process. First, individual principals are becoming frustrated as they see themselves unable to revitalize the power of their peers who are frightened. Their energy becomes sapped and they start to withdraw to the confines of their school, where they are relatively insulated. In the process, of course, their morale becomes lower as they survey the futility of their situation. But the problem, ultimately, will not be confined to them and their feelings of discontent at having no basis of power. Eventually, it would seem, the system will become infected with its own virus. That is, as school principals fail to mobilize and assert themselves, the implicit message they will communicate is that they will remain compliant and open to coercion by higher authority. Perhaps the message even includes their willingness to be coerced, as long as their job security in some form is maintained. The most vital principals, those who provide a spark for the system, will find it difficult to work productively under these conditions and, as was indicated earlier, this is now occurring to some extent with several of the people in our group. They are discontent and want to get out. If they do indeed leave, the system will have succeeded in depriving itself of the very people who can supply the negative entropy on which it depends for its vitality.

There is no inference in all this, of course, that this potential cycle of events is part of some master strategy to get people to resign. But then, there doesn't have to be. In an unplanned-for way, and in the name of economy and "tightening things up," the situation will simply become too emotionally toxic for many people.

When the scene shifts to the individual school buildings where our principals hold sway, their reactions were different with two exceptions. The majority sensed that their position was a powerful one and that they enjoyed feeling that they had strong influence over their day-to-day work lives. A fascinating insight, about the impact that achieving a sense of power in a school has, was provided by John as he contrasted his position in an inner city high school with the change that occurred when he accepted his current position in a suburban school. Reacting to Paul's frustration over his loss of power, John said:

> I felt very much like you do when I was principal at Southern. I felt I didn't have any power. I had no viable parent group that would go down and pound the door down for things we needed at school. I had no board members' children in my school. I really became discouraged. Anything I wanted was always put off with, "Well, we're only going to keep that building open for another year or two." In the meantime, things were dying. They told me what teachers I had to take. I had very little say in hiring and firing or transfers. Supervisors would come in and say that this was the way it has to be. I could rant and rave but I never seemed to be successful at that.
>
> In my new school I sense a lot of power. In fact, I don't know how to use it. That's one of the things I'm going to have to learn. I've got a large parent group and they're extremely vocal and concerned about educational issues. This concept of power—I'm just beginning to appreciate it. I enjoy, now, the feeling of running my school much more so than I did at Southern because I feel I'm more in command. I'm really the guy that makes the decisions. At Southern, I never had it, I just never had it!

It's almost as though moving from a situation where he felt like a functionary to one over which he had mastery has given John a new lease on his professional life. It's also interesting to note his insight as he talked about needing to learn how to use power now that he has it. There is a certain humility to that point that is attractive, because it suggests clearly that the issue is not power for the sake of power. Rather, it's a sense of having control and influence over one's life—or an essential part of it. And perhaps this is the central issue. Levinson (1968) calls it the need for mastery, the need to feel that one has control over one's environment, and that it's not the other way around. When this need is not fulfilled, particularly for the kind of principals studied here, the effects are debilitating, draining and lead to discontent. For example, listen to Ed as he reacted to John's story of having been powerless at Southern:

> That's amazing to me because I live in autonomy. I feel what happens in my building is my responsibility—instructional programs, staff, budget, transportation—you name it. I function autonomously and I have a great deal of power. I can't envision a situation without it. I don't think I could stand it.

And Marie chimed in:

> Yeah, I could envision myself that way but I couldn't handle it.

And then George, who sees himself having more and more of his power taken away by his new superintendent:

> If I could retire tomorrow, I would.

And then Paul who, though he doesn't want to retire, is seriously considering another career for himself because he sees his prerogatives so reduced that the excitement of the job has diminished greatly:

> I think a good deal of my discontent is over loss of power. I mean a loss of power in the sense that I don't have anywhere to fight. The population's changing, the neighborhood's changing, and the school system's changing and I have no control over any of it. What I have to do now is try and eke out enough supplies for the kids. That's not very exciting.
>
> A few years ago everything was creative. Everybody was trying to do something and there was power in the sense that you had to deal with conflicting groups to see if you could bring something off. That's gone now and it seems like we're just trying to exist.

The concern that these principals have about power and the lack of it, then, is very clear. It is not as if they were "jungle fighters," a type of organizational manager whose goal is power for the sake of power (Maccoby, 1976). They do not experience ". . . life and work as a jungle . . . where it is eat or be eaten, and the winners destroy the losers" (p. 47). To the contrary, none of them seemed concerned at all with self-aggrandizement, or that their organizational life was one big win-lose game, although they certainly have won and lost their share of battles. What really is at the heart of things seems to be two factors. First, they have a notion of the kind of school they want to develop and, second, they need to have the power to do it, relatively unfettered by external constraints. They are activists and as such, quite simply, must have the freedom to act. Without that kind of freedom it seems as though they wilt. Power is, indeed, an energizer for them and if they don't have as much of it as they need, they lose part of their sense of being.

Constraints on Emotionality

In one sense, people who are school principals operate under constraints on their behavior that are similar to those that the executive of any enterprise must confront. That is, the managerial role carries with it a mythology that suggests that managers are supposed to be rational at all times, be able to separate their feelings from their thoughts, and to keep themselves under control at all times.

The same set of constraints does not hold, in the case of industry, for production workers or their immediate supervisors. It is not forbidden for them to show their anger, for example. They can swear at each other and it is permissible. The phrase "got chewed out" by the boss is a common one, illustrating as it does the freedom that people who "work" have to deal with their emotionality, particularly when it is negative. Similar circumstances hold in schools. Though it certainly isn't encouraged, it is not considered a major role aberration for a teacher, on becoming angry with a class or a student, to release his/her anger by yelling from time to time. It is only when the frequency or intensity of such behavior exceeds whatever informal norms have been established that other teachers or the principal might become upset.

The same freedom, however, does not hold for principals. If anything, they operate under more constraints than do managers in the private sector. For one thing, public officials, which principals are, are expected to behave with more decorum than their private sector counterparts. This is, perhaps, an unreasonable expectation, but it is the case. Second, they are "professionals" and so must behave in a "professional" manner. It's not clear, of course, what that means precisely but, for sure, it excludes the free expression of emotions, whatever they happen to be. Third, although schools are complex organizations, they are not highly compartmentalized. Thus, if a principal explodes at a teacher in his/her office, that principal can be assured that the incident will not remain in the office. It will be all over the school shortly, and the chances are good that at least some of the students will also have learned of its occurrence. The principal's seeming indiscretion will soon, then, become public property as the youngsters tell the tale at home.

When we introduced this general condition of work to our group of principals, it seemed to strike a resonant chord. They talked first about their anger, then their needs for warmth, and concluded with their feelings of not being able to display their own humanity, in general terms, while they are at school. The following is some of the discussion as it occurred:

Marie:

Every now and then my hostility seeps out because it's not appropriate for me to have a temper tantrum, much as I would like to have one at times.

Ed:

Bullshit!

Marie:

(laughing) You know, it's loss of control.

Paul:

I respond to that. It's frustrating just not being yourself. And Ed, I hear you saying, "Well, why not be yourself?" For me the answer is that, as an administrator, you take on a certain responsibility. What you do affects a wider variety of people than yourself. There's many a day that I envy a teacher, who has run into a frustrating situation, who can come into my office and throw a temper tantrum. And I know full well that when I have thrown temper tantrums the clean-up afterwards is not worth the release at the time. So I begin to restrict myself. I think, What would be an appropriate way of responding to the anger I feel for the situation? What would be appropriate in terms of the flak I would have to take from someone coming in who needs to express it?" I guess I find that as an administrator I don't get my needs satisfied on the job in terms of releasing myself. So I find other answers.

Ed:

I guess I'm not saying that you always have to communicate the feelings you have on the job. But it's important to be aware of them. I agree with your appropriateness comment. There are times when it's very appropriate for me to be angry and to show my anger and, damn, I better be or I'll be hanging on to that anger when I leave the building. And that's no good. Other times it's inappropriate and I have to deal with that in a different way.

What I'm saying is that it's okay to have feelings. A lot of people say, in the role of the principal, "I have responsibility for this building. I should not have feelings. I should not be angry."

It's really an issue of one's basic humanity. Teachers say to me, for example, that they can't be friends with kids. They have to be "teacher." It's an either/or situation with them, either being a teacher or being human or either I'm an administrator or a human being. It really isn't so. Appropriateness is a good word.

Paul:

> I know that when I stub my toe it's appropriate for me to say "Damn!" I think if I stub my toe *on the job* I would think about whether I say "damn" or not. That's a restriction that frustrates me.

Our question of how they deal with their needs for warmth gave rise to the following discussion:

Paul:

> It's with the kids. I've consistently found that the most expressive area for me is with kids. If I want to hug somebody I really get off on that—the interaction with the children—which is why I thought I was in education.
>
> That's not to say you can't be warm with staff. Today we played volleyball. I thought that was important because when we do that we're all in another role, and it helps build morale, particularly in a year like this when everybody's down and we don't know whether the school is going to last. You make avenues for doing that. But there are problems with warmth. I have problems having friends on the staff.

Marie:

> Yeah, me too.

Paul:

> I tend to shy away from that. I think friends find it harder for you to change roles. If you take a job as an administrator, you have to accept the fact that a time will come when you have to call the shots, when you'll have to say you're not satisfied with what's going on. I know I try not to come on too strong in those situations. And if it's someone you have a personal relationship with, it becomes even more touchy. If I come down hard on a friend, I have a tendency to want to make it up. If it's a staff member who's not a personal friend, I leave it and simply expect that fair is fair.

George:

> I had an interesting insight about this. We've had teaching interns for a number of years. I found that my relationship with the interns was always a lot different than it was with any other new teacher. There was one particular intern. We had a particularly high regard for each other and we talked about it. What it came down to, was that I knew I'd never have to hurt that person. I'd never have to evaluate them or get rid of them.

And quite naturally, it seems, the discussion drifted to one that dealt with the problems that principals have simply in being themselves as they preside over a school:

John:

Don't you get the feeling sometimes, I know I do, that you're not allowed the luxury of your feelings? I think it's really the way I was trained into the position. You don't have the luxury of being rattled; you're supposed to be decisive; you're supposed to be under control. I guess sometimes it's acting; because you don't always have the answer and you're not really running under control. Sometimes you're running out of fear. But yet the image of control has to be consistent. At times I walk out of that building at night and it's very frustrating.

Marie:

Drained.

John:

Yeah, sometimes you're just not allowed the privilege of behaving like you really want to.

Marie:

Like walk across the desk and get flippy. That's what I'd like to do someday.

George:

Sometimes my flippiness will just come out. Like at times I'll go over to the air raid cord in our office and just yank it. I guess I do it about once a year after the kids have left. Everyone shrieks. It's stupid but it makes me feel good.

If I get mad I try to tell the person I'm mad. I don't seem to feel as bound by the role as you do. If something scares me I'll say, "Hey, that idea scares me and this is why."

Marie:

The first year I was on the job I felt I had to be under very tight control and that I was being watched so carefully. Every weekend I would get on a plane and just go somewhere. It wasn't that I went and did flippy things or anything like that. It was just that I could sit with a group of people who didn't know who I was and wouldn't care anyhow. It was down time. I could just be me. I was tired, wiped out.

George:

I see myself pretty much in a box, pretty much self-contained. It's the small town stuff. Wherever I go I'm known for what I am and I can't get that need for friendliness satisfied. But somehow things work out. I haven't gone crazy yet.

Marie:

It's the same with me. I don't make friends in that town. And there are some days when I'm so sick and tired of that goddamn school and everybody in it that I won't even go to the local grocery store. It's mostly emotional drain. It's dealing with kids who are upset or parents who are in tears. You have to have tight control. I handle the situations effectively but it takes a lot out of me. Also, I guess it's that I'm highly visible in the town. I'm very aware of it and I'm not comfortable with it. And I'm a single female and that makes me much more visible. I'm aware that people know me, whom I don't know, and that people watch me that I don't know are watching me. You know, I get the stories back. And they are so way out, so ridiculous. And I know I'm susceptible to it all, but it's the one thing that will get me out of it all. I want my own world and I want to be able to share it with a few people whom I choose. Being public property is uncomfortable.

Ed:

I'm a bit different in the role. What you see and hear right now is basically what I am at school. School is my livelihood, not my life. In school I tend to be as warm, human, and genuine as I can be in that role.

The question I ask my teachers quite frequently is, "How do you allow the children in your classroom to nourish you?" Because I've seen them drained at the end of the day, and yet they have to re-plenish themselves and come back the next day. I ask myself the same question, "How do I allow the teachers in my building to nourish me?" Dammit, if I can't get hold of that and find some way of allowing them to do that then I, too, am going to feel drained. And like Paul, I get a lot from the kids, but I also have three or four teachers in the building that I really feel close to. I can sit down with them, reverse roles and say, "Look, this is the way I feel—listen." The big question is, who helps the helper? The helper, in many ways, has no one to turn to.

This dialogue speaks rather eloquently to the human concerns that these school principals have about themselves in their jobs. It also speaks, for the most part, to the loneliness of the position and points out a serious lack in the thinking and planning of school districts relative to providing support systems for school principals. How curious it is that schools—organizations whose raison d'être is the development of people—seem to ignore the problems and needs of those people whose responsibility it is to see that the job gets done. Double messages get sent. One is usually articulated clearly, "Pay attention to, try to understand, and deal with the learning and emotional needs of children." One that is unarticulated but clear nonetheless is, "Make it on your own. You can expect little or no help from the system relative to your own needs as a human being." It is not, of course, that there are no school districts that provide this help. There may, indeed, be some. It is abundantly clear, however, that if such arrangements do exist in some districts, they are aberrations from the norm.

People could take a hard-nosed position about the emotional problems that these principals face as they try to deal with themselves and the demands of the job. "Tough," the response might be. "That's part of the job. If they didn't know it when they became principals, they should have." But that view misses the point. That is, the test of a good principal is not the extent to which he/she can endure emotional stress. If that was all there were to it, we could simply select people who were terribly thick-skinned and had little or no insight into or caring about their own needs, precisely the kind of person who should not be a principal. Further, our group of principals could not, by any stretch of the imagination, be considered weak or complaining. To the contrary, they exhibited a tremendous amount of personal strength among them, and they talked about the concerns they had for themselves as people and the people with whom they work.

The job of a school principal is emotionally taxing. It wears people down. The wonder of it, from our position as professors, is that they continue to do what they do with enthusiasm—and that they seem to have fun doing it.

15

Toward a Theory
of Leading a School

INTRODUCTION

The choice of the title for this chapter was deliberate with regard both to the concept to be discussed—leading rather than administering—and the use of the verb form "leading" rather than the noun "leadership."

The focus on leading rather than administering stems from the manner in which Katz and Kahn (1966) differentiate three basic types of organizational leadership behaviors. These types are ". . . (1) the introduction of structural change, or policy formulation, (2) the interpolation of structure, i.e., piecing out the incompleteness of existing formal structure, or improvisation, and (3) the use of structure formally provided to keep the organization in motion and in effective operation, or administration" (p. 308). Administration, or administering, then, is a type of organizational leadership behavior which has as its goal the maintenance of things as they are on the assumption, perhaps, that the system will produce what it is intended to produce if things are simply kept running smoothly. In the case of the schools, this assumption would mean that they are structured in a functional manner, that the teachers are all competent, and that the curriculum and teaching methodologies employed are functional and relevant to the learning needs of the students. What remains for the principal to do, under this assumption of school organization and functioning, is precisely to be an administrator, to keep things running.

This concept of the principal's role—administrator qua administrator—has led to numerous hyperbolic and somewhat hostile caricatures of principals, all of which undoubtedly contain some kernel of truth. "My principal spends most of his time at his desk counting lunch money." "The only time I hear from my principal is when he comments that the shades in my room aren't drawn evenly." "My principal spends most of her time ensuring that the light bulbs are free from dust." "My principal's main function is to make sure the kids form even lines when they go into school in the morning." Underlying comments as these, though they are exaggerated and hostile, seem to be pleas by teachers for their principal to become a more valued part of the school organization and not merely to conceive of his/her role as focusing on "administrivia."

The principals described in this book obviously did not see themselves as organizational maintainers, as people whose job it was primarily to use the "structure formally provided to keep the organization in motion and in effective operation." Obviously, they had to perform certain routine administrative functions. But the way they described themselves, their interests, their joys and frustrations, shows that they focused their energy and time on other types of things. They were proactive in trying to make the school in which they worked a different place from the one they found. To use the Katz and Kahn formulation, it seems for the most part that they were engaged in interpolating the structure. They used it, frequently testing the boundary lines of their authority and influence, to make the structure work for them and their needs. What seemed to be at issue for most of them, most of the time, was not "We can't do that because things aren't done that way." Rather, the issue appeared to be simply "How should we go about doing it?"

In a way, then, we depart from the notion of equating administration qua administration with organizational "leadership," and thus entitled this chapter as we did. That is, although it is critically important for organizations to be kept in motion, merely to do so is not to be equated with the exercise of leadership. The process of leading involves attempting to influence the behavior of others to do things differently. The process of administering, keeping things going, may involve influence attempts. But such attempts, according to our scheme of things, would be directed at ensuring that organizational members—in this case, teachers and students— do not deviate from established norms in any significant way so that structured operating procedures and interpersonal relationships would not be upset.

We chose to use the verb form "leading" rather than the noun "leadership" in the title of this chapter for a reason that may seem to be more a matter of semantic nit-picking than one of substance. What is at issue is a tendency in education, in the social sciences, and in government to reify —to take ideas, processes or abstractions, give them names, and conceive of them as *things*, for example, progressive education, basic education, individually guided education, accountability, clinical supervision, and so forth. Once *things* have been made out of *ideas* then certain procedures must be followed before people can say that they are doing the "thing." For example, in order to engage in true clinical supervision a supervisor must follow certain steps or else he/she is not doing "it." No matter that the supervisor may be able to help a teacher do an intensive clinical diagnosis of his/her teaching and plan action on the basis of that diagnosis by other means. If the procedures prescribed as those associated with clinical supervision—the thing—have not been followed, then it is not clinical supervision.

Jerry Harvey (1975) has put the issue in a more powerful perspective. In writing about the field of organization development (another reified idea) he says:

> For me, organization development as a capitalized noun does not exist. I don't think it exists as a noncapitalized noun, either. This contention comes essentially from Bion's (1974) assertion that the way one can render a powerful idea impotent is to institutionalize it in the form of a word which restricts its meaning or in the form of an organization which accredits it (p. 5).

In agreement with Harvey's position, the concern in this chapter is not with a thing called leadership, but with trying to explain the dynamics of the process of leading—the principal exerting influence in a school setting. Thus the title of this chapter starts with the words "Toward a Theory . . ." The use of the word theory here is similar to that employed by Cremin (1976) as he analyzed public education in the 1976 John Dewey lectures. He used the term theory ". . . in its common sense meaning as a systematic description or general state of a field" (p. x). Thus the balance of this chapter proposes some tentative notions that make sense, rather than a statement of fact or a set of rules.

Any attempt to explain and analyze the behavior of an individual must conceive of that behavior as a function of the person's perceiving and interacting with a particular situation. This statement of the classic Lewinian (1951) formula (B = P,S) (Behavior equals Person, Situation), provides the backdrop for this discussion. It makes the point that in order to account for the ability of a school principal to exercise influence in a school attention must be given not only to the principal as a person but also to the structure and dynamics of the school as an organization and to the larger social system (the school district) of which the particular school is a part.[1] The discussion will not be a full-blown analysis of schools as organizations (for such an analysis see Bidwell, 1965), but will focus on those facets of school organizational life that have a direct impact on the school building principal—his/her emotionality and ability to exert influence or lead.

SCHOOL SYSTEMS—THE LARGER SETTING

In somewhat of a tongue-in-cheek metaphor (Blumberg, 1974), school system organization has been likened to the structure of a feudal kingdom. There is a castle and a king. Spread out through the kingdom are numerous

1. The broader community context is omitted from this discussion, while acknowledging its impact on the schools and, ultimately, on the behavior of principals. The nature of our data does not permit discussion of the diffuse linkages involved between community and school.

estates, each of which is presided over by a duke or a baron. The function of the king is to provide overall direction for the kingdom, to see that peace is kept within each of the surrounding estates, and to help resolve problems and conflicts that may arise between dukes or barons who, at regularly scheduled intervals, pay fealty to the king. On occasion, if there is trouble in a particular estate—with the people who work in it or the populace in general—the king will call the particular duke or baron to account for an explanation, and may offer some of his own resources to help resolve the problem. Or, the king may think that the person involved is unfit to rule, despite his/her title, and remove that person for incompetency.

The ruler of each estate, besides being charged with keeping the peace and paying fealty, has the responsibility for organizing the estate for both work and protection within the general guidelines that emanate from the castle. The specifics, however, are left up to each individual ruler, and as long as the peace is kept and due obeisance given to the king, there is rarely any trouble.

The metaphor, of course, is only that—a symbolic way of picturing reality that may be incomplete, vague, and somewhat imprecise. Nevertheless, when it was tested out with groups of teachers and principals, their reactions of nods, smiles, and ensuing discussion have indicated that the description doesn't miss the mark by very much.

The metaphor of schools as feudal kingdoms is, then, an amusing and useful tool for communication. People do seem to find it easy to understand and relate to it. However, it hardly rates as a highly sophisticated concept when it comes to describing the complexities of organizational life in schools. One such concept has been discussed at length by Weick (1976). It deals with the proposition that organizations may not be composed of tightly woven networks of relationships, and that it may be more productive to think of them as loosely coupled systems. By loose coupling it is Weick's intention:

> . . . to convey the image that coupled events are responsive, but that each event also preserved its own identity and some evidence of its physical or logical separateness. Thus, in the case of an educational organization, it may be the case that the counselor's office (central office)[2] is loosely coupled to that principal's office. The image is that the counselor (superintendent and other central office personnel) and the principal are somehow attached, but that each retains some identity and separateness and that their attachment may be circumscribed, infrequent, weak in its mutual effects, unimportant and/or slow to respond . . . loose coupling also carries connotations of impermanence, dissolvability, and tacitness all of which are potentially crucial properties of the "glue" that holds organizations together (p. 3).

2. Parentheses inserted by the current authors.

The notion of loosely coupled relationships between and among positions in school organizations can be expanded to suggest that the relationships between subsystems within the organization are, likewise, loosely coupled. That is, the relationship between the Central Office as a system and an individual school is a "sometime thing." In large districts the Central Office, for example, is frequently referred to by the amorphous title of "downtown." "The decision got made 'downtown' or 'someone downtown' spread the word" communicates the loosely connected and tentative nature of the relationship. Even more pronounced is the looseness of the couplings that exist among individual schools in a system. The feudal metaphor spells this out clearly. Each school is a more or less self-contained fief. Its concerns are its own constituents and its own territory. It is only on rare occasions that anything more than ritualistic socializing or committee work takes place beyond the territory. The relationships that exist among principals are transitory and seem to be based mostly on interpersonal liking. When they are in contact with each other, the issues generally concern interpretation of Central Office policy. There is practically never a voluntary joining together on problems of mutual program development.

Crucial to understanding this situation is recognizing that what is at issue is *not* the personality of principals. No data suggests that they are predisposed to be "loners." On the contrary, casual observations reveal that they are fairly gregarious individuals. Rather, the issue is that the behavioral conditions that have been described seem largely to be a function of the goals, values, and structure of the system. For instance, there is no eleventh commandment that says to school principals, "thou shalt not consult, collaborate, or join forces with other principals in your system." Such behavior seems simply to reflect the prevailing role expectations (which are ambiguous to start with) held for principals. Further, if such behaviors are not an explicit dimension of the principal's role, it follows that the rewards a principal may expect for engaging in them are likely to be low if present at all. The system, then, which is loosely coupled to start with, reinforces itself by its priorities, though this reinforcement is not by design. Rather, no one ever gives much thought to it.

The purpose here is not to criticize school systems or to suggest ways in which they could change. Rather, given that what has been described here is a fairly accurate, if brief, description of the reality of school system structure, what are the implications of this situation for the work life of the principal?

From our interview data and our observations of principals at work, three primary characteristics of the principal's role seem to emerge from the nature of the system: (1) they operate under conditions of *ambiguity* relative to their relationships with other administrators outside of their school, whether or not these administrators are in the Central Office or in school buildings, (2) their position is one of relative *isolation*, particularly with regard to work relationships with other principals, and (3) they experience a sense of *powerlessness* deriving from (1) and (2) relative to their ability to exert influence on the larger system. Further, the work life of a school principal, particularly with respect to others in the larger system, seems to be congruent with Weick's observation that a characteristic of loosely coupled relationships is that they ". . . are somehow attached, but that each retains some identity and separateness, and that their attachment may be circumscribed, infrequent, weak in its mutual effects, unimportant and/or slow to respond" (p. 3).

It doesn't take much imagination to create a scenario of the effect that the circumstances just described might have on the behavior and emotionality of a person who has just been appointed to a principalship. There would be an initial testing period during which time the principal seeks answers to numbers of questions. A sample of them would be: What is the system like? To whom can I talk? Whom can I trust? How do I get things done? Where do I get support? How much freedom do I have? Then, depending on the answers and the personality of the principal, there will probably be some attempts to reach out, to establish relationships with other principals. But, these attempts will not be successful, except in a transitory way. As a result the ambiguity will be reduced and both the sense of isolation and powerlessness will be increased.

The upshot of it all is that the principal's energies get turned inward to his/her school which is, perhaps, precisely the way it should be. That is, although the feudal or loosely coupled structure couldn't have been created by deliberate design, it does seem to have the effect of pushing people away from involvement in the larger system to an almost exclusive focus on the individual school as the center of attention.

The piper, of course, must be paid. Although the nature of the system does seem to narrow the principal's focus of energy and locus of control to his/her school, it also results in some costs, both to the system and to the individuals involved. The costs for the individuals stem primarily from their feelings of isolation and relative powerlessness to exert influence beyond the boundaries of their schools. For some, the singular fact of being isolated from meaningful work relations with peers may create an emotional drain for which they must somehow compensate. This lack of integrated work relationships among principals may additionally result in their being deprived of personal and professional stimulation and learning experiences, which may be important both to their own private sense of themselves and to the enthusiasm and skill with which they perform their jobs. The sense of powerlessness also takes its toll. It results in frustration for some, and in a sense of comic cynicism for others. For example, we have observed principals on the receiving end of what they knew were unworkable—in some cases, quite unrealistic if not irrational—policies. They simply took the position that someone "downtown" had nothing else to do and so a new policy was promulgated to deal with a problem that, from the point of view of the principal, was not a problem. So they smile, talk about highly paid Central Office functionaries who don't have much to do, and go about their business of subverting the policy or paying no attention to it.

The system, too, incurs some costs. Its losses derive, once more, from the sense of isolation and powerlessness that it has induced into the principals. That is, the system tends to cut itself off from the *collective* wisdom and deliberative ability of its principals. It is important to note the emphasis on the word collective. The issue is not that individual principals are not involved in matters pertaining to their school. Rather, they tend not to be involved in broad educational policy and program matters that affect the total system. The problem is not really one of authoritarianism on the part of the Central Office, although this may be the case in some circumstances. It seems more to be a question of behavioral and attitudinal norms that develop as a function of organizational structure.

The intention of the preceding discussion has been to describe some central features of school system structure that rarely receive the attention they deserve, and to highlight some important consequences of this structure for the everyday work life of the school principal. In addition, recent contacts with Central Office administrators reveal that they too are concerned about the effects of the system on principals and about the system's capacity to effectively deal with these problems. Thus, what has been described here seems to fit the model system and its operation. When aberrations occur, they seem to be a function of the personalities involved rather than instances of any type of impactful structural change.

THE SCHOOL BUILDING SYSTEM— A SETTING OF IMMEDIACY

We have implied throughout the preceding discussion that the affect of the larger school system setting on the principal's behavior is relatively diffuse and nonimmediate. Though the norms of the system make an impact on the principal, their pressure is felt in subtle ways. Further, the role demands that the larger system puts on the principal are of a global, long-term variety, not for day-by-day or hour-by-hour interaction. Although there are certainly times when the Central Office exerts pressure calling for an immediate response by a principal, the demands are infrequent, and tend not to be an everyday or every week occurrence, particularly in larger systems.

The principal's relationship and interaction with the human system of his/her immediate school building is in contrast, quite different. It is a setting of immediacy; that is, the role demands placed on the principal by members of the school building system—teachers, students, custodians, parents—are frequent and varied during the course of a day, and call for

quick responses. Principals rarely have the luxury of prolonged con-
templation of the actions they take during a school day. Irate parents
cannot be told to come back in a day or two because the principal has
other things to do. Nor can a teacher who is upset because his/her classroom is out of control be put off with "go get a good night's sleep and
it will be better tomorrow." To the contrary, the principal is pressured or
expected to act immediately, even if the action involves something as
simple as listening.

The notion of a "setting of immediacy" connotes a reactive stance on
the part of the principal and, indeed, this is so. Potentially large segments
of a principal's day are spent in reacting to situations that arise, in most
cases, unpredictably. Principals never know, for instance, when the telephone will ring, when a parent will come into school, when a teacher
will become disturbed, or when some youngsters will engage in fighting
or cut classes. Some principals are completely exhausted at the end of a
day from having dealt with one problem after another from the moment
they arrived in school till the moment they leave. Then there are some
principals who, perhaps to protect themselves from the emotionally
draining experience of continually reacting to human problems, spend
much of their time in their office dealing with routine paper and pencil
matters. What seemed to separate the school principals whom we interviewed from most of their colleagues, however, is that though they do
deal with immediate demands on their time, and they do take care of
administrative details, the essence of their own role definition was that it
was proactive. Their position seemed to be that they were educational
leaders; that it was their job to make an impact on the school; and that
they had a personal stake in making it a place conducive to better teaching
and learning.[3]

To help understand the occurrence of this attitude of proactivity in a
setting that puts a high priority on reactivity—immediacy of response—
we turn next to a discussion of some systematic organizational characteristics of schools, which are related to the ability of a principal to adopt
and maintain a proactive position regarding the faculty and the educational program. The point of this discussion is similar to the one that was
made earlier concerning the larger system of which the individual school
is a part. It is not possible to understand the behavior of a person in a
particular role unless attention is also paid to the social (and sometimes
physical) environment in which that behavior occurs.

In many ways, schools as organizations mirror the characteristics of the
larger system. Thus, what follows will deal, at times, with some of the

---

3. We suspect there are few, if any, principals who would not choose to look at
themselves in this light. Our experience suggests, however, that the incidence of
actualizing this proactive stance is not a common one. In fact, as we have discussed
this book with colleagues and friends, indicating the kind of principal we were
studying, the most common reaction was "where did you find them?"

issues that were raised in the prior analysis of that larger system. It will be pointed enough, however, so that the repetition has value.

THE SCHOOL'S SENSE OF THEIR INSTITUTIONAL BEING[4]

It is probably true that aside from governmental institutions, few systems have come under more attack from a wide spectrum of groups than have the schools. For example, conservatives complain that there is not enough emphasis on the basics; liberals criticize because the schools do not offer sufficient alternatives; newspaper editorials focus on too much permissiveness; blacks attack the schools because they don't take into consideration black children; and public advocacy groups take the schools to task for not adequately paying attention to the needs of handicapped youngsters.

For our purposes, the substance of these attacks is less important than their effect. One observable effect is the creation of a sort of siege mentality in many schools. It's as though administrators and teachers find it continually necessary to be on their guard. In addition, there seems to be a spill-over effect of distrust that is directed at strangers, at people who are not directly involved on a daily basis in trying to do the job of schooling, whatever that job may be. Perhaps a more important result, though, of these criticisms and attacks, is that legitimate or not, they induce a feeling of goal ambiguity among the teachers and administrators who work in the schools. "What is it we are all about? I thought I once knew, but now I'm not so sure," is a not uncommon reaction of school people. These reactions typify what Laing (1969) has referred to as a condition of ontological insecurity, a person's being unsure of himself/herself and his/her essential raison d'être.

Laing, a psychiatrist, focuses his concerns on problems of individuals, not organizations. It seems that the concept of ontological insecurity may well be transferred from the analysis of an individual to that of an organization. Speaking of individuals, Laing suggests:

> We can say that in the individual whose own being is secure in this primary experiential sense, relatedness with others is potentially gratifying; whereas the ontologically insecure person is preoccupied with preserving rather than gratifying himself: the ordinary circumstances of living threaten his *low threshold* of security. If a position of primary ontological security has been reached, the ordinary circumstances of

4. The following discussion of school organization dynamics is adapted from A. Blumberg, "School Organizations: A Case of Generic Resistance to Change," a paper presented at the International Conference on Social Change and Organization Development, Dubrovnic, Yugoslavia, February, 1977.

life do not afford a perpetual threat to one's own existence. If such a basis for living has not been reached, the ordinary circumstances of life constitute a continual and deadly threat (p. 44).

Laing uses the concept of ontological insecurity to account for individual psychoses. The transfer of the concept to the schools does not suggest that they are psychotic or that there are such things as psychotic organizations. However, the behavior of schools as organizations frequently communicates a strong sense of insecurity as to what it is they are all about. This does not necessarily mean that individual teachers or administrators are not ontologically secure. But the whole is different from the mere sum of the parts, and it is the whole that is of concern here.

There is a point in Laing's comment that is fundamental to his analysis. It is the suggestion that a condition of ontological security promotes a situation in which relatedness with others is potentially gratifying. In contrast, a condition of ontological insecurity creates conditions where the organism's thrust is on preservation, on scanning the environment for potential threats even if the environment is filled largely with the ordinary circumstances of living. As one or the other of these conditions gets translated into interpersonal or group situations, the behavior that becomes evident takes on the character of a psychological movement *toward* or a movement *away from people* (Horney, 1945). It is not difficult to sense when people perceive a circumstance to be potentially gratifying and interact and become involved with each other, or, the obverse, when they perceive a threat and enact avoidance behavior. A digest of some personal experiences relative to the schools may clarify this point.

Like many of our colleagues, we have held untold numbers of conversations and work sessions with individual administrators and teachers outside the immediate context of the school as an organization. These situations usually have been pleasant and productive. It was as though the people involved wanted to relate, wanted to work, learn, or change. On the other hand, there have been many occasions where we have attempted to work on similar problems within a particular school, but have found the experience much different. We were confronted with lethargy, defensiveness, and an attitude that might be best expressed as "ho hum." The startling thing was that the same people were involved in several of these cases.

Why the difference between our experiences with individuals and with organizations? It is only possible to speculate, of course, but the differences may be related to the notion that the individuals involved were fairly secure in their sense of being as an individual as opposed to an institutional insecurity of being. That is, the individuals seemed not to be threatened by the prospect of new relationships for themselves. As they behaved under the constraints of institutional identity, they seemed to be much less willing to engage in thinking about prospective change. There may be a myriad of other factors that enter the picture—factors that may be related to our own lack of skill, or at times, inability to communicate adequately, or factors that may attach to the system's previous experience with people from the outside. Nevertheless, over and over again the school systems and faculties, by their behavior, communicate that they are unsure of their essential institutional being and react accordingly.

These points are not made to administer a spanking to the schools with the admonition to them to behave and "be secure." To the contrary, they are raised descriptively to suggest that the phenomenon of leadership in the schools cannot be fully understood without also understanding that would-be leaders of schools will probably have to work within the context of ontologically insecure organizations.

ORGANIZATIONAL VALUE SYSTEM

Schools, like other organizations, are permeated by a value structure. Some of the values are explicit and committed to writing, for example, the valuing of each child's individuality. The values that impact most strongly on a system and on those who participate in it are the values implicit in the day-to-day behavior of organizational members. They can be learned best by the outsider through unobtrusive observation, and are reflected, for example, by teachers as they talk about what concerns are uppermost in the minds of administrators and supervisors. Over and over again the theme that gets repeated is, "Are things going smoothly?" An implicit and pervading value in schools, then, is keeping the peace. Concurrent with the value of peace-keeping is that of loyalty. In schools it is very important for school principals to be loyal to their Central Office administrators and for teachers to be loyal to their principals—at least publicly.

The problems for leaders in a school system that places a high priority on peacefulness and loyalty are great. The process of creative leadership, of change that makes a difference, is not necessarily a peaceful business. It may also involve some disloyalty in the sense of creating a facade of maintaining things as they are, thus communicating loyalty (and hopefully a peaceful scene), while simultaneously attempting to restructure ways of thinking and acting and, in the process, perhaps creating a not so peaceful scene.

The system pressures to maintain peace and display loyalty are reinforced in the schools by another system value reflected in the types of changes that are supported and encouraged. Those changes tend to be additive and usually take the form of a newly developed technique or a shift in methodology that does not disturb the basic elements of the system. Changes that receive little support or encouragement are those that require reconceptualizing and/or restructuring some aspect of the system

—the curriculum or the manner in which the school is organized, for example.

Watzlawick, Weakland, and Fisch (1974) place a conceptual distinction on these two types of change and refer to them as change of either first or second order. First order changes involve the rearrangement or substitution of parts of a system without disturbing the fundamental structure of a system. When first order changes are the basis of new programs, the results may indeed achieve some illusions of basic change. What is left untouched, however, is the framework through which people conceptualize their tasks and their relationships with others.

A second order change involves interventions in the system that enable the people in it to transcend their present frame of reference relative to the problems they are confronting. The issue is to create conditions that foster a reformulation of problems so that they may be viewed in new and creative ways. When second order changes are successfully induced into a system the results are qualitatively different in comparison to the results of a first order change.

Two brief examples will help clarify the difference between first and second order change. Inservice training programs are, for the most part, examples of change efforts of the first order. As a rule, they deal with methodological innovations that are perceived as substitutions for current methods or "add-ons." In either event, if the changes are adopted and implemented, they rarely involve a change in the way the teacher's role or the school organization is conceptualized. By contrast, the development and implementation of a flexible modular schedule in a school would be a second order change. The task structure of the organization is radically altered with the effect that teachers, in no small measure, are required to rethink and, perhaps, reconceptualize their role and functioning.

All this, of course, is not to suggest that all first order change is bad and only second order change is good. The issue is, however, that schools *do* seem to place a value on first order change. What does indeed get communicated is that first order change is acceptable. It is not apt to disrupt things. In Sarason's terms (1971) it does nothing to disturb the "regularities" by which schools operate. Second order change, on the other hand, tends to be viewed as relatively undesirable for it contains the potential for disruption of the regularities; it also usually requires a heavier investment of system resources, particularly people's time.

There are many cases that illustrate the point. They may be found in individual classrooms or in school buildings. For example, an elementary school teacher had decided to restructure her classroom, to change it from a teacher-centered interaction plan to one where the locus of interaction would be among the students. The result was highly satisfactory to the teacher. The students seemed highly involved. There was much discussion among them and a lot of "doing." There was also more noise in the classroom than there had been formerly. The principal of the school took a dim view of this. He saw it as disruptive to the peaceful scene for which the school had been noted, and he made his views known to the teacher. The classroom was restructured to its original (more peaceful) form.

A high school principal wanted to restructure the decision-making process in the school from what was a unilateral mode to one that heavily involved the faculty. The plan was put into effect, but it failed. The explicit message from the teachers was "you get paid to administer, we get paid to teach." At issue, in this case, was the fact that a change in the decision-making structure would involve the learning of new skills, a heavy commitment of time, and a thorough rethinking of the meaning of collegial governance of the school. The costs appeared too great for perceived benefits.

These brief examples are not offered by way of criticism, but as illustrations to help explain and understand the manner in which the value system of schools fosters the stability, some would call it inertia, of schools as organizations. Part of this resistance to second order change can probably be attributed to the public character of the schools. They are quickly susceptible to parental and community pressure. After all, everybody has been to school. Thus everybody "knows" how they should be run. When a youngster comes home from school and tells his/her parents of something new that is happening, and possibly of his/her discomfort or bewilderment, the principal is apt to have a questioning or complaining parent at the doorstep in short order. Caution, indeed, becomes the better part of valor. Life for all is simply easier if efforts to change do not disturb the regularities of the system, do not interfere with smoothness of operation.

To some extent, of course, these points are true of any social system. Reconceptualization of problems and restructuring of settings are not easy processes and they do disrupt things. The issue goes beyond the idea that second order change, for example, is not easy. What is involved is the central and powerful normative value-thrust of the schools—to maintain what presently exists in smooth running order.

ORGANIZATIONAL STRUCTURE OF THE SCHOOL

The structure of the larger school system has been characterized here (following Weick, 1976), as much more loosely coupled than tightly woven. This patterning of relationships appears to hold for the individual school organization as well, at least in most of the cases we've observed. What occurs between a teacher and a principal relative to the teacher's work, for example, or what occurs between a teacher and his/her students has no necessary relevance for events that develop elsewhere in the school. Further, the relationship between the principal and the teacher is also loosely coupled, and the common ground that might relate them in a combined effort is hard to discern. Weick approaches this circumstance in his discussion of the relationship between intentions and action:

> There is a developing position in psychology which argues that intentions are a poor guide for action, intentions often follow rather than precede action, and that intentions and action are loosely coupled. Unfortunately, organizations continue to think that planning is a good thing, they spend much time on planning, and actions are assessed in terms of their fit with plans. Given a potential loose coupling between the intentions and actions of organization members, it should come as no surprise that administrators are baffled and angered when things never happen the way they're supposed to (p. 4).

The comment above is, perhaps, another way of saying that "the road to hell is paved with good intentions." The suggestion is strong that the very nature of schools as organizations places major constraints on the ability of a principal to influence the school as an organization or the individual members of the faculty, in a way that, as Weick noted, administrators (and others, too) find baffling.

In a paper written prior to Weick's, Blumberg and Schmuck (1972) spoke more specifically to some school structural patterns that systematically create barriers to efforts to induce change in the school as an organization. Their analysis nicely parallels Weick's notion of schools as loosely coupled systems. It includes a concern with the individuated nature of the teacher's role and the dyadic nature of the principal's role.

INDIVIDUATED NATURE OF TEACHER'S ROLES

In Woodward's terms (1958) teaching is a single unit or small batch type of technology. The teachers have responsibility for total production within the classroom including planning, operating, and evaluating. Even though specialized roles develop around areas of psychological and subject matter competence, for most purposes, how well one teacher does his/her job is not related directly to how well another teacher does his/her job, even when they are working with the same students. At least the effect of one teacher's work on another's work is not easily perceived. Indeed, the teacher's role in the classroom tends to be organizationally nonintegrative. Teachers can do what is expected of them, for the most part, without ever communicating with one another. It seems reasonable to think that this lack of integrativeness of teachers' roles has influenced the development of norms of low collaboration in the school. Perhaps a better term for these norms is "acollaborative." While school staffs are not necessarily against collaboration and integration, the point is that such norms tend not to be at all salient in most schools.

The primary orientation of a teacher to his/her school, then, is one of individuation, and not in the direction of what might be called organizational membership. The school for a teacher is the building in which he/she teaches. It is not the social organism that provides the goals, the relationships, and the setting within which a teacher channels his/her efforts to produce something in consort with others. Because there often is little concern on the part of teachers with the school as an organization, the idea of devoting energy to improving the organization seems vague and irrelevant. This would be true especially of a teacher who is having a satisfactory experience even as the walls of the school come tumbling down.

DYADIC NATURE OF PRINCIPAL'S ROLE

The single unit or small batch technology that encourages individuated teacher's roles also has influence on administrative behavior. The principal is confronted with the nonintegrative norms of the staff, and his/her behavior often reinforces these norms. As in the case of the teachers, the principal's view of the school tends to be oriented toward interpersonal relations and not toward the organization as a whole. Thus, the principal's concerns for change and development move him/her in the direction of improving communications with individuals and not with organizational norms and group problem solving. The principal tends, from this point of view, to be an organizational manager who has only a limited view of the concept of the organization.

On a behavioral level, what seems to happen is that principals make many decisions with only an occasional consultation with teachers as a group. The principals spend a large amount of their time developing good relationships with individual teachers, not with groups of teachers. The norms of school staffs legitimize and sanction this way of working; it is not the fault of the principal alone. With the exception of adherence to system-wide policies, each school tends to be the private domain of the principal and the noninterdependent teachers. The principal's socialization into that role began when he/she was still a teacher. What was learned in that situation often tends to be repeated when a teacher becomes a principal. In this way, the organizational pattern of dyadic relationships with individual teachers on the part of the principal is circular and reinforced.

The principal who would lead a school, then—who would help teachers do a better job, induce changes into the curriculum when appropriate, and create a searching, collaborative and open organization—is confronted with an organization which, though bearing similarity to organizations that are structured in a hierarchical manner, is also markedly dissimilar in some crucial ways. Organizations in the private sector and many governmental agencies seem to have more of a sense of their institutional being, seem to be more ontologically secure than schools. While they value a peaceful scene and loyalty, these values seem not to be as all-pervasive as they are in the schools.[5] Although there are many loose couplings in them, because their mission tends to require more in the way of functional integration of tasks—more relating of individuals and work groups to each other in order to produce a product—they tend to be much more tightly woven than are the schools. It is essential, for example, in an industrial concern, for the sales department to coordinate its needs with the manufacturing department which, in turn, depends heavily on the purchasing department—and so on up and down and across lines. A similar situation does not exist in the schools where the activities of one teacher do not markedly affect those of another. In point of fact, the major structural interdependency that is common to all schools has to do with promotion through the grades. It is trite and perhaps extreme, but nonetheless true, to make the point that in order for second grade teachers to do their jobs, first grade teachers must certify and promote their pupils into the second grade.

All this is not to suggest that schools are organized in a manner that is structurally dysfunctional. It may be, to the contrary, that they are organized in precisely the best way possible. After all, schools in their present form have existed many years and though there have been many criticisms of schools and what they do, few of these criticisms have to do with the way they are organized to perform tasks. The issue, then, goes back to the principal, the nature of the demands that are placed on him/her that emanate from the organizational structure and value system, and the kinds of personal needs system and skills that might enable a person to lead.

This discussion of the problem of the principal's role in leading a school may appear to retrogress from current theory and research on the process of group or organizational leadership. The study of this process was early-on concerned with personality traits. As research into the traits of leaders proved inadequate for predicting who would perform well in a leadership position and who wouldn't, the emphasis of study shifted to conceiving of leading as the ability of a person to have certain sensitivities to individuals and groups combined with ability to perform particular functions that would enable the group to reach its goal. Further, it was assumed that these sensitivities and abilities were widely spread among

5. This may in part be related to the fragility of the schools as social systems. That is, they are fragile in the sense that precisely because they are relatively nonintegrative they are very vulnerable to pressures induced by the external environment.

people, were not the property of a select few, and, thus, the process of leading could be shared among the members of a group, depending on what was required at a particular moment in time. This view is one of democratic group process.

So far so good. The notion of egalitarianism in group or organizational functioning is one that appeals to peoples' value systems. Indeed, university training programs in educational administration stress the notion of training would-be school principals in the attitudes and skills of shared and functional leading. However, our observations of the field and our interviews with the people whom we have described in this book strongly suggest to us that in our concern to make schools "democratic" we have neglected the person of the one who is supposed to guide this process. The change in our thinking noted above, then, is one that moves away from a pure process notion of leading and focuses, initially, on the character and predispositions of the principal. Our study has led us in the direction of thinking that there are certain definable personality and behavioral differences between those principals who are able to make a difference in their schools and those who are not.

The idea of a "great man or woman" view of the principal who would lead is not advanced to suggest a new Machiavellianism. Rather the concept is this: It seems to be true that most people can learn the necessary attitudes and skills that enable a group of people to function adequately. And it seems to be true that groups can learn to accept influence from a variety of people and to assign group functions accordingly. What seems not to be true, is that *anyone* can assume the role of leading an organization—a school—in the direction of making itself better than it is. Other things besides democratic functioning have to occur and the suggestion here is that these other things start with the character of the person involved.

This position takes on added weight when thought is given to the low degree of structural complexity that is typical of schools as organizations. Schools, particularly elementary schools, are hierarchically very flat, having typically only a one-step separation between teacher and principal. Secondary schools may be somewhat more complex as they usually have hierarchies of three steps (teacher-department head-assistant principal-principal). Even in secondary schools, however, the functional hierarchy is quite flat. Department heads tend not to have or assume great power and assistant principals usually function as staff officers with specialized duties, not as next in line to the principal in decision making. The effect of this situation is to make the principal *the* central figure in the school. He/she is the only person in the school who has legitimated access to its total functioning, thus the centrality of the position. The remainder of this chapter thus focuses on the person of the principal as he/she functions within the school as an organization and interacts with the individuals who work in it.

What follows, then, is a discussion of some focal characteristics that appear necessary for the principal who would lead. These characteristics have been inferred primarily from our talks with the principals in our study, although we have certainly been influenced by discussions with teachers and from observations of principals in action.

Principals who lead seem to be highly *goal oriented* and to have a keen sense of *goal clarity*. The two go hand in hand. It is not enough to have clear goals, if these goals do not provide a continuous source of motivation. Further, the substance of the goals is important. Even though all the principals interviewed had different (though in several cases, related) images of what they wanted to see their schools become, none of them conceived of this image simply as maintaining things the way they were. As was noted earlier, it would probably be most difficult to uncover a school principal who did not espouse clear, substantive goals. It seems clear, though, that in most cases the mere espousal of goals substitutes for continual action in the service of those goals. Such was not the case with our interviewees. These people were continually alert for opportunities to make things happen, and if the opportunities didn't present themselves, they created them. Thus the principal must be capable of making his/her goals operational both through long-term strategy *and* day-to-day actions. It is of little worth to be able to articulate his/her aims if he/she has no notion of how to go about implementing them.

Principals who lead appear to be characterized by a relatively high degree of *ontological security*. Their sense of themselves as people and what it is they are about seems rather highly developed. It is not a matter of question to them. This facet of the leading principal's life enables him/her to confront day-to-day relations with others both inside and outside the system boundaries without feeling threatened. The superintendent does not become a figure to be treated with kid gloves. Parents are not seen as sources of threat, but as people who are concerned and may have something to offer. New ideas are welcomed and tested, not brushed aside as potentially upsetting to the school. This is another way of saying that the principal who is secure with his/her own sense of being is able to be open with self and with others, and is able to permit and encourage the testing of a wide variety of new ideas. If the new idea fails, it is simply seen as an idea that didn't work, and does not have consequences for the integrity of the people involved.

Building upon this last point, part of the character of principals who lead is that they seem to have a rather *high tolerance for ambiguity*. In a system that is as loosely coupled as the schools, the ability to tolerate a large amount of ambiguity relative to both the task and to relationships with others would appear to be highly important. Theoretically, this quality may well be related to the individual's ontological security. That is, if the system is ambiguous and a principal's self-security is low, then the ambiguity is likely to become a source of high personal tension. If he/she can't turn to himself/herself, and the system itself does not provide solid ground, the resulting situation will tend to be anxiety provoking. One would expect principals whose tolerance for ambiguity is low to avoid specifically those situations and ideas that might contain the seeds of productive change in a school precisely because those situations and ideas may create more ambiguity. Also, such principals probably would spend a great deal of time in routine administrative affairs, not attempting to lead.

Principals who lead appear to have a marked tendency to *test the limits* of both the interpersonal and organizational systems that they encounter. They seem to be proactive copers and confronters. It is as if they were continually searching and probing in order to establish greater degrees of freedom for themselves and their school. That is, they seem prone to taking risks, but they are not suicidal risk takers in the sense of embarking on projects which, if they fail, would result in catastrophe. They have a feel for the possible, but they define the possible after they test the limits of the situation, and not by way of a priori assumptions about what can or cannot be done. This latter point is a critical one. Sarason (1971) speaks to it when he notes the "regularities" of school system operation; ways of doing things that have developed over time, for which there is no particular rationale except the integrity of the regularity itself. That principals who lead don't accept the stonelike quality of these regularities can be illustrated by the example of one principal who wanted to build a regular weekly time for grade team meetings into the schedule. The widespread assumption was that it couldn't be done because the "regularity" specified that children had to be in school for a certain number of hours each day. He tested the limits—and it was done. Children were dismissed an hour and a half early one day a week.

A companion notion to that of testing limits is that principals who lead apparently are *sensitive to the dynamics of power* in both the larger system and in their own school. Although they don't conceptualize the system with the words "loosely coupled," they seem to understand the behavioral phenomena that result from loose coupling—for example, the difficulty of arriving at collective decisions that result in desired action. They understand the necessity for seeking out sources of power in the informal network of relationships in the school system, and they appear to be adept at cultivating these sources. It is not so much that they are political people, though they may be, as it is that they understand and are able to work with the requirements of the situation. They are aware of the need to establish alliances outside their schools in order to get things done or, if this proves unfeasible, to establish a power base in their own school that will enable them to make successful demands on the larger system.

Principals who lead seem to approach problem situations from a highly *analytical perspective.* They're able to stand back for a moment and not become immediately consumed by the problem situation itself. It seems to be a question of their initial impulse when confronted by a problematic situation. Is the impulse to try and objectify the problem, analyze it into its focal issues (some of which may be interpersonal) or is the impulse to deal centrally with the interpersonal aspects of the problem and secondarily with its substance? The inferences we drew from our talks with our principals was that analyzing the substance of things comes first. Thinking through the consequences of the analysis on personal, interpersonal, and organizational outcomes is second. They're first concerned with figuring out what is happening; then comes concern for the meaning and consequences of it all.

A characteristic of principals who lead seems to be that they behave in ways that enable *them to be in charge of the job* and *not let the job be in charge of them.* They are not pawns of the system. They seem to be adept at playing the games on which their survival depends, but they don't let the game playing consume too much of their energy. These principals seem to be well aware of the minimum requirements on them to perform routine administrative functions, and they seem able to fulfill these requirements with dispatch, thus freeing themselves for more exciting (for them) activities.

A somewhat different perspective on the principal who would lead concerns the interpersonal need system of these principals and the basis upon which they approach their job. The discussion, which reflects the theoretical formulation of interpersonal needs developed by Schutz (1958), derives both from our interviews with these principals and some casual research we have engaged in from time to time.

Schutz suggests that each individual has an interpersonal relations orientation that is composed of a mix of three focal needs: needs for inclusion, control, and affection. Further, each of these has two dimensions: one that deals with expressing the need behaviorally towards others and one that is suggestive of what the individual wants behaviorally from others. A person may have, for example, high needs to be included by others in activities, but a low need to include others in his/her activities. Our data suggests several notions regarding the interpersonal needs make-up of principals who would lead:

1. They appear to have high needs to control a situation and low needs to be controlled by others. They rather like being in charge of things, proposing ideas, and initiating action. They strongly dislike it, and tend to reject it, when constraints are proposed on their prerogatives, or their freedom of action and initiative is restricted in any way. They prefer to find their own solutions to ambiguous problems than to be told how to do it by others, particularly their organizational superiors.

2. These principals seem to have rather high needs to include others in projects or in problem solving, and moderate to high needs to want others to include them. Part of their analytic stance toward

problem solving is to make sure that those who are to be involved in the consequences of decisions be involved in making them. Thus, they are not "loners," controlling things and making decisions from the confines of their office. More often than not they are found out in their school talking with teachers and with students. It is fairly important for them to be asked by others to join in working on projects, and they tend to become upset at not being involved by others, particularly when they think they have some expertise that is germane to the problem under consideration.

3. Principals who lead tend to have rather high needs both to express warmth and affection towards others, and to receive it. It is not so much that they are "warm fuzzy-wuzzies" to the exclusion of anything else. Clearly, this is not the case. But, when they interact with teachers in their school, there is a large amount of friendliness and good-natured fellowship. These principals are not standoffish.

How do these principals compare, relative to their interpersonal needs, with those who might be categorized as not leading? A data base for making such a judgment is not available. However, Schutz (1967) did report data on a sample of 104 school administrators simply as a normative example. On the whole, the mean scores were quite moderate and distinctly different from our hunches about our own small group. Something out of the ordinary seems to be operating among those principals who lead.

The intent of this chapter has been to recast our thinking about the process of leading a school. We suggested that the nature of schools as social systems requires that renewed attention be given to the person of the principal and we offered a number of propositions concerning the character and style of some principals who engage in leading. This chapter has not been a plea to return to a trait theory of leadership. However, we do suggest that in our headlong rush toward the greater development of social technology as the answer to the problems of creating more productive learning environments in the schools, we may have neglected the essential humanity of the people who preside over them. And this humanity is, after all, much of what schools are all about.

A final point is in order. It might be possible to infer a prescriptive tone out of the foregoing discussion of the characteristics of school principals who are somehow able to induce creative influence on their schools, and in a deliberate fashion, to lead. Description, not prescription, has been the intent. To the extent that our observations have credibility, and we believe they do, they constitute a basis for further study and action.

16

Review, Implications, and Conclusions

This final chapter addresses the difficult task of bringing the discussion and analysis of these eight principals to a close. While it is clear from the preceding examination of the day-to-day work world of these men and women that the elementary and secondary schools of today seem different in many ways from those we and our parents attended, in many respects both the problems and the general responsibilities of principals have not changed a great deal. A reading of Willard Waller's *Sociology of Teaching* (1932) and Dan Lortie's *Schoolteacher: A Sociological Study* (1975) reveals that, indeed, many of the issues and problems confronting school people in the early twentieth century are still here today. The enduring character of the school organization is in many respects both a blessing and a curse. Although the characteristics of the containing community and the values and attitudes of the major participants in schools have changed drastically during the past half century, the basic relationships among the actors in those systems have not changed substantially, nor have the organizational structures and basic operating procedures of schools been altered in any substantial degree. In many respects, although some things have changed, much remains the same.

The closing remarks in this chapter have been organized into three major parts. First, the eight thumbnail sketches, the analyses of these data, and the theoretical statement in the previous chapter are reviewed briefly. A discussion of the implications of these observations for school district staff development and university training programs is the focus of the second part of this chapter. The third portion is devoted to recommendations relevant to teachers desiring to become principals, elementary and secondary principals themselves, school district superintendents and personnel responsible for the personal and professional development of school principals. And, finally, suggestions are offered for university professors involved in studying and training school administrators generally, and principals in particular.

251

REVIEW

As we indicated in our introduction, we weren't sure what we'd find in our exploration of the on-the-job behavior of some school principals who seemed by all reports to be out of the ordinary. We were curious regarding the observations they would have of themselves and their respective school situations. We thought, perhaps, that by talking with them we might acquire a more complete understanding of the principal's work world, of the similarities and differences in their experience and in their responses to the demands of the job.

As we tried to grasp the significance of and understand the information they provided us with during our interviews with them, it became clear to us that each of these men and women brought something different with them, a unique quality, as they approached and dealt with the problems of their respective schools. We were able to distinguish among these principals in terms of the idiosyncratic perspectives each of them held toward life generally and their work situation in particular. While many of the problems they faced were similar in type and magnitude, the variations in the perspectives they held appeared to be the major factor relating to the differences in their approaches to the job, in their conceptions of what was critically related to effectiveness in the principalship. The central life interests of these eight men and women were to a great extent realized in the world of work, their principalships.

While it is difficult to capture completely the nuances and full implications of their perspectives in a single phrase or word, we found ourselves distinguishing among them and referring to their dominant work orientations with rather rich descriptors: The Politician; The Humanist; The Broker; The Catalyst; The Juggler; The Organizer; The Rationalist; and The Helper. Each of these people, because of their distinctive and idiosyncratic views, approached the demands and problems of the principalship in different ways. The central thrust of their effort to solve a particular problem or introduce some desired change in their respective schools was guided by one overriding concern or another, depending on their orientation to work.

Paul, The Politician, was typically concerned with the distribution and exercise of power vis-à-vis actors in his school and community. John, The Humanist, was primarily interested in the welfare and proper treatment of the students, teachers, and parents associated with his school situation. Fred, The Broker, wanted more than anything else to ensure that the various groups and individual participants in his school and surrounding community were sufficiently apprised of and put in contact with the resources necessary to solve problems as they arose. He prided himself and indeed spent much of his time as a "linking agent" between and among various groups that had or could have an impact on his school. Joan, The Organizer, saw herself as a prime mover in getting new initia-

tives off the ground through her inclination to put together all the necessary pieces needed to accomplish particular objectives. She not only
planted new ideas in people's minds but also organized and operationalized
the resources and processes required to achieve desired goals. In this
respect she differed from Marie, The Catalyst, whose major thrust was to
move continuously throughout the organization and stir people to action.
Her view seemed to have as a central focus the idea that any kind of
"positive action" was better than no action at all. She did not, however,
seem to take it upon herself to be the principal actor involved in organizing the resources needed to move things beyond the idea stage. Rather,
she preferred to leave this to others in her system, usually those most
closely tied to the problem about which she'd been busy stirring people to
action.

George, The Juggler, was guided by an overriding concern that the
children in his charge receive the very best education possible, including
in his notion of education *all* of what happens in school, not merely academic activity. This orientation shaped his problem-solving behavior, regardless of whether the issue was a class scheduling problem, a teacher
morale issue, a rainy graduation ceremony, or an individual student disruption. Fran, The Rationalist, attached primacy to clear communications,
role specification, and delineation of authority amongst herself and her
administrative staff. She was extremely sensitive to the ambiguity of
language that both she and others used to describe problems and prescribe
solutions, or to refer to one or another school actor or situation. As a
consequence, her approach to school problems, her general demeanor as
a principal, reflected her concern for clarity—clarity of language, of relationships, of functions, and responsibilities. Ed, The Helper, focused
his principalship on helping others help themselves. His concern with the
individual growth and maturation of his faculty and the children in his
school permeated all that he did. The psychological health and emotional
strength of participants in his school guided most of his actions.

While we were struck by the clear differences among these eight
people, and the subsequent differences in their approaches to the demands
of the principalship, we were not so surprised to find that there was a
great deal of similarity among the problems they faced on a day-to-day
basis. As was suggested at the beginning of this chapter, schools are in
many ways not much different today from what they were like even fifty
years ago. It was not surprising, therefore, to find that the character of
the problems and issues concerning these men and women did not differ
much from one school to another. Although there were some variations
in the size and the magnitude of problems experienced, these were more a
function of differences in social context and community situation than
they were of anything generic to the schools themselves, which is in part
due to the similarity of school organizational structures and basic role
relations. Stripped of particularistic social, economic, and racial distinc-

tions, the eight schools being served by these principals were extremely similar relative to organizational configuration, instructional objectives, group norms, and role relationships among participants. They were correspondingly similar relative to the nature of the problems and issues that confronted the principals on a day-to-day basis. Thus, while there were clear wrinkles of differences related to economic, racial, and social context, the basic problems related to issues of resource allocation, control and coordination of personnel, conflicting role expectations of participants, goal ambiguity, and the distribution of power and authority were common to each. The magnitude of these several problems varied depending on the character of the school community (the economic, social, and racial composition), the size of the school itself, and the age of the students (elementary or high school). Beyond this, the situations these principals faced were essentially similar.

IMPLICATIONS

As we reflected upon our analyses of these data several critical issues continued to nag at us. One is that, with the exception of The Helper, who had received extensive training in Gestalt theory and technique, none of the other seven principals were able to articulate any sort of comprehensive conceptual framework or theory of schools or administration guiding their performance. While we suspect they each have a tacit (Polanyi, 1967) understanding of the particular attitudes, values, behaviors, ideas, and skills requisite to effectiveness on the job, none of the principals except The Helper was able to explicate clearly the basis for their beliefs and actions. While this ability in and of itself is not necessarily a critical factor related to success on the job, when such understanding *can* be articulated *and* enacted, performance is enhanced. The character of their graduate training and the related administrative certification procedure may be related to this problem.

A second issue concerns these principals' relations to other principals and the overall attitude taken toward them by their superiors. Without exception, these principals perceive themselves to be very lonely and isolated from their peers, and feel generally ignored by their superiors as long as they're able to "keep the peace" in their school. As noted in a previous chapter, Fred was neither visited by a superior nor called upon to account for his performance until two years after his appointment to the position —and this was his *first* administrative appointment!

In terms of their relations with other principals, it was generally noted that although it would be desirable to collaborate and interact more frequently with their peers, such activity was rare and clearly not the rule. With the exception, perhaps, of cooperation growing out of a friendship developed in another context, the relations of these principals to their colleagues tended not to be characterized by helping, sharing expertise, or otherwise relying on one another for anything. This circumstance seemed to be attributable in part to the organizational condition of having to (a) compete with one another in obtaining already scarce resources from the school district central administration, and (b) bargain away less desirable teachers not clearly incompetent enough to be fired—horse trading teachers to the extent that one or another principal would inevitably end up with some other principal's reject. More importantly, perhaps, the lack of collegiality may be attributed to a value system inherent in schools as organizations—not putting a very high premium on the benefits of fostering personally and professionally supportive relationships among teachers, principals, and other adult actors in schools.

Exacerbating this general set of circumstances was the physical isolation of principals from one another. The only sanctioned occasions for getting together were usually district administrative staff meetings held once a month; otherwise they kept pretty much to themselves and their school staffs and suffered unnecessary stress and frustration as a result. This problem seemed especially acute in small district settings where the population of principals was lower to begin with and, frequently, there would be only several elementary schools, a single junior high school, and a senior high school. Principals in both large and small districts spoke of their peers as if they were located on another planet!

If school districts are bent on burning-out or killing-off whatever talented principals might be in their midst, these circumstances would seem to provide the key. All the principals interviewed expressed a similar concern for higher-quality and more frequent interaction with their peers. They saw it as a critical factor related to their general level of motivation and psychological health. The lack of having someone to talk to who experiences similar problems was, indeed, seen as a major frustration. Developing a mechanism to accomplish this would seem to offer multiple pay-offs. In addition to gaining an understanding and appreciating sounding board, it is likely that their related phenomena of loneliness, lack of collaboration, and sharing of expertise would be affected as well.

In a related way, and implicit in the reports of the principals with whom we talked, there seemed to be no systematic or continuous effort by the school districts to develop the skills and talents of their building principals. Presumably it was either assumed that such development was unnecessary to their well-being and continued effective functioning or, perhaps, that they would simply develop on their own! The results of this neglect by their respective districts were several missed opportunities for not only directly providing services to those principals needing and wanting help in a particular area, but also using the talents and special skills of some principals to help others so that the egos and sense of self-worth of these "helping" principals could be bolstered. There's no reason why every principal in a district can't be treated as a special resource of some sort. It was clear, from talking in depth with these eight principals, and from casual conversation and observation with many of the school principals and superintendents we come in contact with in the course of our work, that a great deal of talent is likely being wasted, and certainly not maximized, in most school districts. Districts need not necessarily look outside of themselves in thinking of beginning an administrator staff development program—the first year's program is probably right there in their own backyard, just waiting to be tapped.

GRADUATE TRAINING

Relative to the implications of our findings for the preparation and training of principals, we found little to suggest that university graduate training had much direct or observable influence on any of these men and women. The possible exception to this is the elementary principal who had very extensively studied Gestalt theory and practice before becoming a principal. It should be noted, however, that this was a personal interest of his, and not part of either a graduate training program for administrators or a requirement for administrator certification. All the others, on the other hand, were involved in a doctoral "training program" in the field of educational administration.

When we asked ourselves what we could point to in the data that might reflect the influence of such extensive graduate training, such as they all had, we found little. Indeed, as was noted earlier, none except The Helper was able to articulate explicitly and clearly a conceptually abstract or theoretical frame of reference guiding his/her on-the-job behavior. However, we are reluctant to suggest that evidence of success in a graduate education program means little in terms of the principalship; if nothing else is clear, it probably is a fair indicator of the intellectual ability of these men and women—a factor which Hemphill, Griffiths, and Frederiksen (1962) found to be related to principal effectiveness. Nevertheless, we were discomforted by the great difficulty they had in explaining to us *what* they did that made them effective administrators, and similarly, they were unable to articulate clearly the reasons *why* they took certain actions. The exceptions to this were instances in which specific situations or problems were the focus. There seemed to be no overarching conception guiding their actions, other than the rather general orientations we were able to identify as a result of our analyses.

In reviewing the data we observed that these eight people did, in fact, hold a number of characteristics in common, the threads, if you will, shaping the fabric of their effectiveness. There were five major strands that we were able to discern clearly. While we're sure this is not the complete picture, we believe these five are critically related to their success on the job:

1. A high level of energy and a willingness to work long hours on a continuous basis. These men and women consistently spent very long hours each day on job-related activity. Some spent as much as fifteen to eighteen hours, on a regular basis, at particular times during the school year.
2. Extremely well-developed expressive abilities. All of these principals had very well-developed interpersonal skills and were able to communicate effectively in face-to-face interaction with a diverse range of individuals and groups.
3. A proactive approach in response to the requirements of the situation they faced as principals. All tended to take the initiative and not wait for the lead from others, except as this would help them achieve their objectives. They were all clearly leaders who felt comfortable and were effective being in charge of things. This is not to say they did everything themselves—they were, however, clearly adept at "getting the ball rolling."
4. All of these principals were very good listeners and observers. Their antennae were always out and highly sensitive to what was occurring both in and around their schools. They were continuously collecting data about their situation.
5. Finally, all of them were very skilled at analyzing and determining the requirements of their school situations, and evaluating alternative courses of action. This was, like their disposition to collect information as they moved through their work world, a continuous process. They were constantly sorting, sifting, categorizing, and interrelating phenomena bearing on the principalship.

Doubtless these five characteristics were not acquired in a graduate training program, although it might be argued that their graduate training enhanced and expanded their abilities in these areas. This could be the case, but it is highly unlikely. The graduate training programs we're familiar with tend not to do a very good job in any of these realms, although many espouse to do so.

What does the foregoing suggest to us about the selection and training of school principals? For one thing, it should be obvious from getting a glimpse of these principals' lives that quite a wide range of people may be effective in the role. It's unlikely that grade point averages, Miller Analogy Tests, Graduate Record Examinations or number of graduate credits will be a reliable predictor of success as an administrator. It is also unlikely that completion of a program of graduate course work in educational administration will be a helpful index to use in selecting an effective administrator, except as it might indicate superior intellectual ability, no doubt an advantage as a principal, but not likely to be sufficient for success on the job. While some administrative internship experiences *may* be a good predictor, more depends on the quality and character of the actual internship experience, not necessarily on the length or the fact of the internship itself. For example, the indication of "internship credit" on a transcript or job application is not by itself likely to be as reliable a predictor as detailed knowledge about the substance of the internship and under whose guidance it occurred. In sum, then, the business of selection and prediction is, at best, a risky enterprise.

What then should be done given these observations? A shift in the assumptions guiding administrator selection may be a key to understanding their professional development and hence the criteria that might effectively be used to select principals likely to succeed on the job. Basically, this shift involves a de-emphasis of formal factors and an increased recognition of informal factors related to acquiring the knowledge and ability necessary for success in the administrative work world. In a sense, those involved in the selection and training of educational administrators, of school principals in particular, have been asking an insufficient set of questions. Attention has been on formal rather than informal indices of competence. The focus has been on number of years of teaching experience, number of previous administrative jobs, number of advanced degrees or graduate credit hours, grade point averages, test scores, and the like. There has been relatively little attention given to assessing the *qualitative* character of people's previous experience as a teacher, graduate student, supervisor, or administrator. The informal learning that occurs as people enact these various roles is probably a major influence shaping their capabilities as a principal. And the informal learning that has occurred is precisely the learning that is at once not adequately assessed, yet is likely to be more highly related than formal learning to success in the administrative work world. Candidates for the principalship, for example, might be asked to explain what they've learned about schools, communities, principals, teachers, and students as a result of their past experience at working in schools. Their answers and any ensuing discussion with a selection team could be very helpful to the group or individual charged with making a hiring recommendation.

The distinction between formal and informal learning involves differences in both the role of the learner and in the content of what is learned (Brim and Wheeler, 1966). In a formal learning situation both the role of learner and the content to be learned are known. In an informal learning situation, usually neither the role of the learner nor the content to be learned is specified. An example of a formal learning situation would be that of a student, an intern, or a new military recruit in training. Even in these instances, as Becker (1951) among others has pointed out, a great deal of informal socialization is likely to accompany the "formal" learning. An example of an informal situation where neither the learner role nor the content to be learned is specified is the case of peer group socialization, as of a new student in the class, or the case of the experienced teacher who moves to a new job. In these instances the learner's role as "learner" is not specified, nor is the actual learning that occurs typically prespecified in any way.

A parallel informal learning situation occurs throughout our lives. What is relevant here concerns what we informally learn in our work setting. The structure of the work setting itself has much to do with what is learned. For example, the quality of a person's experience as a teacher may have very different learning outcomes for different individuals, depending on the character of the setting itself. One teacher may be assigned to a single classroom teaching situation in which he/she is responsible for a specific group of children for the entire day. Another teacher, in another situation, may be required by the job description to attend to multiple groups of students and to team with or otherwise deliberately coordinate effort and communicate with other teachers on the staff. These are both teaching experiences, but they are qualitatively different in their structure and in what a teacher might informally learn as a result of engaging that role. In the one where the teacher is assigned responsibility for one group of students for the entire day, there is little or no opportunity for interaction with other teachers. In the other situation, a major part of the job requires continuous interaction and exchange with other teachers. The potential for increasing, or at least practicing, his/her skills at working face-to-face with adults is greater in the second situation than the first. If one of the requirements of the principalship is skill at working effectively with adults, the teacher in the second example would, all other things being equal, stand a greater likelihood than the first teacher of being successful at fulfilling this requirement of the principal's role. However, informal learning opportunities such as the one just noted don't always result in learning by a participant.

The old adage, "experience is the best teacher," speaks to this point. The relation of "experience" to ability is frequently oversimplified and often only partially understood. It's the quality, the nature of the experience, that counts. Another point is that what is learned informally through "experience" at an early stage in a teacher's career may indeed *not* be functionally relevant or appropriate to the role demands at a later stage in the career. Interning as a high school vice principal in charge of student discipline probably teaches more about what principals prefer *not* to do than what "effective" principals in fact do. A third issue concerns the timing of "experience." When most people talk about "experience being the best teacher," they're typically referring to experience *in the role itself*, and not to role-related learning, which may have occurred as the result of experience in previous, but different, roles. This is certainly a relevant and important dimension. The very important informal learning that has accrued as a result of experience in *former* roles and settings is often ignored. This sort of previous informal learning is critical and should not be overlooked. Teachers, while active in the teaching role, for example, unwittingly accrue both useful *and* inappropriate conceptions of the principalship. If administrator selection procedures deliberately reflected upon the nature of what "informal" learning may or may not have occurred, then such procedures would stand an improved chance of facilitating a good match between a candidate's capabilities and the requirements of the school principal's role. While this is often not a criteria used, in those cases where such an effort is made to assess the relevance of prior experience, much "informal learning" data about an individual can frequently be examined and evaluated.

Like it or not, school districts are thus very much involved in the "training" of principals. The informal on-the-job learning that accrues to teachers, supervisors, and administrators can be ignored (as it usually is), or utilized. This is not to suggest that it be "formalized." Rather, it is necessary to understand that learning does occur both formally *and* informally, and that the quality and nature of the work situation of a particular individual may or may not provide opportunities to acquire the knowledge, skills, and attitudes needed to perform well in subsequent roles. If principals must be able to work well with adults in face-to-face situations, then provisions have to be made for principals and aspiring principals to work at tasks and activities that offer them the chance to acquire and practice the requisite interpersonal and problem-solving skills. If principals need to have a grasp of "the big picture" vis-à-vis the school district organization and community, then provisions should be made for job experiences and assignments that serve to broaden their view of the school, the community, and problems attendant to the principalship (see Davies, 1962; and Cronin and Horoschak, 1973, regarding experience in the field and the training of administrators).

In the training and selection of principals, *both* their formal *and* informal learning should therefore be taken into consideration. Certification, advanced graduate work, an excellent teaching reputation, and a personable and likable manner are no guarantee of effectiveness as a principal. Asking evaluative questions regarding the informal learning and practice opportunities attendant to previous work experience as a teacher, supervisor, or whatever, is likely to yield critical information regarding the degree of understanding and ability a prospective principal has of the demands characterizing the principal's work world.

What does this mean for university training programs, given that there is rarely little direct correspondence between formal course work and on-the-job capability as an administrator? Although there is substantial validity to this observation, we do not advocate doing away with graduate study. The problem, rather, is the expectation that is implicit in reference to university "training" programs. The data provided by the principals we studied suggests rather strongly that they were not "trained" for their jobs by a graduate preparation program per se. Indeed, they do not even seem to share a very extensive or systematic body of special knowledge as a result of their involvement in a graduate training program in educational administration.

What good, then, is graduate course work relative to learning how to be a successful school administrator? As it is presently conceived, it's probably not much good to anyone, least of all teachers and supervisors working toward administrative certification. In part, this is a function of the degree of investment by students in their graduate study. Most students desiring to become administrators accrue the necessary graduate credits on a part-time, piecemeal basis. In those instances where there has been an effort to interrelate and focus the graduate work into a more integrated and holistic program of study, it is still attended to rather superficially—and for good reason. Two hours of sitting in a graduate class once each week for a semester does not begin to have the impact upon an individual that comes with full involvement in the "blooming buzzing confusion" of the day-to-day work world of schools. The "formal" graduate work just does not compare to the power of the "informal" learning that occurs in the work setting—where the role of learner is not specified and where the process and content of learning usually occurs without the awareness of the individual affected. The net result is that graduate course work as it is presently engaged does not have much impact on prospective administrators vis-à-vis their on-the-job effectiveness. The major exception here may be specific courses in law, negotiations, supervision of instruction, curriculum development, and the like (see, for example, Byrne's et al., 1978, analysis of the 1965 and 1978 surveys conducted by the National Association of Secondary School Principals). However, these courses neither individually nor collectively serve to train men and women for the day-to-day requirements of the principalship, nor do they provide any sort of comprehensive, coherent, and systematic frame of reference as a guide to action. They represent a lot of bits and pieces, but not a coherent whole. Indeed, some of the skills learned for success in graduate courses may be entirely dysfunctional as far as performance on the job is concerned (Bridges, 1977).

So what contribution might graduate programs make to preparing educational administrators? There are two: one concerns the acquisition of a substantive body of knowledge about schools as organizations; the other concerns learning five specific skills requisite to success in an executive, leadership role. The rudiments of both can best be learned through full-time university study for at least one year, preferably for a period of eighteen to twenty-four months; once learned, they can be improved and expanded through use in "live" settings such as the principalship.

March, 1976, after reviewing the nature of educational organizations, managerial work, and the comparative advantage a university has relative to developing certain analytical skills germane to successful management, argues that educational administrators can benefit from training in five different skill areas. Although March's ideas will not be addressed in depth here, the five skills he discussed are worth noting for the reader. Briefly, they include:

1. The analysis of *expertise*. The management of knowledge.
2. The analysis of *coalitions*. The management of conflict.
3. The analysis of *ambiguity*. The management of goals.
4. The analysis of *time*. The management of attention.
5. The analysis of *information*. The management of inference (March, 1976, pp. 121–22).

These skills are important to success in the principalship. They are mentioned here as a specific focus of graduate study precisely because they are not the sorts of skills one is likely to acquire systematically and informally in a work setting, although it is very likely that an individual will have had some previous experience and will have already "informally" learned something about each of these problems of management.

Acquisition of a systematic knowledge base regarding the nature of school organizations, and individual and group behavior in such settings, is the second contribution a graduate school might make to the preparation of educational administrators. A fundamental theoretical and empirical understanding of the complexities of leadership in such settings seems paramount if school principals are expected to be effective. This knowledge combined with the complement of special skills learned formally and informally would increase the chances a principal has of being successful and contributing to the educational and organizational well-being of the teachers and children in his/her charge. The work of the University Council for Educational Administration, for example, has been influential in integrating knowledge from the behavioral and social sciences into the curricula of some graduate training programs for educational administrators (Culbertson, Farquhar, Gaynor, and Shibles, 1969).

CURRENT STAFF
DEVELOPMENT/PROFESSIONAL
IMPROVEMENT EFFORTS

In similar fashion, it seems apparent that central office personnel in school districts need to attend more deliberately and carefully to the challenge and potential of staff development of middle managers, elementary and secondary principals in particular. Any effective program aimed at developing administrative talent must capitalize on both the formal and informal learning opportunities that already exist in most school districts, for both principals and those aspiring to that position. We don't believe any additional financial commitments would be necessary to achieve a situation wherein principals, supervisors, and other administrators were encouraged to meet and exchange ideas and talents, and thereby draw upon one another for special contributions to solving organizational, personnel, or community relations problems. The talent is usually there—the challenge is to mobilize it in a creative and effective manner.[1]

Numerous efforts at administrator staff development have blossomed across the nation during the last decade. The American Association of School Administrators, for example, has developed an extensive national program of inservice development and professional training workshops focusing on a range of problems and issues germane to the principalship. Various state level associations have also recently become very active in developing and sponsoring staff development programs for administrators. The Association of California School Administrators, for example, published a notebook in 1975 that describes six successful models of California programs designed to train administrators in school management skills. The Colorado State Department of Education has also been active in promoting administrative renewal programs aimed at middle managers. In 1975 Brainard issued a report describing how Colorado school districts can organize a collegial team to design a renewal program based on participants' needs. In a related report, Brainard (1973) explains how a single administrator can serve as a catalyst in bringing together other administrators to develop their own self-improvement programs. These and many other descriptions of staff development programs (Blakeslee, 1975; Canadian Teachers' Federation, 1975; Day and Jenkins, 1975; Devaney and Thorn, 1975; Doob, 1974; Higley, 1974; Klopf, 1974; Lutz and Ferrante, 1972; National Education Association, 1975; and Seldin, 1975, to mention a few) are available from the ERIC Clearinghouse on Educational Management.

Byrnes, Klopf, Scheldon, and Blake (1975) describe a program specifically designed to help elementary principals become educational leaders. This staff development effort took a developmental approach, which provided a lot of peer and staff support and encouraged principals to cooperate in analyzing school situations and helping one another to develop their leadership capabilities. With its emphasis on continuous needs assessment and feedback by participants themselves, it departed from the traditional one-shot workshop approach to staff development that characterizes most inservice programs in the field of education. Participants were unanimous in evaluating the program as having been a significant growth experience enhancing their capabilities as leaders.

---

1. In this connection, it scarcely needs to be said that situations in which principals are pitted against each other in haggling over scarce resources, or in horsetrading incompetent staff, have no place in a school system. These activities, though they may be functional from one perspective, simply exacerbate an already unfortunate situation.

In another noteworthy effort related to the challenge of increasing principals' effectiveness, the Atlanta Public School System joined the University Council for Educational Administration in using federal support provided by the Emergency School Assistance Program to identify and elaborate specific performance objectives for principals. Many of the concepts and instruments developed during the course of the project are discussed by Culbertson, Henson, and Morrison (1974). As a guide to staff development, this work provides an array of ideas that can both serve as a basis for designing staff development programs for administrators and as a focal point for staff development training by participating principals. Specific attention is given to problems related to decision making, organizational change, human relations and morale, improving the instructional program, and evaluating school processes and products.

There have been other notable efforts to design staff development programs for principals based on the idea of specifying competencies and performance objectives that can, in fact, be learned and evaluated. In a departure from much of the prescriptive literature that merely exhorts principals to be more effective leaders (but frequently fails to specify what knowledge, beliefs, or behaviors are actually needed to achieve that objective), is the work by McCleary and his associates (1976) at the University of Utah. Numerous preservice certification and inservice staff development programs of this nature (see, for example, Ellett, Payne, and Perkins's (1976) description of the Georgia Principal Assessment System or Erlandson's (1978) discussion of accountability and competency-based education for administrators) have emerged during the past five or six years. A major contribution of these programs, in addition to their utility for university professors and school districts involved in training and improving the performance of educational leaders, is their recognition of the complexity of the principalship, and the difficulties inherent in identifying competencies and developing staff development modules that are both relevant and effective.

Argyris and Schön's (1974) recent developments focusing on increasing the leadership effectiveness of business executives offer another valuable exploration of the problems inherent in efforts to increase a person's professional effectiveness. Like many effective staff development programs, their model incorporates the principles of specificity, evaluation, and direct feedback on learning and behavioral outcomes to participants. While the focus is in a context that differs in many respects from the situation of elementary and secondary school principals, many of their ideas have direct applicability to field-based staff development efforts in education.

A final example is Rubin's (1978) work on the inservice education of teachers. Although the focus is on trends, processes, and prescriptions for enhancing teacher effectiveness, many of the ideas raised are equally appropriate to staff development efforts aimed at increasing the leadership performance of principals and other school administrators. Much of value can be gleaned by understanding the nature of the successes and failures of staff development and inservice education programs for teachers. Administrators need not repeat the mistakes made in the past. This might seem obvious on the face of it, and thus silly to mention. However, educators have a major tendency not to look to the past as a basis for information for present and future work. The ideas raised by Rubin and other contributors to his book offer a valuable framework useful in guiding administrator staff development efforts.

This brief mention of some of the work that has been undertaken to improve staff development programs in education is just a small sample of the growing body of literature on these matters available for those wishing to take advantage of the opportunities to develop programs to increase principals' effectiveness. Many of these ideas can be implemented at little or no cost to a school district, or to a principal bent on initiating a personal program of self-development.

RESEARCHABLE QUESTIONS

In addition to these recommendations related to issues bearing on the selection and training of school principals, here are a number of suggestions for those interested in studying the principalship. Many researchable questions can be derived from the observations made by these eight principals. The emotional toxicity of the principal's work world, the loneliness and lack of interaction with other principals, the ideas of the principalship as a role in a "feudal kingdom," the immediacy of the setting, the attitude of proactivity, and the like, all suggest points of departure for exploring the world of the principal and contributing to the understanding of administrative behavior.

For example, is there any relationship between a principal's on-the-job effectiveness (using a variety of criterion measures) and the frequency, intensity, and nature of that principal's contacts with peers? How do we develop reliable and valid measures of the emotional toxicity of a principal's work environment? In what ways does the emotional toxicity of a principal's work environment affect his or her motivation? What kinds of support systems reverse the "burn-out" process? In what ways does a school system's value structure inhibit or support proactive behavior on the part of principals? Or, is proactiveness mostly a personality variable relatively unaffected by normative structures?

While researchers might productively examine these and related questions, as for example Forsyth and Hoy (1978) do in their study of isolation and alienation in educational organizations, the field of educational administration can also benefit from systematically collected empirical descriptions of the actual on-the job behavior of school principals and superintendents. Qualitative efforts paralleling the work of Wolcott (1973) promise increased understanding of the work of school administrators and of phenomena attending their job performance. Although this work offers a glimpse of the variety of perspectives principals bring to their work, in-depth case studies of individual principals may yield insights on both the appropriateness of the concepts suggested here and their fuller meaning for the effectiveness of principals. While empirical description of the work of principals will not by itself advance theory underlying the study and practice of educational administration, the availability of such data can provide researchers with a basis for generating theory and developing researchable problems bearing on the principalship.

In addition to research questions growing out of the data reviewed in the preceding chapters, there are other areas of inquiry that can and should be systematically pursued. The principalship and the individuals fulfilling that role may vary in important ways in different school settings, at different school levels, and at different points in time across the principal's career. For example, are there observable and critical differences in principalships located in what might be termed placid versus turbulent school environments? What features of the principalship endure across the elementary, middle, and high school levels; what features characterize one level but not another? Do principals' orientations to their role change as they move through the early, middle, and later career stages? Are the job-related problems identified as important early in a principal's career also identified as important at a later stage? Do general role orientations change or remain fairly constant over the years?

Another set of researchable problems which might be fruitful to study involves comparing and contrasting effective and ineffective principals along any one of a variety of dimensions, including the nature of their interpersonal relations with teachers, their locus of control vis-à-vis day-to-day school operations, and their level of psychological, emotional, and physical health. While the criterion used to discriminate between more and less effective principals might be fairly sophisticated and could involve the administration of a set of rigorously validated instruments measuring organizational or administrative effectiveness, it might be as simple as asking for nominations from the superintendent, central office staff, teachers, or parents. The differences between principals and the consequences of these differences for principals as well as for those whom they serve through their office need to be more completely understood.

A third general approach to studying the principalship might involve comparisons between the role of principals and the roles of administrators in other occupational settings. Which aspects of the role are similar and different across occupations? In what ways is the principalship role similar to and different from managerial and leadership roles in nursing, social work, medicine, civil service, business, government, and the military? Within the field of education, how does the work of the school principal compare with the work of community college administrators, college deans, or those managing and leading adult and continuing education programs?

While there are many research questions that can be asked, there remain some practical constraints influencing research on the principalship, not the least of which are limited financial resources to support such research. One suggestion involves the potential we see for piggybacking research and staff development efforts. If events in the future parallel those of the past, which is highly likely, it is likely that more financial resources will be given by schools and government agencies to support administrator inservice and staff development programs than to support research on the principalship. If this prediction is accurate, one of the alternatives researchers and students of the principalship might explore is to design staff development or inservice training programs in a way that permits the investigation of some of the research questions posed here. For example, assuming that effective principals have well-developed analytical and interpersonal skills, it might be possible to build a set of research questions and data collection and analysis procedures into a staff development project designed to improve the analytical and interpersonal skills of principals. With a little creative planning and imagination, personnel responsible for the staff development effort could design the project in a way that facilitates both research and staff development/training objectives.

With declining school enrollments, increasing sentiment among professional educators for field-based training, and the continuing public press for accountability, the time may be ripe for school officials to invest in establishing a school district capability for systematic research, development, and evaluation. There is an increasing pressure to use dwindling resources more effectively—and not merely to do less of the same old thing. More creative use of supervisory personnel and a re-allocation of existing instructional resources may yield enough resource "slack" in the system to permit the development of a small but effective cadre of research, development, and evaluation personnel.

For example, in one school system school closings have produced a situation that has resulted in the development of what has been termed the "co-principal." That is, principals from schools that have been closed have been "teamed" with principals in schools that remain open. While it can be argued that assigning additional administrative personnel to a single school will permit more effective control and coordination of the work in a given school, it is doubtful whether it is the best way to use "excess" principals. A possible alternative, for example, would be to group them within a single office in the school district and charge them with the responsibility for developing and implementing a systematic program of staff development, research, and evaluation.

Whatever the catalyst or means, additional research on the principalship is needed, particularly at the middle and high school levels. The fact remains that even though the principalship has been in the past and will continue to be a crucial influence on what happens in schools, too little is known about the men and women assigned to this position and their role in guiding and developing educational programs in our nation's schools.

CONCLUSION

As we stated at the outset, our approach to increasing our understanding of men and women in the principalship deviates in many ways from the work of other researchers. We did not set out to test the validity of any particular concepts or hypotheses bearing on the principalship, but instead sought to capture and understand the substance of what selected principals would have to say about their role, what they did, and to the extent possible, why they reported behaving as they did. In our analysis of their responses to the rather general questions we raised in our interviews, we've identified a number of issues bearing further study. In the process, we've acquired a fuller understanding of the complexity of the principalship and the range of approaches to the demands of that role.

Leading schools effectively requires expressive abilities, tolerance for ambiguity, vision and initiative, skills at collecting and analyzing data, and a great deal of physical energy and psychological strength. Each of the people we studied reflect these characteristics in varying combinations. Additionally, we've observed that each principal approached the demands of their work world in idiosyncratic and behaviorally distinct, but functionally equivalent ways. Their perspectives clearly differentiated them as individuals, which suggests that there are many roads to effectiveness as a principal. This is so because schools are highly ambiguous organizations, structurally very similar, yet peculiar according to variations in the social, racial, and economic characteristics of the containing community. The problems met by principals vary in magnitude but are generally of the same category from one school to another. In a very real sense, by design or not, a principal develops a school in his/her own image.

As described by the men and women portrayed in this book, the school principalship can be a very challenging and rewarding experience, quite different in many ways from teaching or instructional supervision. School principals can make a real difference in the lives of children and teachers, and the role of principal offers many opportunities for satisfying the personal and professional growth needs of individuals willing to assume the responsibilities of leadership in education. The principalship desperately needs men and women having a vision that carries them beyond merely maintaining things as they are; it needs men and women with the confidence and strength to build a school environment that releases rather than restrains the educational potential of children, teachers, and other members of the school community.

Our nation's schools need leaders who care about children and teachers and who are willing and able to involve themselves in developing school work settings in a way that is both personally satisfying and educationally beneficial to the constituents being served. However, it takes more than caring. If such leadership is to be effective, people assuming the responsibilities and challenges of the principalship must also possess sufficient educational, organizational, and interpersonal know-how to cope satisfactorily with the many demands of the role. Being a nice person just isn't enough.

As the images of the men and women discussed in these pages have demonstrated, an effective principal must be willing to take a few risks, must make informed choices that judiciously use the human and technical resources available, and must clearly understand and be able to use the vast opportunities for change inherent in the principalship. Those who see this potential, *and act upon it*, can indeed make a much needed contribution to improving our nation's schools—to creating the kinds of learning and working environments we long for as professional educators.

References

AMERICAN ASSOCIATION OF SCHOOL ADMINISTRATORS. *The American School Superintendency*. Washington, D. C.: American Association of School Administrators, 1952.

"Annual Cost of Education Index." *School Management* 18 (1974):16–37, 63.

ARGYRIS, C. *Personality and Organization*. New York: Harper & Bros., 1957.

——. *Interpersonal Competence and Organizational Effectiveness*. Homewood, Ill.: The Dorsey Press, 1962.

——. *Increasing Leadership Effectiveness*. New York: John Wiley, 1976.

ARGYRIS, C., and SCHÖN, D. *Theory into Practice. Increasing Professional Effectiveness*. San Francisco: Jossey-Bass, 1974.

ASSOCIATION OF CALIFORNIA SCHOOL ADMINISTRATORS. *Strategies for Administrative Staff Development: Operations Notebook 13*. Burlingame, Calif.: Association of California School Administrators, 1975.

AUSTIN, D. B., and BROWN, H. L., Jr. *Report of the Assistant Principalship*. Washington, D. C.: National Association of Secondary School Principals, 1970.

BECKER, H. S., GEER, B., HUGHES, E. C., and STRAUSS, A. *Boys in White: Student Culture in Medical School*. Chicago, Ill.: University of Chicago Press, 1961.

BIDWELL, C. E. "The School as a Formal Organization." In *Handbook of Organizations*, edited by J. G. March. Chicago: Rand McNally, 1965, pp. 972–1022.

BION, W. *Attention and Interpretation*. New York: Basic Books, 1974.

BLAKESLEE, Jean C. "Individualized Inservice Training." *Catalyst for Change* 4(2) (Winter 1975):4–8.

BLUMBERG, A. *Supervisors and Teachers*. Berkeley, Calif.: McCutchan Publishing, 1974.

BLUMBERG, A., and SCHMUCK, R. "Barriers to Organizational Development Training in the Schools." *Educational Technology*, October 1972, pp. 30–34.

BRAINARD, E. "Individualizing Administrator Inservice Education." *Thrust for Education Leadership* 2(5) (April 1973):29–33.

——. *The Colorado Department of Education and the Development of School District Based Administrator Renewal Programs*. Denver: Colorado State Department of Education, 1975.

BRIDGES, E. M. "The Nature of Leadership." In *Educational Administration: The Developing Decades*, edited by L. L. Cunningham, W. G. Hack, and R. O. Nystrand. Berkeley, Calif.: McCutchan Publishing, 1977, pp. 202–230.

BRIM, C., and WHEELER, S. *Socialization after Childhood: Two Essays.* New York: John Wiley, 1966.

BRYNE, D. R., HINES, S. A., and McCLEARY, L. E. *The Senior High School Principalship,* Vol. I: The National Survey. Reston, Va.: Association of Secondary School Principals, 1978.

BYRNES, J. C.; KLOPF, G. J.; SCHELDON, E. S.; and BLAKE, S. M. *Report of the Program for the Development of the Elementary School Principal as an Educational Leader.* New York: Bank Street College of Education, 1975.

BUTTON, H. W. "Doctrines of Administration: A Brief History." *Educational Administration Quarterly* 2(3) (Autumn 1966):216–24.

CANADIAN TEACHERS' FEDERATION. *Continuing Education for Teachers.* Bibliographies in Education No. 53. Ottawa, Ontario: 1975.

CARROLL, P. A. "Central Life Interests and Sources of Attachment to Work Among School Administrators." Ph.D. dissertation, Syracuse University, 1978.

CREMIN, L. *Public Education.* New York: Basic Books, 1976.

CRONIN, J. M., and HOROSCHAK, P. P. *Innovative Strategies in Field Experiences for Preparing Educational Administrators.* University Council for Educational Administration Monograph Series, Number Eight. Danville, Ill.: Interstate Printers and Publishers, 1973.

CROSS, Ray. "A Description of Decision-Making Patterns of School Principals." Paper presented to American Educational Research Association, February 1971.

CULBERTSON, J. A.; FARQUHAR, R. H.; GAYNOR, A. K.; and SHIBLES, M. R. *Preparing Educational Leaders for the Seventies.* Columbus, Ohio: University Council for Educational Administration, 1969.

CULBERTSON, J. A.; HENSON, C.; and MORRISON, R. *Performance Objectives for School Principals: Concepts & Instruments.* Berkeley, Calif.: McCutchan Publishing, 1974.

DAVIES, D. R. *The Internship in Educational Administration.* Washington, D. C.: The Center for Applied Research in Education, 1962.

DAY, B. D., and JENKINS, J. W. "North Carolina's K-3 Staff Development Program." *Educational Leadership* 32(5) (February 1975):326–30.

DEAN, S. E. *Elementary School Administration and Organization.* U.S. Office of Education Bulletin No. 11. Washington, D. C.: Government Printing Office, 1960.

DEPARTMENT OF ELEMENTARY SCHOOL PRINCIPALS, NATIONAL EDUCATION ASSOCIATION. *The Elementary School Principalship in 1968.* Washington, D. C.: National Education Association, 1968.

DEVANEY, K., and THORN, L. *Exploring Teachers' Centers.* San Francisco: Far West Laboratory for Educational Research and Development, 1975.

DOOB, H. S. *Internship Programs in Educational Administration. An ERS Report.* Washington, D. C.: Educational Research Service, 1974.

DUBIN, R. "Industrial Workers' Worlds: A Study of Central Life Interests of Industrial Workers." *Social Problems* 3 (1956):131–42.

ELLETT, Chad D.; POOL, J. E.; and HILL, A. S. "A Time-Motion Study of Principals in Thomas County, Georgia." *CCBC Notebook,* Vol. 4, No. 1, 1974.

ELLETT, C.; PAYNE, D. A.; and PERKINS, M. L. "The Relationship of Principals' Competencies and Meaningful School Outcome Measures: Field Test of the Georgia Principal Assessment System." *CCBC Notebook* 5(3) (May 1976): 13–32.

ERLANDSON, D. "The Meaning of Accountability: CBAE Comes of Age." *CCBC Notebook* 7(3) (May 1978):2–5.

FEATHERSTONE, J. Testimony quoted by the Senate Select Committee on Equal Educational Opportunity, February 19, 1970, p. 305. Washington, D C.: Government Printing Office, 1970.

FORSYTH, P. B., and HOY, W. K. "Isolation and Alienation in Educational Organizations." *Educational Administration Quarterly* 14(1) (Winter 1978): 80–96.

FOSKETT, J. M. *The Normative World of the Elementary School Principal.* Eugene, Ore.: Center for the Advanced Study of Educational Administration, University of Oregon, 1957.

FREEMAN, J., and HANNAN, M. "Growth and Decline Processes in Organizations." *American Sociological Review* 40 (1975):215–28.

FROMM, E. *Escape from Freedom.* Rinehart & Co., 1941.

GOLDHAMMER, K.; BECKER, G.; WITHYCOMBE, R.; DOYEL, F.; MILLER, E.; MORGAN, C.; DELORETTO, L.; and ALDRIDGE, B. *Elementary Principals and Their Schools—Beacons of Brilliance and Potholes of Pestilence.* Eugene, Ore.: Center for the Advanced Study of Educational Administration, University of Oregon, 1971.

GORTON, R. A., and McINTYRE, K. E. *The Senior High School Principalship,* Volume II: The Effective Principal. Reston, Va.: National Association of Secondary School Principals, 1978.

GROSS, N., and HERRIOTT, R. E. *Staff Leadership in Public Schools: A Sociological Inquiry.* New York: John Wiley, 1965.

GROSS, N. C., and TRASK, A. E. *The Sex Factor and the Management of Schools.* New York: John Wiley, 1976.

HARVEY, J. "Eight Myths OD Consultants Believe In . . . and Die By!" *OD Practitioner* 7(1) (1976):1–5.

HEMPHILL, J. K.; GRIFFITHS, D. E.; and FREDERIKSEN, N. *Administrative Performance & Personality.* New York: Bureau of Publications, Teachers College, Colombia University, 1962.

HIGLEY, J. "Inservice Training for Staff and Administrators." *School Leadership Digest Series,* Number 8, 1974.

HORNEY, K. *Our Inner Conflicts.* New York: W. W. Norton, 1945.

HOY, W. K., and MISKEL, C. G. *Educational Administration: Theory, Research, and Practice.* New York: Random House, 1978.

KAHN, R. L., WOLFE, D. M., QUINN, R. P., and SNOEK, J. D., in collaboration with R. A. Rosenthal. *Organizational Stress: Studies in Role Conflict and Ambiguity.* New York: John Wiley, 1964.

KATZ, D., and KAHN, R. *The Social Psychology of Organizations.* New York: John Wiley, 1966.

KLOPF, G. J. *The Principal and Staff Development in the Elementary School.* Princeps Series: Occasional Paper No. 4. New York: Bank Street College of Education, 1974.

KNEZEVICH, S. *The American School Superintendent.* Washington, D. C.: The American Association of School Administrators, 1971.

———. *Administration of Public Education.* New York: Harper & Row, 1975.

LAING, R. *The Divided Self.* New York: Pantheon Books, 1969.

LEVINSON, H. *Organizational Diagnosis.* Cambridge, Mass.: Harvard University Press, 1972.

———. *The Great Jackass Fallacy.* Boston: Division of Research Graduate School of Business Administration, Harvard University, 1973.

———. *The Exceptional Executive: A Psychological Conception.* Cambridge, Mass.: Harvard University Press, 1968.

LEVINSON, H.; PRICE, C.; MUNDEN, K.; MANDL, H.; and SOLLEY, C. *Men, Management and Mental Health.* Cambridge, Mass.: Harvard University Press, 1962.

LIKERT, R. *The Human Organization.* New York: McGraw-Hill, 1967.

LIPHAM, J. M., and FRANCKE, D. C. "Non-Verbal Behavior of Administrators." *Educational Administration Quarterly* 2(2) (Spring 1966):101–09.

LIPHAM, J. M., and HOEH, J. A., Jr. *The Principalship: Foundations and Functions.* New York: Harper & Row, 1974.

LORTIE, Dan C. *Schoolteacher: A Sociological Study.* Chicago: The University of Chicago Press, 1975.

LUTZ, F. W., and FERRANTE, R. "Emergent Practices in the Continuing Education of School Administrators." ERIC/CEM-UCEA Series on Administrator Preparation, Columbus, Ohio: The University Council for Educational Administration, 1972.

MACCOBY, M. *The Gamesman.* New York: Simon and Schuster, 1976.

MARCH, J. G. "American Public School Administration: A Short Analysis." *School Review* 86(2) (February 1978):217–50.

———. "Analytical Skills and the University Training of Educational Administrators." In Walter D. Cocking Lectures: *The NCPEA Series of Prominent Papers in Educational Administration,* edited by J. D. Herring and R. E. Klimes. Berrien Springs, Mich.: Center for Studies and Services in Education, Andrews University, 1976, pp. 87–162.

MARCH, J. G., and OLSEN, J. P. *Ambiguity and Choice in Organizations.* Bergen: University Press of Norway, 1976.

MARIN, P. "The New Narcissism." *Harper's,* October 1975, pp. 45–56.

MASLACH, C. "Burned Out." *Human Behavior,* September 1976, pp. 16–21.

McCLEARY, L. Annotated Bibliography on Competency-Based Education for Administration. *CCBC Notebook*: University of Utah, 1976.

MEYER, J. W., and ROWAN, B. "Institutionalized Organizations: Formal Structure as Myth and Ceremony." *American Journal of Sociology* 83 (September 1977):340–63.

NATIONAL ASSOCIATION OF ELEMENTARY SCHOOL PRINCIPALS. *The Assistant Principalship in Public Elementary Schools, 1969: A Research Study.* Washington, D. C.: National Association of Elementary School Principals, 1970.

NATIONAL EDUCATION ASSOCIATION OF THE UNITED STATES. *The Elementary School Principalship in 1968: A Research Study.* Washington, D. C.: National Education Association, 1968.

———. *Needs Assessment for Inservice Education.* Washington, D. C.: Division of Instruction and Professional Development, 1975.

ORZACK, L. H. "Work as a Central Life Interest of Professionals." *Social Problems* 7 (1959):125–32.

PETERSON, V. T. "Response to Mandate: Organizational Implementation as a Loosely-Coupled Adaptation Process." Ph.D. dissertation, Stanford University, 1976.

PIERCE, P. R. "The Origin and Development of the Public School Principalship." Ph.D. dissertation, University of Chicago, 1934.

POOL, J. E. *A Compilation of Competencies as Derived from the Literature: Research Report No. 1.* Athens, Ga.: University of Georgia, 1974.

POLANYI, M. *The Tacit Dimension.* New York: Doubleday, 1967.

ROE, W. H., and DRAKE, T. L. *The Principalship.* New York: Macmillan, 1974.

RUBIN, L. *The In-Service Education of Teachers: Trends, Processes, and Prescriptions.* Boston: Allyn and Bacon, 1978.

SARASON, S. *The Culture of the School and the Problem of Change.* Boston: Allyn and Bacon, 1971.

SCHUTZ, W. *FIRO.* New York: Holt, Rinehart, 1958.

———. *The FIRO Scales Manual.* Palo Alto: Consulting Psychologists Press, 1967.

SELDIN, P. "The Twenty Day Program." *Clearing House* 49(4) (December 1975):175–78.

SENATE SELECT COMMITTEE ON EQUAL EDUCATIONAL OPPORTUNITY. Toward Equal Educational Opportunity: The Report of the Senate Select Committee on Equal Educational Opportunity, February 19, 1970. Washington, D. C.: Government Printing Office, 1970.

SMALL, J. F. "Initiating and Responding to Social Change." In *Performance Objectives for School Principals: Concepts and Instruments,* edited by J. A. Culbertson, C. Henson, and R. Marrison. Berkeley: McCutchan Publishing, 1974, pp. 18–53.

STEELE, F. *The Open Organization.* Reading, Mass.: Addison-Wesley, 1975.

WALLER, W. W. *The Sociology of Teaching.* London: Chapman and Hall, 1932.

WATZLAWICK, P.; WEAKLAND, J.; and FISCH, R. *Change.* New York: W. W. Norton, 1974.

WAYSON, W. W. "A New Kind of Principal." *The National Elementary Principal* 50(4) (February 1971):9–19.

WEICK, K. "Educational Organizations as Loosely Coupled Systems." *Administrative Science Quarterly* 21 (March 1976):1–19.

WOLCOTT, H. F. *The Man in the Principal's Office: An Ethnography.* New York: Holt, Rinehart, and Winston, 1973.

WOODWARD, J. *Management and Technology.* London: Her Majesty's Stationery Office, 1958.

Index